THE CHILDREN'S

BIBLE

IN COLOUR

THE CHILDREN'S BIBLE

IN COLOUR

The Old Testament and
the New Testament

HAMLYN

INTRODUCTION

The Bible tells the story of God's dealings with men, beginning with the creation of the world. The parts of the Bible are called "books", such as the Book of Ruth or the Book of Kings. The word "Bible" comes from a Greek term meaning "the books", since the Bible is really a library in itself, containing many volumes. These books were written in the course of a thousand years by many authors in many places, under the guidance and inspiration of God. Most of the Old Testament books were originally written in Hebrew. The books of the New Testament were written in Greek.

Each book was meant for a special purpose. Some of them are historical, telling the story of God's chosen people, the children of Israel. Others are prophetic, speaking of things which are still to come, of the hidden things in God's plan for us. Others were written to teach wisdom or give advice. One of them, the Book of Psalms, is simply a collection of sacred hymns once used in the Temple worship. Others are almost novels and even contain love stories, such as that of Ruth, or tell of heroes who saved their people, like Moses.

Starting with the beginning of the world, the story of the Bible covers several centuries and lands, teaching generation after generation that there is a divine plan in history and a purpose in human life; and today, as in every age, the Gospels are the fabric with which the house of Christian faith is built.

THE EDITORS

First Edition 1964
Seventeenth impression 1979
Published by
The Hamlyn Publishing Group Limited
London · New York · Sydney · Toronto
Astronaut House, Feltham, Middlesex, England
by arrangement with Western Publishing Company, Inc.
© Copyright 1963 Western Publishing Company, Inc.
© Copyright 1962 by Fratelli Fabbri, Milan
ISBN 0 601 07131 X
Printed in Czechoslovakia
51154/17

The Publishers with to express their appreciation to Dr Samuel Terrien, Th. D.,
for his invaluable assistance in the preparation of this book.
This book has been designed and edited by *Editions Graphiques Internationales*.
The illustrations have been executed by Fabbri Studios,
under the direction of Sandro Nardini and Aldo Torchio.

the
OLD
TESTAMENT

CONTENTS

THE CREATION AND THE PATRIARCHS

The Creation

The first day

In the beginning God created the heavens and the earth. The earth was without form and empty. Darkness was everywhere and in the darkness the spirit of God moved upon the face of the deep.

GOD SAID: "Let there be light," and there was light.

God saw that it was good and he separated the light from the darkness. God called the light Day and the darkness he called Night.

And there were evening and morning: the first day.

The second day

GOD SAID: "Let there be a sky in the midst of the waters and let it divide the waters from the waters." Then God made the sky and he separated the waters above from the waters below.

God called the sky Heaven. And there were evening and morning: the second day.

The third day

GOD SAID: "Let the waters under the heaven be gathered together in one place, and let the dry land appear." And it was so. God called the dry land Earth, and the waters he called Seas. And he said:

"Let the earth bring forth grass, and yield plants bearing seed, and trees bearing fruit." The earth did so and God saw that it was good.

This was the third day.

The fourth day

GOD SAID: "Let there be lights in the sky of heaven to divide the day from the night. Let them be for signs and for seasons, for days and for years. Let them be for lights in the sky of heaven to give light upon the earth." And it was so.

God made two great lights, the greater light to rule the day, and the lesser light to rule the night. He also made the stars and set them in the sky of heaven to give light upon the earth, to rule over the day and over the night, and to divide the light from the darkness. God saw that it was good.

This was the fourth day.

The fifth day

GOD SAID: "Let the waters bring forth in great numbers moving creatures that

have life, and let birds fly above the earth in the open sky of heaven."

So God created great whales, and every living creature that moves. These the waters brought forth in great numbers. He created the birds, and saw that all this was good.

He blessed the creatures and said:

"Be fruitful and multiply, and fill the waters in the seas. Let the birds also multiply on earth."

This was the fifth day.

The sixth day

GOD SAID: "Let the earth bring forth creatures of all kinds, cattle and creeping things and beasts of the earth." The earth did so and God saw that this was good.

"Let us make man in our image, after our likeness, and let him have power over the fish of the sea and the birds of the air, over the cattle, over all the earth and over everything that moves on the earth."

So God created man in his own image. In the image of God he created man and woman. Male and female created he them. And he blessed them and said to them:

"Be fruitful and multiply. Fill the earth and have power over the fish of the sea and over the birds of the air, over every living thing that moves upon the earth.

"Behold, I have given you every plant bearing seed and every tree yielding fruit which is upon the face of the earth. They shall be your food. To every beast of the earth, to every bird of the air, to everything that creeps upon the earth and has life, I have given the grass and the plants for food." And it was so. God saw everything that he had made, and it was very good.

This was the sixth day.

The seventh day

The heavens and the earth were finished and filled with life. On the seventh day God rested from his work and all that he had made. God blessed the seventh day and made it a holy day, because on that day he had rested.

This is how the Lord God made the earth and the heavens, and every plant before it was in the earth, and every tree of the field before it grew. And when God had made man, a mist had gone up from the earth, and had watered the whole surface of the ground. The Lord God had formed man of the dust of the ground, and had breathed into him the breath of life, and man had become a living soul.

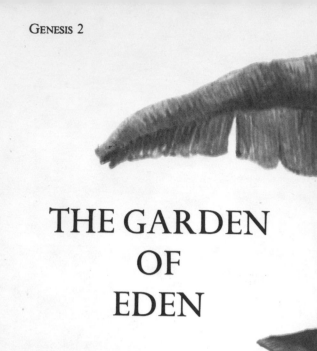

THE GARDEN OF EDEN

G OD planted a garden in the east, in Eden, and there he put the man whom he had formed. Out of the ground the Lord made trees of every kind to grow, both those that are pleasant to the eye and those that are good for food. In the middle of the garden he planted the tree of life, and the tree of knowledge of good and evil.

A river flowed out of Eden to water the garden, and beneath the garden the river divided and became four rivers. The first was called Pison; the name of the second was Gihon, the third Hiddekel, and the fourth Euphrates.

God took the man and put him into the garden of Eden to care for it and keep it. And God commanded the man, saying:

"Of every tree in the garden you may eat freely, except for the tree of knowledge of good and evil. Of this, do not eat, for in the day that you eat of it, you shall surely die."

Then the Lord God said:

"It is not good that the man should be alone. I will make a companion for him."

But first God brought every beast of the field and every bird of the air, which he had made out of the earth, to

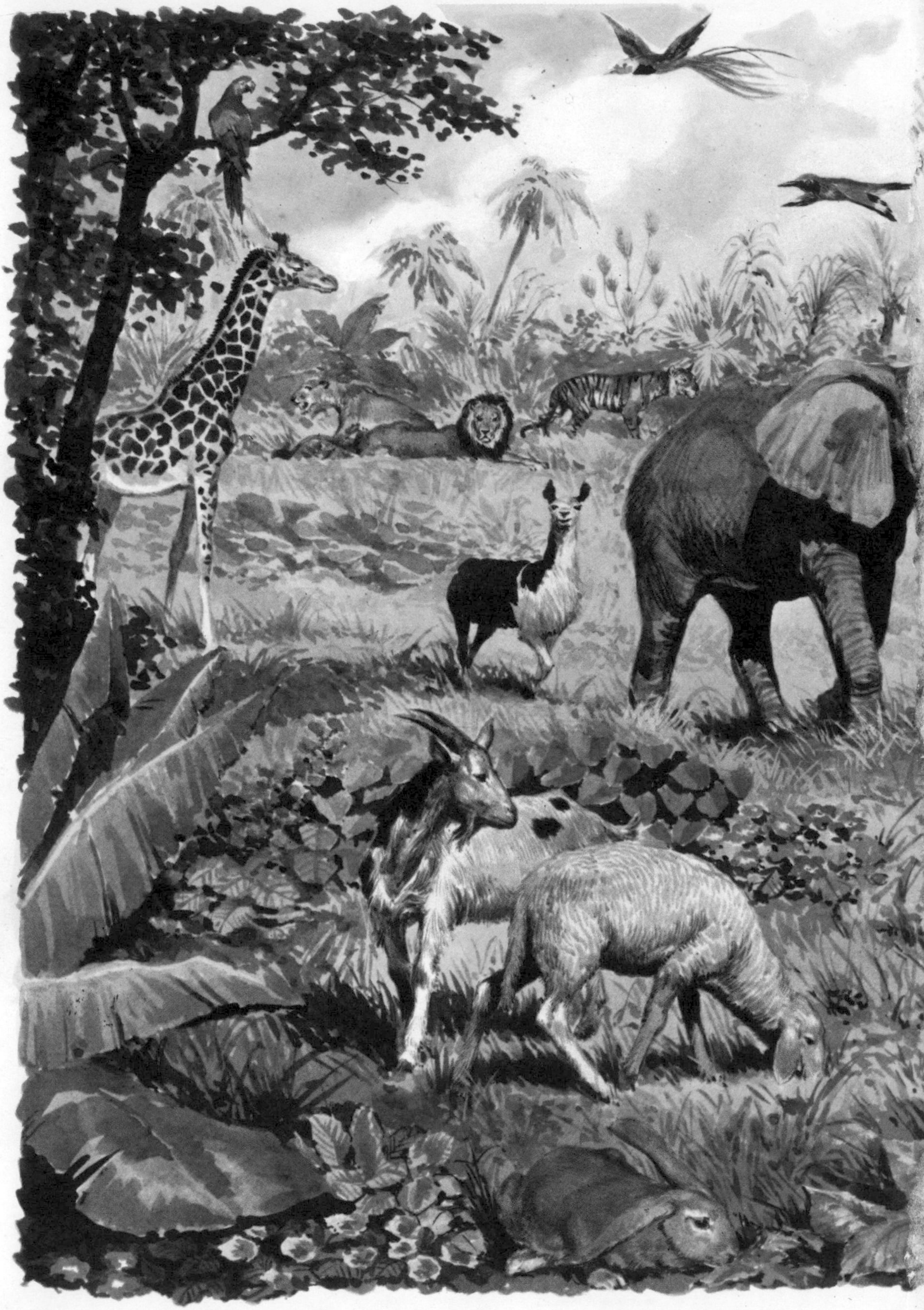

man, to see what he would call them, and what man called each creature, this became that creature's name. Man gave names to the cattle, to the birds of the air, and to every beast of the field. But for himself, man did not find a companion.

So God put man into a deep sleep and as he slept, God took one of his ribs. This rib the Lord God made into woman, and he brought her to man, who said:

"This is now bone of my bones and flesh of my flesh. Her name shall be Woman, because she is taken out of Man." And the man and the woman were naked but they were not ashamed.

THE SERPENT IN THE GARDEN

HE most cunning of the beasts which the Lord had made was the serpent, and the serpent said to the woman: "Did God forbid you to eat the fruit of the trees of the garden?"

The woman said: "We may eat the fruit of the trees of the garden, except the tree which is in the middle of the garden.

"Of this God said, 'You shall not eat of it nor touch it, lest you die.'"

"You will not die," said the serpent. "God knows that the day you eat of the fruit your eyes shall be opened and you will be like gods, knowing good from evil."

The woman looked at the tree and saw that it was pleasant to the eye and good for food. She felt it was to be desired because it would make one wise.

So she picked some of the fruit and ate it, and she gave some also to her husband who was with her, and he ate it.

Then the eyes of both of them were opened, and they knew that they were naked. So they sewed fig leaves together to cover themselves.

In the cool of the day the Lord walked in the garden. The man and the woman heard the voice of the Lord and hid themselves from his presence, among the trees of the garden.

The Lord God called to man saying: "Where are you?"

"I have heard your voice in the garden," said man. "I was afraid, because I was naked, and I hid myself."

"Who told you that you were naked?" asked the Lord God. "Have you eaten the fruit of the tree from which I commanded you not to eat?"

Man said: "The woman whom you gave me to be with me, gave me fruit of the tree and I did eat."

The Lord God said to the woman: "What is this you have done?"

"The serpent tempted me," said the woman, "and I ate."

THEY ARE DRIVEN FROM THE GARDEN

The Lord God said to the serpent:

"Because you have done this, you are cursed above all cattle and above every beast of the field. You shall crawl on your belly and eat dust all the days of your life. I shall make the woman your enemy and her children the enemies of your children.

They shall wound you in the head and you shall wound them in the heel."

To the woman he said:

"I will multiply your suffering. You shall bring forth your children in sorrow and for happiness you shall depend on your husband, and he shall rule over you."

To the man he said: "Because you listened to the voice of your wife and ate of the forbidden fruit, the ground shall be cursed beneath you. In sorrow

you shall eat of it every day of your life. Thorns and thistles it will bring forth for you, and you shall eat the grass of the field. By the sweat of your brow you will earn your bread until you return to the earth, for out of the earth you were taken: dust you are and to dust you shall return.''

The Lord God then made coats of skin for the man and his wife, and clothed them.

And the Lord God said:

''Behold, the man is like one of us now, knowing all things. If he were to put out his hand and eat also of the tree of life, he would live for ever.''

Therefore the Lord God sent man out of the garden of Eden, to till the ground from which he was made. He drove him out, and placed cherubim to the east of the garden of Eden, and a flaming sword which turned in every direction to guard the path to the tree of life.

CAIN AND ABEL, SONS OF ADAM

ADAM named his wife Eve, and she became the mother of all who lived. She gave birth to Cain and said: "The Lord has given me a boy." Then she gave birth to Abel.

Abel became a keeper of sheep and Cain became a tiller of the ground. One day it came to pass that Cain brought some of his harvest as an offering to the Lord, while Abel brought the fattest and choicest of his lambs. The Lord was pleased with Abel and his offering but with Cain and his offering he was not content. Cain was angry and his face fell.

And God said to him:

"Cain, why are you angry? Why are you crestfallen?"

Cain made no answer but later when they were in the fields together, he rose up against his brother and killed him.

And God said to Cain: "Where is Abel your brother?"

"I do not know," said Cain. "Am I my brother's keeper?"

"What have you done?" said God. "The voice of your brother's blood cries out to me from the ground. The earth itself which has received your brother's blood from your hand, now cries out against you. You shall be cursed and from now on, whenever you till the ground, it will not yield its strength to you. A fugitive and a vagabond you shall be on the earth."

"My punishment is more than I can bear," said Cain to the Lord. "Behold, you have driven me out this day from the face of the earth, and from your face I shall hide. I shall be a fugitive and a vagabond on earth, and whoever finds me shall slay me."

"But on whomever kills Cain," said God, "revenge shall be taken seven times over."

And the Lord set a mark upon Cain, so that anyone finding him would not kill him.

After that, Cain went out from the presence of the Lord, and dwelt in the land of Nod, to the east of Eden.

And later in the land of Nod, Cain took a wife and she gave birth to a son who was named Enoch. And Cain built a city and named it after Enoch. From Enoch are descended those who have tents and cattle and those who play upon the harp and the pipe.

Meanwhile Eve gave birth to another son. She called him Seth, for God had given him to her in place of Abel. And in Seth God blessed Adam with a son who resembled his father. Adam lived to a very great age and Eve bore many more sons and daughters.

Thus men began to multiply on the face of the earth and many generations were descended from Adam and Eve. And in the ninth generation there was a descendant named Noah. Noah was a just man, the best of all the men of his time, and he lived by God's rules. He had three sons, named Shem, Ham and Japheth.

NOAH AND THE ARK

"You shall do this because I shall bring upon the earth a great flood which shall destroy every living thing. But with you I will make a promise and the promise shall be called a covenant. You shall enter the ark with your sons, and your wife, and your sons' wives with you.

"Of every living creature upon the earth you shall bring into the ark two of each sort to keep them alive with you. They shall be male and female. Birds of all kinds, cattle and every creeping thing, two of every animal in creation shall come to you for you to keep them alive.

"And take with you some of every kind of food that is eaten. Gather it up, and it shall be food for you and the creatures that are with you."

HE Lord saw that men had become very wicked and that in their minds and their hearts there was only evil. He regretted that he had made man on earth and in his heart he grieved very deeply.

And God said to Noah:

"The end of all flesh is before me. I will destroy all living things on earth for because of them the earth is filled with evil and violence.

"Make an ark of cypress wood," commanded the Lord. ' Make rooms in the ark, and cover it inside and out with pitch. Make it in this fashion: the length of the ark shall be four hundred and fifty feet, the breadth of it seventy-five feet, and the height forty-five feet. You shall put a window in it and in its side you shall put a door. The ark shall have three decks: a lower, a second and a third.

THE GREAT FLOOD

Noah had lived to a very great age when the flood of waters came upon the earth.

And God said to Noah:

"Come into the ark, you and all who are with you. Seven days from now, I will cause it to rain upon the earth for forty days and forty nights. And every living thing I have made, I will destroy from the face of the earth." And Noah did all that the Lord had commanded him.

He entered the ark with Shem and Ham and Japheth, his sons, his own wife and the wives of his sons. Birds and beasts and creeping things of every kind came to Noah and went into the ark, two by two, the male and the female, as God had commanded.

Then the Lord shut Noah in the ark, and the waters of the flood were upon the earth. All the fountains of the great deep were broken up and

the windows of heaven opened. The rain fell upon the earth forty days and forty nights. The waters swelled and lifted the ark above the earth.

The flood spread and the waters continued to rise upon the earth. And the ark floated upon the face of the water. The waters rose higher and higher upon the earth until all the high mountains under heaven were covered. Forty-five feet more did the waters rise above the high mountains and they were indeed covered.

Every living thing that moved upon the earth died: birds, cattle, beasts, every creeping thing that creeps upon the earth, and every man. All in whose nostrils was the breath of life, every man and every living thing which was upon the face of the ground were destroyed. Only Noah and those who were with him remained alive.

God remembered Noah and every living creature with him in the ark. God caused a wind to pass over the earth and to quiet the waters.

THE ARK COMES TO REST

The fountains of the deep and the windows of heaven were stopped and the rain from heaven was restrained. The waters receded for a hundred and fifty days so that in the seven month on the seventeenth day of the month, the ark rested on the mount of Ararat. And the waters continued to decrease until the first day of the tenth month when the peaks of the mountains were seen.

At the end of forty days Noah opened the window of the ark and sent out a raven, which flew to and fro. He also sent out a dove to see if the waters had dried from the ground anywhere. The dove found no rest for the sole of her foot, and she returned to the ark, for the waters still covered

the earth. So Noah put out his hand and took her back into the ark.

He waited seven more days and once again he sent out the dove. The dove came back to him in the evening and, when she did so, there was in her mouth a freshly plucked olive leaf. So Noah knew that the waters had receded from the face of the earth.

Noah waited still another seven days before he sent out the dove. This time the dove did not return.

The water had dried from the earth, so Noah opened the window of the ark. He looked out and saw that the ground was dry.

God spoke to Noah, saying:

"Take with you the birds, the cattle, and every living thing that is with you, that they may breed and raise their young and multiply upon the earth."

So Noah went out, and his sons and his wife and his sons' wives with him. Every beast, every creeping thing and every bird went out of the ark.

And Noah built an altar to the Lord and offered him burnt offerings of every clean beast and every clean fowl.

The Lord smelled the sweet odour and said in his heart:

"I will not curse the ground any more for man's sake. Nor will I ever again strike down every living thing as I have done. As long as the earth remains, seedtime and harvest, cold and heat, summer and winter, day and night will never cease."

God blessed Noah and his sons and said to them:

"Be fruitful and multiply, and re-plenish the earth. The fear and the dread of you shall be upon every beast of the earth and upon every bird of the air, upon all that moves on the earth and upon all the fishes of the sea. Every moving thing that lives shall be food for you. As once I gave you the green plants, now have I given you all these things."

And God continued, saying:

"Behold, I make my promise to you, and to your children after you, and to every living creature that is with you, and to every living beast of the earth. To the birds and the cattle and all who come out of the ark, I promise that never again will all flesh be cut off by the waters of a flood, nor will a flood destroy the earth.

"This promise is a covenant which I make between myself and you and every creature that is with you, throughout all generations without end.

THE RAINBOW

"I set my rainbow in the cloud and this rainbow shall be a token of the covenant between me and the earth.

"And it shall come to pass when I bring a cloud over the earth, that the rainbow shall be seen in the cloud. I will look upon it, and I will remember the everlasting covenant between me and you and every living creature upon the earth."

And Noah lived a long time after the flood and was a very old man when he died.

Sons were born unto the sons of Noah after the flood, and they went forth and were the fathers of the nations of the earth.

THE TOWER OF BABEL

AFTER God made the covenant with Noah, Noah's descendants increased greatly and one generation succeeded another.

People at this time the earth over were of one language and one speech. And as men journeyed eastwards, they entered a plain in the land of Shinar, where they settled. They said to one another:

"Come, let us make bricks and bake them thoroughly." They used bricks for stone and they had slime for mortar.

And they said: "Let us build a city, and a tower whose top may reach up to heaven. Let us make a name for ourselves lest we be scattered abroad upon the face of the whole earth."

God came down to see the city and the tower which the children of men were building, and said:

"The people of the earth are one people and have only one language. If they begin to do this, nothing will restrain them from doing whatever they conceive. Let us go down, therefore, and confuse their language so that they may not understand one another's speech."

So God scattered them abroad upon the face of the earth, and they left off building the city. And the name of the place is Babel, for there it was that the Lord made a confusion of the language of the earth, and it was in this manner that the Lord scattered the people over the face of the earth.

GOD'S PROMISE TO ABRAM

IN the land of Haran, there lived a man called Abram. Abram was the son of Terah who was descended from Shem. Terah and his family had returned to Haran after living in Ur, when one day God said to Abram:

"Leave your country, and your kinfolk, and your father's house, and go to a land that I will show you. I will make of you a great nation, and I will bless you and make your name great. I will bless those who bless you, and curse those who curse you, and through you all the families of the earth shall be blessed."

So Abram heeded what the Lord had said and departed; he was seventy-five years old when he left Haran. With him he took Sarai his wife, and Lot his brother's son, and all their goods and cattle, and the people they had gathered in Haran. And they went into the land of Canaan.

And they passed through Canaan to Shechem in the plain of Moreh which was occupied then by the Canaanites. At Shechem God appeared to Abram and said:

"This land I will give to your people."

And Abram built an altar to the Lord at Shechem. Then Abram moved and came to a mountain to the east of Bethel where he pitched his tent with Bethel to the west and Ai to the east. Here too he built an altar and called upon the name of the Lord before continuing his journey to the south.

There was famine in the land, so Abram continued to Egypt and lived there until the famine was over. Then he returned to the place between Bethel and Ai where he had built an altar and there he again called on the name of the Lord.

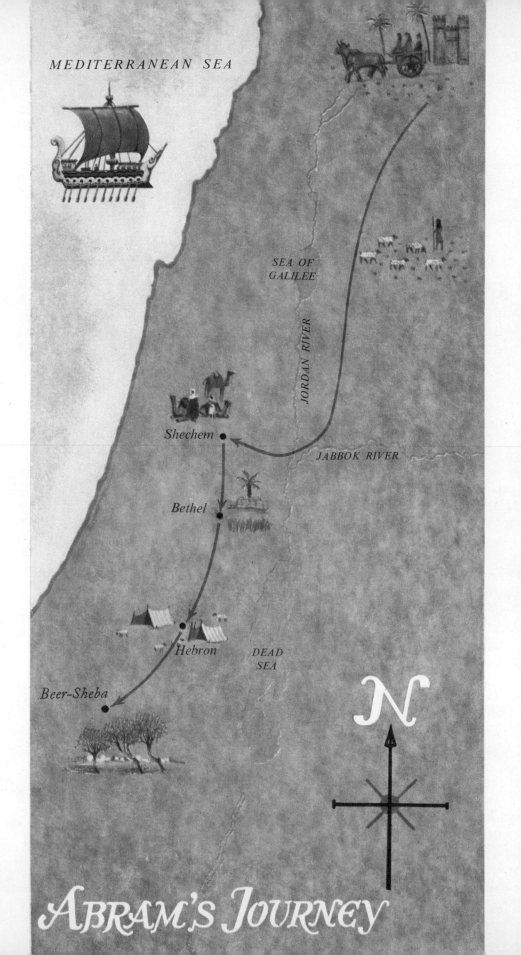

MEDITERRANEAN SEA

SEA OF
GALILEE

JORDAN RIVER

Shechem

JABBOK RIVER

Bethel

Hebron

DEAD
SEA

Beer-Sheba

N

ABRAM'S JOURNEY

ABRAM AND LOT

and they separated one from the other.

Abram lived in the land of Canaan and Lot lived in the cities of the plain and pitched his tent near Sodom.

And when Lot had departed, God said to Abram:

"Lift up your eyes now, and look northward, southward, eastward and westward. For all the land which you

 BRAM was very rich in cattle, in silver and in gold, and Lot who travelled with him was also very rich, having flocks and herds and tents. The land was not able to support them all; they could not live together in one place and there was trouble between the herdsmen of Abram and the herdsmen of Lot. There were Canaanites and Perizzites also living off the land, so Abram said to Lot:

"Let there be no trouble between you and me, nor between your men and my men, for we are relatives. Is not the whole land before you? Separate yourself, I beg you, from me. If you choose the left hand, I will go to the right. Or if you move to the right then I will go to the left."

Lot lifted his eyes and looked out over the whole plain of Jordan, and saw how well the land was watered everywhere. It was like the garden of the Lord and like parts of the land of Egypt.

So Lot chose for himself all the plain of Jordan. He went towards the east, see I will give to you and to your descendants for ever. And I will make your descendants as the dust of the earth, so that if anybody could count the dust of the earth, he would also be able to count your descendants.

"Arise, walk through the land, the length of it and the breadth of it, for to you I will give it all."

Then Abram moved his tent and went and dwelt in the plain of Mamre which is in Hebron, and there he built an altar to the Lord.

Soon afterward, there was war in the land and Lot and his possessions were captured and taken from Sodom. Abram rescued Lot and his goods and his people, and restored them.

"To your children and to all your children's children, I have given this land, from the river of Egypt to the Great River, the river Euphrates. All the people who dwell within it, I have delivered to you."

ABRAHAM IS NAMED

When Abram was ninety-nine years old, the Lord appeared to him and said:

"I am the Almighty God. Walk in my ways and be perfect. I will make my covenant with you, and your people shall increase greatly."

Abram knelt down, his face to the ground, and God talked to him, saying:

"My covenant I shall keep with you. No longer will you be called Abram; from you shall many be descended. Your name shall be Abraham for I have made you a father of many nations. I will keep my covenant with you and my covenant shall be everlasting with you and your descendants through all generations. Your line shall prosper and from it shall arise nations and kings. To you and to them I will give the land of Canaan, in which you are a stranger, as an everlasting possession, and I will be their God.

"As for Sarai, your wife, you shall call her no longer Sarai, but her name shall be Sarah. I will bless her, and from her you shall have a son. She shall be a mother of nations and of kings."

Abraham bowed down and laughed to himself, saying:

"Can a man a hundred years old have a son? And Sarah, a woman of ninety, can she have a child?"

Then God said:

"Sarah, your wife, shall bear a son, and you will call him by the name Isaac. With him and with his children after him will I make my everlasting covenant."

But the nation that shall oppress them I will judge, and afterwards they shall emerge with great possessions.

"You yourself shall go to your fathers in peace, and be buried in a good old age. Your children shall return here in the fourth generation."

When the sun was down and it was dark, behold, a smoking furnace and a burning lamp passed between the pieces of the offering.

And on that day God made a covenant with Abram, saying:

THE THREE ANGELS

And it came to pass that when Abraham was sitting in the door of his tent in the plains of Mamre, the Lord appeared to him in the form of three angels in the heat of the day. Abraham raised his eyes and saw three men standing before him. He ran to meet them and bowed to the ground, saying:

"My Lords, if I have now found favour in your sight, do not pass away, I beg you, from your servant. Let a little water be fetched and wash your feet and rest yourselves under the tree. I will bring bread to refresh you. Comfort your hearts, then you may go on your way."

They said to him: "Do as you have said." So Abraham hastened into the tent where Sarah his wife was and said:

"Quickly, make three measures of fine meal, knead it, and bake cakes upon the hearth."

Then he ran to the herd and fetched a good and tender calf, and

gave it to a young man to prepare.

Abraham then took butter and milk, and the calf, and set the food before the men. He stood by them under the tree while they ate.

"Where is Sarah, your wife?" they asked him.

"There, in her tent," he said.

And one of the men said, "Sarah your wife shall have a son."

Sarah, standing in the tent doorway behind him, heard this. She and Abraham were old and they were beyond the time for having children.

Sarah therefore laughed to herself.

Then God said to Abraham:

"Why did Sarah laugh, saying she is too old to have a child? Is there anything the Lord cannot do? At the appointed time, Sarah shall have a son."

Sarah denied that she had laughed, for she was afraid. But God said:

"No, you did laugh."

The Lord did as he had promised, and Sarah bore Abraham a son in his old age at the time chosen by God, and Abraham called the son Isaac, a name which means 'He will laugh.'

A WIFE FOR ISAAC

MANY years later, Abraham was very old and the Lord had blessed him in all things. One day Abraham said to the eldest servant of his house, who managed all that he had:

"Give me your hand, I pray you. I will make you swear by the Lord, the God of heaven and the God of earth, that you will not choose a wife for my son from the daughters of the Canaanites, among whom I dwell. But you will go to my country and there among my own people you will choose a wife for my son Isaac."

"What if the woman that is chosen will not be willing to follow me to this land?" said the servant. "Must I take your son back again to the land from which you came?"

Abraham said to him: "Beware, above all, that you do not take my son there again. The Lord God of heaven, who took me from my father's house and from the land of my people, made a covenant with me, and said to me: 'To your children will I give this land.'

"He shall send his angel before you, and you shall choose there a wife for my son. If the woman does not willingly follow you, then you shall be freed from your oath. Only do not take my son to that land."

So the servant gave his hand to Abraham, his master, and swore to do as he had been told.

ABRAHAM'S SERVANT DEPARTS

Then the servant took ten of his master's camels, for all the goods of his master were in his care, and he departed.

He went to Mesopotamia to the

city of Nahor. There he made his camels kneel down outside the city, beside a well of water, at the time of the evening when the women went out to draw water.

Then he prayed:

"O Lord, God of my master Abraham, I beg of you, send me good fortune today, and show kindness to my master, Abraham. Behold, I stand here by the spring, and the daughters of the men of the city are coming to draw water. Let it come to pass that the girl to whom I shall say: 'Let down your pitcher, so that I may drink,' and who will say to me: 'Drink! And I will give your camels a drink also,' let this girl be the wife you have chosen for your servant Isaac. By this I shall know that you have shown kindness to my master."

Before he had finished speaking a young girl appeared. She was Rebekah, whose father was the son of Nahor, Abraham's brother. She carried her pitcher upon her shoulder. The girl was very fair to look upon, young and unmarried.

She went down to the well, filled her pitcher, and came up.

REBEKAH AT THE WELL

Abraham's servant ran to meet her and said: "Let me drink a little water from your pitcher."

And she said: "Drink, my lord."

Then she quickly lowered the pitcher upon her hand and gave him a drink. When she had finished giving him a drink, she said: "I will draw water for your camels also, until they have finished drinking."

She hurried and emptied her pitcher into the trough, ran to the well to draw water, and drew it for all his camels. The man held his peace, wondering whether the Lord had made his journey successful or not.

As the camels had finished drinking, he took out a golden ear-ring of half a shekel weight and two bracelets for her hands, also of heavy gold. "Whose daughter are you?" he asked. "Tell me, I beg of you. Is there room in your father's house for me to spend the night?"

She said to him: "I am the daughter of Bethuel, the son of Milcah and Nahor. Of both straw and food we have enough, and also room to lodge in."

Then the man bowed down his head and worshipped the Lord, saying, "Blessed be the Lord, God of my master Abraham, who has not kept his mercy and his truth from my master. The Lord led me on the way to the house of my master's brother."

The girl ran on to her mother's house, and told these things.

LABAN, REBEKAH'S BROTHER

Now Rebekah had a brother, and his name was Laban. When he saw the ear-rings and the bracelets upon his sister's hands, and when he heard the words of Rebekah his sister, Laban ran out and found the servant of Abraham standing by the camels at the well.

Laban said:

"Come in, you whom the Lord has blessed. Why do you stand outside? For I have prepared the house, and there is room for the camels."

So the man came into the house, and Laban unharnessed the camels and gave them straw and feed. He brought water to wash the man's feet and the feet of the men who were with him.

They set meat before the man to eat, but he said: "I will not eat until I have told my errand."

"Speak on," said Laban.

The man said: "I am Abraham's servant. The Lord has blessed my master greatly, and he has become great. The Lord has given him flocks and herds, silver and gold, menservants and maidservants, camels and asses. And Sarah, my master's wife, bore a son to my master when she was old, and to him he has given all that he has."

Then the servant told how Abraham had sent him to find a wife for Isaac, and how the Lord had led him to Rebekah. "And now if you will deal kindly and truly with my master, tell me. If not, tell me also, so that I may know which way to turn."

Then Laban and Bethuel answered and said: "All this comes from the Lord. We cannot say anything to you, bad or good. Behold, Rebekah is here before you; take her and go. Let her be your master's son's wife, as the Lord has said."

When Abraham's servant heard their words, he worshipped the Lord, bowing himself to the earth. And he brought out jewels of silver and jewels of gold and clothing, and gave them to Rebekah. To her brother and her mother he also gave precious things.

They ate and drank, he and the men that were with him. They spent the night and rose up in the morning. Then he said: "Send me back to my master."

Rebekah's brother and her mother said: "Let the girl remain with us a few days, at least ten. After that she shall go with you."

"Do not hinder me," he said to them. "The Lord has made my errand successful. Send me away, that I may go to my master." "We will call the girl and ask her," they said.

They called Rebekah and said to her: "Will you go with this man?"

"I will go," she said.

So they sent away Rebekah their sister, and her nurse, and Abraham's servant, and his men. They blessed Rebekah, and Rebekah arose with her maidens, and they rode upon the camels and followed the man. And the servant took Rebekah and went his way.

ISAAC AND REBEKAH

Isaac went out of his dwelling in the south country to walk in the field, at the end of the day. He lifted his eyes and, behold, he saw the camels were coming.

Rebekah lifted her eyes and saw Isaac. She lighted from her camel and said to the servant: "Who is this man walking in the field towards us?"

"It is my master's son," said the servant.

Thereupon, she took a veil and covered herself. The servant told Isaac everything he had done. Then Isaac brought her into the tent of Sarah, his mother. Rebekah became his wife, and he loved her.

ESAU AND JACOB

L ATER when Isaac was three score years old, Rebekah bore him twin sons. The firstborn had red hair all over like a hairy coat. They called him Esau. His brother they called by the name of Jacob.

The boys grew. Esau became a cunning hunter, a man of the out-of-doors, but Jacob was a plain man, dwelling in tents. Isaac loved Esau, because he liked to eat his venison, but Rebekah loved Jacob.

One day Jacob was boiling a thick soup, when Esau came from the field. Esau was faint with hunger and said to Jacob:

"Feed me, I pray you, some of that good lentil soup, for I am faint."

"Sell me this very day your birthright," said Jacob. For Esau, being the elder, was to inherit their father's goods.

"I am at the point of death," said Esau. "What good will this birthright do me?"

But Jacob said, "Swear to me this day."

So Esau swore to him, and sold his birthright to Jacob. Then Jacob gave Esau bread and the lentil soup. Esau ate and drank, then he rose up and went his way.

Thus Esau threw away his birthright.

REBEKAH AND JACOB PLOT AGAINST ISAAC

When Isaac was old, his eyes became dim, so that he could see no longer. He called Esau, his elder son, and said to him:

"My son."

"Here I am," said Esau.

"Look now," said Isaac, "I am old, I do not know the day of my death. Take your weapons, your quiver and your bow, go out to the field and get me some venison. Make me savoury meat, such as I love, and bring it to me that I may eat, so that my soul may bless you before I die."

Now Rebekah was listening and heard what Isaac said to Esau, his son. Esau went to the field to hunt for the venison and to bring it home.

Then Rebekah spoke to Jacob her son, saying:

"Behold, I heard your father speak to Esau, your brother, saying, 'Bring me venison and make me savoury meat, that I may eat, and bless you before the Lord before my death.' Now, therefore my son, obey my voice and do as I command you.

"Go now to the flock and fetch me from it two good kids of the goats, and I will make them into savoury meat for your father, such as he loves. You shall take it to your father, that he may eat, and that he may bless you before his death."

Jacob said to Rebekah, his mother:

"Behold, Esau my brother is a hairy man, and I am a smooth man. Perhaps my father will feel me, and I shall seem a deceiver. I shall bring a curse upon myself, and not a blessing."

But his mother said to him:

"Upon me be the curse, my son. Only obey my voice and go and bring the kids to me that I may prepare them."

So he went and brought them to his

mother, and his mother made a savoury meat, such as his father loved.

Then Rebekah took the best robes of her elder son Esau, which were in the house, and put them upon Jacob her younger son. With the skins of the kids she covered his hands and the smooth of his neck.

Then she put into the hands of Jacob the savoury meat, and the bread she had prepared.

So Jacob went to Isaac and said: "My father."

And Isaac said: "Here I am. Who are you, my son?"

"I am Esau, your firstborn," Jacob said to his father. "I have done as you told me. Arise, I beg of you, sit up and eat of my venison, so that your soul may bless me."

But Isaac said to his son: "How is it that you found it so quickly, my son?"

"Because the Lord your God brought it to me," said Jacob.

Still Isaac said to Jacob:

"Come near, I beg of you, so that I may feel you, my son, and know whether you are really my son Esau or not."

Jacob went near to Isaac his father, and Isaac felt him and said:

"The voice is Jacob's voice, but the hands are the hands of Esau."

He did not recognize him, because his hands were hairy like the hands of Esau his brother, so he blessed him. Once more he said:

"Are you really my son Esau?"

"I am," said Jacob.

Then Isaac said: "Bring it near to me, and I will eat of my son's venison, that my soul may bless you."

Jacob brought the food close to him, and he ate. He brought him wine, and he drank.

Then Isaac said to him:

"Now, come near and kiss me, my son."

Jacob came near and kissed him. Isaac smelled the smell of his robe and blessed him, saying:

"See the smell of my son is as the smell of
a field which the Lord has blessed!

May God give you of the dew of heaven
and the fatness of the earth,
and plenty of corn and wine.

Let people serve you,
and nations bow down to you.

Be lord over your brothers,
and let your mother's sons bow down
to you.

May every one who curses you be cursed,
and blessed be those that bless you!"

Now it happened, as soon as Isaac had finished blessing Jacob, and when Jacob had scarcely left Isaac his father, that Esau his brother came in from his hunting. He also made savoury meat and brought it to his father.

"My father," he said, "please rise up and eat of your son's venison, so that your soul may bless me."

Then Isaac his father said to him: "Who are you?"

"I am your son, your firstborn, Esau."

Then Isaac trembled all over and said:

"Who is he then, he who prepared venison and brought it to me, and I ate of it before you came and have blessed him? Yes, and he shall be blessed."

ISAAC DISCOVERS THE PLOT

When Esau heard the words of his father, he cried out with a great and bitter cry, and said to his father:

"Bless me, even me, also, O my father!"

But Isaac said:

"Your brother came with cunning and has taken away your blessing."

Esau said:

"Is he not rightly named Jacob, for he has taken my place twice? He took away my birthright, and, behold, now he has taken away my blessing."

Then he said: "Have you not saved a blessing for me?"

Isaac answered and said to Esau:

"Now, I have made him lord over you, and all his brothers I have given to him for servants. I have provided him with corn and wine. What is there I can do for you, my son?"

Esau said to his father:

"Have you only one blessing, my father? Bless me also, O my father!"

Esau lifted up his voice and wept. Then Isaac his father answered and said to him:

"Behold, your dwelling shall be far from the
fatness of the earth,
and far from the dew of heaven from above.
By your sword shall you live,
and shall serve your brother;

Then, it shall come to pass when you shall
have power,
That you shall break his yoke from off your
neck!"

Therefore Esau hated Jacob, because of the blessing with which his father had blessed him, and Esau said in his heart: "The days of mourning for my father are near. Then I will slay my brother Jacob."

These words of Esau, Rebekah's elder son, were told her and she sent for Jacob, her younger son.

"Now your brother Esau," she said to him, "wants to be revenged upon you and kill you. Therefore, my son, obey my voice and rise, flee to Laban, my brother, at Haran. Stay with him a few days, until your brother's fury turns away from you and he forgets what you have done to him. I will send for you to come home again."

Isaac called Jacob, and blessed him. Then he commanded him, saying:

"You shall not take a wife among the daughters of Canaan. Arise, go to Padan-Aram, to the house of Bethuel, your mother's father, and take a wife there from among the daughters of Laban, your mother's brother. God Almighty bless you, that you may inherit the land where you are a stranger and which God gave to Abraham."

And Isaac sent Jacob away.

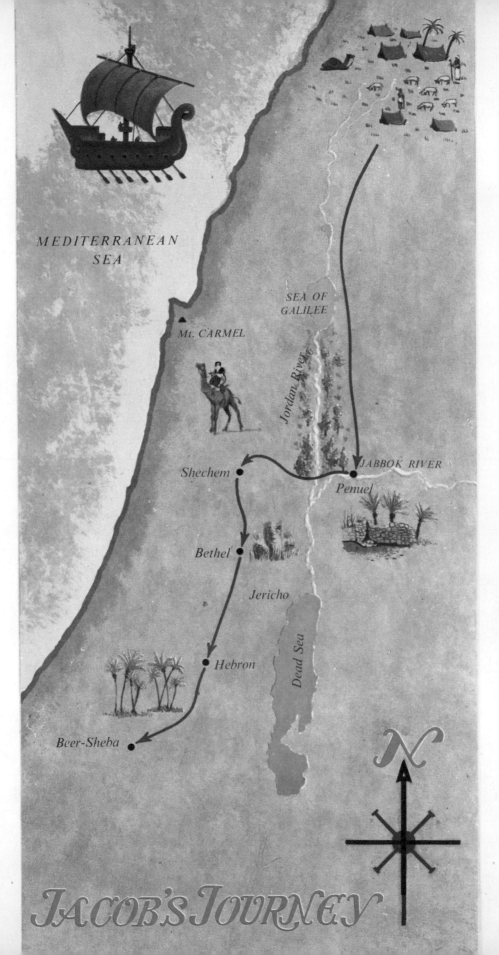

MEDITERRANEAN
SEA

Mt. CARMEL

SEA OF
GALILEE

Jordan River

JABBOK RIVER

Shechem

Penuel

Bethel

Jericho

Dead Sea

Hebron

Beer-Sheba

N

JACOB'S JOURNEY

JACOB'S FLIGHT AND DREAM

JACOB set out from Beersheba and started towards Haran. He came to a certain place and had to stay there all night, because the sun had set. Taking one of the stones from the ground, he placed it under his head for his pillow, and lay down in that place to sleep.

Jacob dreamed, and in his dream he saw a ladder set up on the ground, the top reaching to heaven, and, behold, angels of God were going up and down on it.

The Lord was standing above the ladder and he said to Jacob:

"I am the Lord God of Abraham, and the God of Isaac. The land on which you lie I will give to you and your children. Your children shall be as the dust of the earth and you will spread abroad to the west and to the east, to the north and to the south. Through you and your children all the families of the earth will be blessed.

"Behold, I am with you, and I will guard you everywhere you go, and will bring you back to this place. For I will not leave you until I have done everything I have promised."

Then Jacob waked out of his sleep and said:

"Surely the Lord is in this place, and I did not know it." He was afraid and said:

"This is surely the house of God, and this is the gate of heaven."

Early in the morning Jacob rose up,

took the stone that he had used as a pillow, set it up for a pillar and poured oil upon the top of it. He called the name of that place Bethel.

Then Jacob vowed a vow, saying:

"If God will be with me, and will guard me in the journey I am undertaking, and will give me bread to eat and clothes to wear, if I return again to my father's house in peace, then the Lord will be my God. This stone, which I have set up for a pillar, will be God's house, and of all that you give to me, O God, I will give a tenth to you."

JACOB AND RACHEL

ACOB went on his journey and came into the land of the people of the East. As he looked he saw a well in a field and three flocks of sheep lying by it. It was the well from which the flocks were watered and a great stone was upon its mouth. When all the flocks were gathered around it, the shepherds would roll the stone from the well's mouth, water the sheep, and then put the stone back upon the well's mouth.

Jacob said to the shepherds:

"My brothers, where are you from?"

"We are from Haran," they said.

"Do you know Laban, the son of Nahor?" he asked them.

They said:

"We know him."

"Is all well with him?" Jacob said.

They said, "All is well with him, and, see, there is Rachel, his daughter, coming with the sheep."

While they were talking. Rachel came with her father's sheep, for she looked after them. And when Jacob saw Rachel, the daughter of Laban, his mother's brother, and saw Laban's sheep, he rolled away the stone which covered the well's mouth and watered the flock of Laban.

Then Jacob kissed Rachel and lifted up his voice and wept. He told Rachel that he was her father's kin and Rebekah's son. And leaving the sheep, Rachel ran and told her father.

Laban hastened out to meet Jacob,

"Because you are my kin, should you work for me for nothing? Tell me, what shall your wages be?"

Now Laban had two daughters. The name of the elder was Leah, and the name of the younger was Rachel. Leah was plain, but Rachel was very beautiful and pleasing to look upon.

Jacob loved Rachel, so he said:

"I will work for you seven years if at the end of that time you give me Rachel, your younger daughter."

Then Laban said: "It is better that I give her to you than to any other man. Stay with me."

So Jacob served seven years for Rachel, and they seemed to him but a few days, because he loved her.

his sister's son, and embraced him, kissed him, and brought him to his house. Jacob told Laban all the things that had happened to him, and Laban said to him: "Surely you are my bone and flesh."

And when Jacob had stayed with him for a month, Laban said to him:

JACOB SEEKS TO LEAVE LABAN

At the end of the seven years, Jacob said to Laban:

"Give me my wife, for I have fulfilled our agreement." And Laban prepared a wedding feast. But that evening in the darkness, Laban brought Leah to Jacob, and he married her, believing she was Rachel. When Jacob discovered that he had been deceived, he said to Laban:

"What have you done to me? Did I not serve you for Rachel?"

Laban said:

"In our land it is not right to marry off the younger before the firstborn. But if you will promise to serve me yet seven years more, I will give you Rachel, too, as a wife."

So Jacob took Rachel as his wife also, as it was the custom in that time for a man to have more than one wife.

He served Laban seven more years. And he loved Rachel more than Leah.

Rachel did not bear any children and was unhappy. But Leah gave Jacob many sons. Then the Lord took pity on Rachel and allowed her to bear a son. And she named her son Joseph.

After twenty years with Laban, Jacob had prospered exceedingly. He had many cattle, and menservants and maidservants, and camels and asses. But he heard the words of Laban's sons, saying:

"Jacob has taken away all that was our father's, and from our father he has all his wealth."

Jacob also saw that Laban was not the same towards him as before. And the Lord said to him:

"Return unto the land of your fathers, to your own land, and I will be with you."

So Jacob called Rachel and Leah

JACOB AND RACHEL DEPART

And when the time came for him to leave, Jacob stole away secretly while Laban was shearing his sheep. He passed over the river, fleeing with all that he possessed, and set his face toward Mount Gilead. On the third day, Laban was told that Jacob had fled. He took his brothers with him, and pursued Jacob for seven days and overtook him on Mount Gilead.

But God came to Laban the Syrian in a dream by night and said to him:

"Take heed that you speak not to Jacob, neither good nor bad."

Jacob had pitched his tent on the mount and Laban and his brothers pitched their tents close by. Then Laban came to Jacob and said: "What have you done? Why did you steal away without my knowledge and carry away my daughters, like war captives? Why did you not tell me so that I could send you on your way with merriment, with tambourines and with harps? You did not allow me even to kiss my grandsons and daughters goodbye. In so doing, you have behaved foolishly. It is in my power to harm you, but the God of your father spoke to me last night, saying: 'Take heed not to speak to Jacob, good or bad.' Now if you left because you are longing to return to your father's house, why then have you stolen my family images?"

Jacob did not know that Rachel had stolen Laban's images, and he answered:

"Search the tents and whatever you may find belonging to you, take it. And if anyone has stolen your family images, let that one not live."

So Laban searched Jacob's tent and the servants' tents, but he did not find the images. Rachel had hidden the images in the trappings of her camel and was sitting upon them. Laban

to the field, where he was with his flock and said to them:

"I see from your father's face that he no longer regards me as he did, but the God of my fathers has been with me. And you know that I have served your father with all my power. Yet your father has cheated me and changed my wages ten times, but never has God allowed him to do me harm.

"The angel of God spoke to me in a dream and said: 'I am the God of Bethel where you anointed the pillar and where you vowed a vow to me. Now arise, go out from this country and return to your own land.' "

Rachel and Leah answered and said to him: "Whatever God has said to you, do."

So Jacob rose up and set his sons and his wives upon camels and he took all his cattle and all his goods, to return to Isaac his father in the land of Canaan.

searched her tent but did not find the images, and Rachel said to her father:

"Let it not displease you that I do not rise in your presence, but I am not feeling well today."

Then Jacob became angry and chided Laban, saying:

"What wrong have I done against you, what sin have I committed that you should pursue me? You have searched all my belongings, but what have you found that was yours? Let it be set down here before my brothers and your brothers and let them judge between us. For twenty years I have been with you: your ewes and your she-goats have done well, and never have I eaten a ram from your flocks. The heat consumed me during the day and the cold by night. Sleep departed from my eyes. I served you fourteen years for your two daughters, and six years more for your cattle, and you have changed my wages ten times.

"Had you not feared the God of my father, the God of Abraham and Isaac, surely you would have sent me away now empty-handed. God has seen my suffering and the labour of my hands, and he rebuked you last night."

Laban answered and said to Jacob:

"These daughters are my daughters, these children are my children, these cattle are my cattle, and all that you see is mine.

"What could I do against my daughters and the children they have borne? Therefore, come, let us make a covenant, and let it be for a witness between you and me."

JACOB AND LABAN MAKE A PACT

Jacob took a stone and set it up for a pillar. Then Jacob said to the men with him:

"Gather stones and make a heap."

They did so and there they ate, upon the heap. Then Laban said:

"Behold this heap and behold this pillar, which I have cast between me and you. This heap is a witness between us. I will not pass over this heap to you, and you shall not pass over this heap to harm me. The God of Abraham and the God of Nahor judge between us."

Jacob swore by the fear of his father Isaac. Then he offered sacrifice upon the mount and called his brethren to eat bread, and they ate and tarried all night on the mount.

Early in the morning Laban rose and kissed his sons and his daughters and blessed them. He departed and returned to his land.

JACOB SENDS MESSENGERS TO ESAU

Jacob went on his way and the angels of God met him.

When he saw them, Jacob said: "This is God's host."

Then Jacob sent messengers before him to Esau, his brother, in the country of Edom. He commanded them, saying: "Thus you shall speak to my lord Esau: 'Your servant Jacob wishes to say to him that he has stayed with Laban until now. He has oxen, asses, flocks, menservants and woman-servants. He is sending to tell this to my lord, that he may find grace in his sight.' "

Later, the messengers returned to Jacob, saying: "We went to your brother Esau, and he is coming to meet you, and four hundred men are with him."

Jacob was greatly afraid and was distressed. He divided into two camps the people that were with him, the flocks, the herds and the camels, saying: "If Esau should come upon one camp and smite it, then the other camp shall be able to escape."

Then Jacob said:

"Deliver me, I pray you, O God, from the hands of my brother, from the hands of Esau, for I fear him lest he will come and strike me, sparing neither mother nor children. Yet you have said to me: 'I will surely do you good, and make your race as the sand of the sea, which cannot be numbered because of its multitude.'"

Jacob spent the night there; then he took from his possessions at hand a present for Esau, his brother: twenty goats and two hundred she-goats, twenty rams and two hundred ewes, thirty milking camels and their young, ten bulls and forty cows, twenty asses and ten colts.

He delivered them to his servants, keeping each drove separate from others. Then he said to the first servant:

"When Esau, my brother, meets you and asks: 'To whom do you belong? Where are you going? And to whom belong these beasts before you?' you will answer: 'They belong to your servant Jacob. They are a present for my lord Esau, and, behold, your servant is behind us.'"

Jacob gave the same order to the second servant, then to the third one, and to all those that were walking behind the droves, saying:

"This is how you will speak to Esau when you meet him."

For Jacob thought:

"I will appease him with the gift that goes ahead of me, and later I will look at his face. Perhaps he will accept me."

The men left with the present, and Jacob spent that night in the camp.

During the night Jacob rose up and took his two wives and his two women servants, together with his eleven sons, and passed over the ford of Jabbok. He sent them over the brook, with everything he owned.

Then Jacob was left alone. All night long he wrestled with an angel. At daybreak the angel said:

"Your name shall no longer be called Jacob but Israel, for you have contended with God and prevailed."

JACOB AND ESAU ARE REUNITED

Jacob lifted up his eyes and, behold, Esau was coming, and with him were four hundred men. Jacob divided the children between Leah, Rachel and the two handmaids. He put the handmaids and their children foremost, Leah and her children came after, and Rachel and Joseph were last.

He went ahead of them and bowed himself to the ground seven times until he was near his brother. Esau ran to meet him, embraced him, and fell on his neck and kissed him, and they wept. Esau looked up and saw the women and the children.

"Who are those with you?" he said.

"Those are the children," Jacob said, "which God has graciously given your servant."

Then the handmaids came near, they and their children, and they bowed themselves. And then Joseph and Rachel came near, and they bowed themselves.

"What do you mean," Esau said, "by all this flock and cattle that I met?"

"These are to find grace in the sight of my lord," Jacob said.

"I have enough, my brother," Esau said. "Keep what is yours for yourself."

"No, I pray you," said Jacob, "if now I have found grace in your sight, then receive my present at my hand, for I have seen your face as

He urged him, and Esau took it and said:

"Let us go and start our journey. I will go before you."

"My lord knows," said Jacob, "that children are tender, and I have the care of ewes and milking cows with their young. Should they be overdriven, even one day, all the flocks will die.

"Let my lord, I pray, go ahead before his servant, and I will follow softly, in step with the cattle before me, and according to what the children are able to endure, until I come to my lord in Seir."

Esau said: "Then let me leave with you some of the men that are with me."

"What need is there?" said Jacob, "Just let me find grace in the sight of my lord."

So Esau departed that day on his way to Seir.

And Jacob went to Shalem, which is in the land of Canaan, and he pitched his tent outside of the city.

He bought the parcel of land, where he had spread his tent, for one hundred pieces of money. There he erected an altar, and called it El-elohe-Israel.

though I had seen the face of God, and you were pleased with me.

"Take, I pray you, the gift that was brought to you, because God has dealt graciously with me, and I have enough."

JOSEPH AND HIS BROTHERS

OW Jacob dwelt in the land where his father had been a stranger, in the land of Canaan. His son Joseph, now a strong and healthy lad, daily fed the flock with all his brothers, the sons of his father's wives. And Joseph brought his father an evil report of them.

Jacob loved Joseph more than all his sons, because he was the son of his old age, so he made for him a coat of many colours.

When his brothers saw that their father loved Joseph more than all his brothers, they hated him, and could not speak to him in a friendly way.

Joseph dreamed a dream and told it to his brothers, and they hated him all the more.

He said to them:

"Hear, now, this dream which I have dreamed. We were in the field binding sheaves, and, lo, my sheaf arose and stood upright, and your sheaves stood around about and bowed down to my sheaf."

Then his brothers said to him:

"Would you indeed be king over us? Would you really rule over us?"

They hated him all the more on account of his dreams, and on account of his words.

He dreamed another dream, and told it to his brothers:

"Behold, I have dreamed another dream," he said. "The sun, the moon

JOSEPH'S BROTHERS ARE ENVIOUS

His brothers were envious of him, but his father remembered the dream.

Now his brothers went to feed their father's flock in Shechem. And one day Jacob said to Joseph:

"Your brothers are feeding the flock in Shechem. Come, I will send you to them."

"Here I am," said Joseph.

"Go, then," said Jacob, "and see whether all is well with your brothers and the flocks, and bring me word again."

So he sent Joseph out of the valley of Hebron, and the boy arrived at Shechem. He was wandering in the field when a certain man found him and asked him:

"What are you looking for?"

"I am looking for my brothers," he said. "Can you tell me where they are feeding the flocks?"

"They went on from here," the man said, "for I heard them say, 'Let us go to Dothan.'"

So Joseph went after his brothers and found them in Dothan.

When they saw him far off, even before he came close to them, they plotted against him and wanted to slay him. They said to one another:

"Behold, here comes the dreamer. Come, now, let us kill him and throw him into a pit. We will say some wild beast has devoured him. Then we shall see what will become of his dreams."

But Reuben heard this, and he said:

"Let us not kill him. Shed no blood. Throw him into this pit here in the wilderness, but do not lay hands on him."

He planned to save Joseph from their hands and to deliver him to his father again.

and the eleven stars bowed down to me."

He told the dream to his father, and his father rebuked him, saying:

"What is this dream you have dreamed? Shall your mother and I and your brothers really come to bow ourselves down to the earth before you?"

JOSEPH IS THROWN INTO THE PIT

So it happened that when Joseph came up to his brothers, they stripped Joseph out of his coat, the coat of many colours which he was wearing. Then they took him and threw him into the pit. The pit was empty and there was no water in it.

Then they sat down to eat bread, but when they lifted their eyes, behold, they saw a caravan of Ishmaelites arriving from Gilead, their camels loaded with spices, balm and myrrh which they were carrying down to Egypt.

Then Judah said to his brothers:

"What will we gain if we kill our brother and conceal his blood? Come, let us sell him to the Ishmaelites, and let us not touch him, for he is our brother and our flesh."

This satisfied the brothers. They lifted Joseph out of the pit and sold him to the Ishmaelites for twenty pieces of silver, and the merchants took Joseph to Egypt.

When Reuben returned to the pit, behold, Joseph was no longer in the pit. Reuben tore his clothes in grief.

Then he went to his brothers and said: "The child is not there, and I, where shall I go?"

The brothers took Joseph's coat, killed a young goat, and dipped the coat in the blood. Then they brought the coat of many colours to their father, saying: "We found this. Do you know whether or not it is your son's coat?"

He recognized it and said:

"It is my son's coat. A wild beast has devoured him. Joseph has been torn in pieces."

Then Jacob tore his clothes in grief, and put on sackcloth and mourned for his son many days. All his sons and all his daughters rose up to comfort him, but he refused to be comforted, and said: "I will go down to the grave, mourning for my son."

Thus his father wept for him.

MEDITERRANEAN SEA

Dothan
Shechem

Nile Delta

On
(Cairo)

Memphis

JOSEPH'S
JOURNEY

Red   Sea

N

JOSEPH IN EGYPT

JOSEPH was brought down to Egypt, and Potiphar, who was an officer of Pharaoh and captain of the guard, bought him from the Ishmaelites.

The Lord was with Joseph, and he became a favoured servant, living in the house of his Egyptian master. His master saw that the Lord was with him, and that the Lord made all that he did prosper in his hands. Joseph found grace in his master's sight and he was made overseer in his house, and all that his master had he put in Joseph's hands.

The Lord blessed the Egyptian's house for Joseph's sake, and the blessing of the Lord was upon all that he had in the house and in the field. So Potiphar left all that he had to Joseph's hands, and he did not even know what he owned, except the bread he ate.

Now Joseph was a handsome young lad, and when he grew up his master's wife cast her eyes upon Joseph and loved him. But he would not love her, and said to her:

"Behold, my master does not even know what is in his house. He entrusted all that he has to my hand. There is none greater in this house than I. Neither has he kept back anything from me but you, because you are his wife. How then could I love you and do this great wickedness, and sin against God?"

Then she went to Joseph's master, and told lies about Joseph, saying:

"The Hebrew servant, whom you have brought to us, came into the house to mock me, and he fled as I lifted my voice and cried."

When the master heard the words of his wife, he was angry and he took Joseph and put him in prison, where the king's prisoners were kept, and there he stayed.

But the Lord was with Joseph and

showed him mercy, and made the keeper of the prison think well of him. So the keeper of the prison put all the prisoners that were in the prison into Joseph's hands, and whatsoever they did there, he was in charge of them.

The keeper of the prison paid no attention to anything that Joseph did, because the Lord was with Joseph, and whatever he did, the Lord made it prosper.

THE TWO DREAMS

Some time later, it happened that the butler of the king of Egypt and his baker offended their Lord Pharaoh, the king of Egypt. In his anger, Pharaoh put them into the house of the captain of the guard, into the prison where Joseph was held. The captain of the guard turned them over to Joseph and he looked after them. They stayed in prison for some time.

Now one night, both the butler and the baker of the King of Egypt dreamed a dream, each of them a different dream. When Joseph came to them in the morning and looked upon them, he saw that they were sad, he said to the men:

"Why do you look so sad today?"

"We have dreamed a dream," they said to him, "and there is no one to interpret it for us."

"Interpretations come from God," Joseph said to them. "Tell me your dreams."

So the chief butler told his dream to Joseph.

"In my dream," he said, "a vine was before me, and on the vine were three branches. It seemed as though it budded and the blossoms shot forth and the clusters grew into ripe grapes. Pharaoh's cup was in my hand. So I took the grapes and pressed them into Pharaoh's cup, and I placed the cup into the hand of Pharaoh."

Joseph said to him:

"This is the interpretation of your dream: The three branches are three days. Within three days Pharaoh will lift your head, he will restore you to your place, and you will place Pharaoh's cup into his hand, as you used to do when you were his butler.

"Only think of me and it shall be well with you, and be kind to me, I beg of you, and mention me to Pharaoh, and get me out of this place. For indeed I was stolen away from the land of the Hebrews, and I have done nothing here to deserve this dungeon."

THE BAKER'S DREAM

When the chief baker saw that the interpretation was good, he said to Joseph:

"I also had a dream and, behold, I had three baskets of white bread on my head. In the uppermost basket there were all kinds of baked goods for Pharaoh, and the birds ate them out of the basket upon my head."

Joseph answered him and said:

"This is the interpretation of your dream: The three baskets are three days. Within three days Pharaoh will call you and hang you on a tree, and the birds will eat your flesh."

On the third day, which was his birthday, Pharaoh made a feast for all the servants. He called for the butler and the chief baker among his servants. Then he returned the chief butler to the butlership again, and the butler gave the cup to Pharaoh. But Pharaoh hanged the chief baker, as Joseph had said.

Yet the chief butler did not remember Joseph but forgot him.

PHARAOH'S DREAMS

WO full years went by, and then it happened one night that Pharaoh dreamed. He stood by the river and, behold, seven fine, fat cows came out of the Nile and they fed in the meadow. Then, behold, seven other cows, thin and scrawny, came up after them out of the Nile and stood by the other cows upon the brink of the river, and the thin and scrawny cows ate up the seven fat and handsome cows. Then Pharaoh awoke.

He slept again and dreamed a second dream. Seven ears of corn came up on one stalk. They were hardy and good and, behold, seven ears, undersized and blasted by the east wind, sprang up after them, and the seven undersized ears swallowed the seven hardy and full ears. Pharaoh awoke and knew it was a dream.

On the next morning, his spirit was disturbed. He sent and called for all the magicians of Egypt, and the wise men of the land. Pharaoh told them his dreams, but there was no one who could interpret them to Pharaoh.

And then the chief butler spoke to Pharaoh, saying:

"Now I remember my faults. Pharaoh was angry with his servants and put me into the prison of the captain of the guard, both me and the chief baker. One night we each had a dream, he and I, each a different dream. There was in the prison with us a young man, a Hebrew, servant to the captain of the guard. We told him our dreams and he interpreted them to us, giving to each of us the meaning of our dreams. And everything happened as he told us, so it did. I was restored to my office, and the baker was hanged."

Then Pharaoh sent for Joseph. They brought him hastily out of the dungeon. He shaved himself, changed his clothing, and came to Pharaoh.

Pharaoh said to Joseph:

"I have had a dream and there is no one that can interpret it. I have heard it said that you can understand a dream and tell its meaning."

Joseph answered Pharaoh, saying:

"It is not in my power. God shall give Pharaoh an answer."

PHARAOH TELLS JOSEPH HIS DREAMS

So Pharaoh said to Joseph:

"In my dream, behold, I stood upon the bank of the Nile, and there came out of the river seven cows, fat and handsome, and they fed in the meadow but, behold, seven other cows came up after them, thin and scrawny, such as I never saw in the land of Egypt for badness. The lean and scrawny cows ate the first seven cows, the fat ones, and when they had eaten them, they still appeared the same. They remained thin and scrawny as in the beginning. So I awoke.

"In my other dream I saw, behold, seven ears of corn come up on one stalk. They were full and good. Then, behold, seven ears, withered, thin and blasted with the east wind, sprung up after them. The thin ears devoured the seven good ears. I told these dreams to the magicians, but they could not interpret them for me."

Joseph said to Pharaoh:

"The two dreams of Pharaoh are one. God has shown Pharaoh what he is about to do.

"The seven good cows are seven years, and the seven good ears are seven years: the dream is the same. The seven thin and scrawny cows that came after are seven years, and the seven empty ears, blasted with the east wind, will be seven years of famine.

"This is the meaning of what I have told Pharaoh: What God is about to do, he is showing to Pharaoh. Behold, there will be seven years of great plenty throughout the whole land of Egypt. And after them will come seven years of famine. All the plenty shall be forgotten in the land of Egypt, and the famine shall consume the land. The plenty will no longer be remembered in the land because of the famine that will follow, for it shall be great.

"The dream was sent to Pharaoh twice because this thing has been decided by God, and God will make it happen soon.

"Now, therefore, let Pharaoh search for a man wise and discreet, and make him a governor over the land of Egypt. Let Pharaoh do this and let him appoint officers over the land, and gather up a fifth of the harvest of the land in the seven years of plenty.

"Let them gather all the food of those good years that come, and lay up corn under the order of Pharaoh, and keep it in the cities. And that food shall be stored for the land to draw on during the seven years of famine which shall come later in the land of Egypt, so that the land may not perish through famine."

The plan seemed good in the eyes of Pharaoh, and in the eyes of all his servants. Pharaoh said to his servants:

"Can we find such a man, a man in whom there is, as in this one, the spirit of God?"

PHARAOH REWARDS JOSEPH

Then Pharaoh said to Joseph:

"Inasmuch as God has shown you all this, there is no one as wise and as discreet as you are. You shall be in charge of my house, and all my people will be ruled according to your word. Only on the throne itself will I be greater than you." Then Pharaoh said to Joseph: "See, I have set you over all the land of Egypt."

Pharaoh took off the ring from his hand and put it upon Joseph's hand. He dressed him in robes of fine linen and put a gold chain around his neck. He made him ride in the second royal chariot, and people cried before him: "Bow the knee!" So Pharaoh made him ruler over all the land of Egypt, and he said to Joseph:

"I am Pharaoh, and without you no man shall lift up his hand or foot in all the land of Egypt. Then Pharaoh gave Joseph the Egyptian name of Zaphnath-paaneah and he gave him for his wife Asenath, the daughter of Potipherah, priest of On.

JOSEPH HAS SONS:
MANASSEH AND EPHRAIM

Joseph was thirty years old when he stood before Pharaoh, king of Egypt. Then Joseph left Pharaoh, and went all over the land of Egypt. In the seven years of plenty, the earth brought forth food in abundance. So during those seven years when plenty

prevailed in the land, Joseph gathered up food and stored the food in the cities. In the same way, he stored up the food of the fields which closely surrounded the cities.

Joseph gathered grain in quantities as great as the sand of the sea: so much that he stopped counting, for it was without number.

Asenath the daughter of Potipherah, priest of On, gave Joseph two sons before the years of famine.

Joseph called the first Manasseh: "Because God," he said, "has made me forget all my suffering, and all my father's house."

And the name of the second was Ephraim: "Because God has made me

fruitful in the land of my affliction."

Then the seven years of plenty in the land of Egypt were ended, and the seven years of poverty began, just as Joseph had said. Famine was in all lands, but in all the land of Egypt there was bread. Then the land of Egypt was famished, and the people cried to Pharaoh for bread and he said to all the Egyptians:

"Go to Joseph, and do as he tells you."

The famine spread all over the face of the earth and Joseph opened all the storehouses and sold food to the Egyptians. The famine was severe in Egypt, but the famine was so severe in other lands that people from all countries came to Egypt to buy food from Joseph.

JOSEPH'S BROTHERS IN EGYPT

 ACOB heard that there was grain in Egypt and he said to his sons:

"Why do you sit and look at one another? I have heard that there is grain in Egypt. Go down and buy some for us there, so that we may live and not die."

So Joseph's ten brothers set out to buy grain in Egypt. But Benjamin, Joseph's youngest brother, did not go with them, 'for harm might befall him,' said Jacob.

So, among the crowds that came to buy grain, came the sons of Jacob, for the famine was in the land of Canaan. Now Joseph was governor of the land. He sold grain to all the people of the land. Joseph's brothers came to him and bowed themselves before him with their faces to the earth.

When Joseph saw his brothers, he recognized them, but he acted as a stranger toward them and he spoke roughly to them, saying:

"Where did you come from?"

"From the land of Canaan to buy food," they said.

Joseph's brothers did not know him, but he remembered the dreams he had dreamed of them, and he said to them:

"You are spies. It is to find out the secret of this land that you have come."

"No, my lord," they said to him, "your servants have come only to buy food. We are true men; your servants are not spies."

And Joseph said to them:

"No, you have come to find out the secrets of the land."

"We are twelve brothers," they said, "the sons of one man in the land of Canaan. The youngest one is with our father now, and one is no more."

But Joseph said again:

"It is just as I said: You are spies. This shall be the proof: By the life of Pharaoh, you shall not go out of here unless your youngest brother comes to this place. Send one of you and let him fetch your brother, and you shall be kept in prison so that it may be proved whether there is any truth in your words. Or else, by the

life of Pharaoh, surely you are spies."

And he put them all together under guard for three days.

The third day Joseph said to them:

"Do this and save your lives, for I am a God-fearing man. If you are true men, let one of you stay bound in the prison where you are kept. The rest of you take grain to feed the hungry in your houses. But bring your brother to me, the youngest one, so that your words are proven, and you shall not die."

And they did so, saying to one another: "Truly we are guilty about our brother, for we saw the anguish of his soul when he pleaded with us, and we would not listen. That is why this distress has come upon us."

And Reuben answered them:

"Did I not tell you: Do not sin against the child? But you would not listen and now we must settle for his blood."

They did not know that Joseph understood them, for he spoke to them through an interpreter. Joseph turned away from them and wept. Then he returned and spoke to them. He took Simeon from them and bound him before their eyes.

Then Joseph ordered servants to fill their sacks with grain, to put every man's money back into his sack, and to give them provisions for the journey. That was how he treated them.

THE BROTHERS RETURN HOME

So they loaded their asses with the grain and started home. But when they stopped at an inn and one of them opened his sack to feed his ass, he spied his money in the mouth of his sack.

"My money is back in my sack!" he said to his brothers.

Their hearts failed them and they were afraid, saying to one another:

"What is this that God has done to us?"

They came home to Jacob, their father, in the land of Canaan, and told him all that had happened.

"The man, who is the lord of the land, treated us harshly and took us for spies, but we said to him: 'We are true men; we are not spies. We were twelve brothers. One is no longer, and the youngest is with our father in the land of Canaan.' Then the man who is the lord of the land said to us:

" 'I will know if you are true men. Leave one of your brothers here with me and take food to feed the hungry in your houses, and be gone. Then bring your brother to me, the youngest, and I shall know that you are not spies but true men. Then I will deliver your brother and you shall trade in the land.' "

Now when they emptied their sacks, behold, every man found his bundle of money in his sack. And when both they and their father saw the bundles of money, they were afraid. Jacob said to them:

"You have taken away my children from me. Joseph is no more, and Simeon is no more, and now you want to take Benjamin away. All these things are against me."

Reuben said to his father:

"You may kill my two sons if I do not bring Benjamin back to you. Put him into my hands, and I will bring him to you again."

But Jacob said: "My son shall not go down with you, for his brother is dead, and he alone is left. If harm should come to him on the journey, you would bring down my grey hairs with sorrow to the grave."

BENJAMIN GOES TO EGYPT

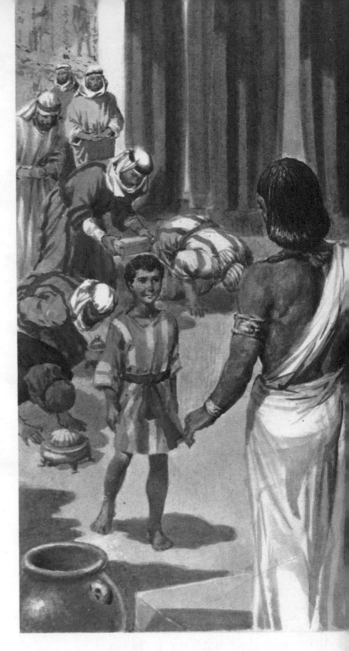

The famine continued in the land. And the time came when Jacob and his sons had eaten up the grain which they had brought from Egypt, and their father said to them:

"Go again, buy us a little food."

But Judah told him:

"If you will send our brother with us, we will go down and buy you food, but if you will not send him, we will not go down, for the man said to us: 'You shall not see my face unless your brother is with you.'"

"Why did you deal so badly with me as to tell the man you had another brother?" asked Jacob.

And they explained:

"The man asked many questions about ourselves and about our family, saying: 'Is your father still alive? Have you another brother?' We answered according to his questions. How could we know that he would say: 'Bring to me your brother?'"

Then Judah said to his father Jacob:

"Send the lad with me, and we shall arise and go, so that we may live and not die, we and you and all our little ones.

"I will be responsible for him, and you may demand him of me. If I do not bring him to you and set him before you, then let me bear the blame forever. If we had not lingered so long surely we would already have been back a second time?"

Their father said to them:

"If it must be so now, do this: Take some of the best fruits of the land in your sacks and carry down to the man presents, a little balm, and a little honey, spices and myrrh, nuts and almonds. Take twice the money in your hands. In this way you will be able to give back the money that was in the mouths of your sacks. It may be that it was an oversight.

"Take also your brother, and go again to the man. May God Almighty grant you mercy from the man, so that he may send home Benjamin and your other brother Simeon. For if I must grieve for my children, it is bitter grief indeed."

And the men took presents, and they took double money in their hand. They took also Benjamin and started off and went down to Egypt. They came and stood before Joseph.

THE BROTHERS ARE TAKEN TO JOSEPH'S HOUSE

Joseph saw Benjamin with them, and he said to the ruler of his house:

"Take these men home, kill some meat, and make it ready, for these men will dine with me at noon."

The servant did as Joseph told him, and took the brothers to Joseph's house.

The men were afraid when they were brought into Joseph's house, and they said: "It is because of the money that was returned in our sacks the first time that we have been brought here, so that he may find fault with us, and fall upon us, and take us for slaves, and seize our asses."

So they approached the steward of Joseph's house, and they spoke to him in the doorway.

"O Sir," they said, "truly we came down the first time only to buy food, but when we went back and opened our sacks, behold, every man's money was in the mouth of his sack, our money in full amount, so we have brought it back with us.

"We have brought other money, too, to buy food. We do not know who put the money in our sacks."

"Peace be with you," said the steward. "Fear not. Your God, the God of your father, gave you the treasure in your sacks. I received your money."

Then he brought Simeon out to them.

The man took the brothers into Joseph's house, and he gave them water to wash their feet, and he gave food to their asses. Meanwhile they prepared the presents to give to Joseph when he came in at noon, for they had been told that they were to eat there.

When Joseph came home, they gave to him the presents which they had brought into the house, and they bowed themselves down to the earth before him.

He asked them how they were, and said: "Is your father well, the old man of whom you spoke? Is he still alive?"

"Your servant, our father, is in good health," they answered. "He is still alive."

And they bowed down their heads respectfully.

Lifting up his eyes, Joseph saw his brother Benjamin, his own mother's son, and he said:

"Is this the youngest brother of whom you told me?" Then he said: "God be gracious to you, my son."

Then Joseph hurried away, for his heart yearned for his brother, and he sought a place to weep. He went into his room and he wept there. Then he washed his face and calmed himself and went out and said: "Serve the food."

JOSEPH DINES WITH HIS BROTHERS

The servants served him separately and the brothers by themselves, and the Egyptians, who ate also by themselves, because the Egyptians could not eat bread with the Hebrews, for that was against the laws of the Egyptians.

The brothers sat before Joseph in order, from the first-born according to his birthright down to the youngest according to his youth. The men looked at one another in wonderment.

Joseph sent servings to them from his table, and Benjamin's serving was five times as much as any of the others.

They drank and were merry with him.

Then Joseph gave orders to the steward of his house, saying:

"Fill the men's sacks with food as much as they can carry, and put every man's money in his sack's mouth. And put my cup, the silver cup, in the mouth of the sack of the youngest, with his grain money."

The steward did everything Joseph had told him.

As soon as the morning was light, the men were sent away, they and their asses. When they had left the city, but were not yet far off, Joseph said to his steward:

"Up, follow the men! When you have overtaken them, say to them: 'Why have you returned evil for good? Is not this the cup from which my lord drinks, and which he uses in making prophecies? In doing this you have done evil!' "

The steward overtook them, and he spoke to them in the words of Joseph. But they said to him:

"Why does my lord say these things? God forbid that your servant should do anything like this. Behold, the money we found in our sacks' mouths, we brought back to you from the land of Canaan. Why then would we steal silver or gold out of your lord's house?

"Let whoever among us is found to have this object die, and the rest of us will be your lord's slaves."

The steward said:

"Let it be as you say. He who is found to have it shall be my slave, but the rest of you shall be blameless."

Then each man speedily put down his sack on the ground, and each man opened his sack. The steward searched, beginning with the eldest and finishing

with the youngest, and the cup was found in Benjamin's sack.

Joseph's brothers tore their clothes in grief; then each man loaded his ass again and they returned to the city.

Judah and his brothers came to Joseph's house and found him there. They fell down before him on the ground. Joseph said to them:

"What is this that you have done? Do you not know that a man like me can see through these things?"

"What shall we say to my lord?" answered Judah. "How shall we speak and how shall we clear ourselves? God has found out the wickedness of your servants. Behold, we shall be my lord's slaves, all of us as well as he in whose sack the cup was found."

"God forbid that I should demand that," Joseph said. "The man in whose hand the cup was found, he shall be my slave. As for the rest of you, go in peace to your father."

JUDAH PLEADS WITH JOSEPH

Then Judah came closer to him and said: "Oh, my lord, I beg of you, let your servant speak a word in my lord's ear, and do not let your anger burn against your servant, even though you are as powerful as Pharaoh.

"My lord asked his servants: 'Have you a father or a brother?' And we said to my lord: 'We have a father, an old man, and in his old age he had a child, a little boy whose brother is dead, and he alone is left of his mother. His father loves him.'

"Then you said to your servants: 'Bring him down to me, that I may have a look at him.' We said to my lord: 'The lad cannot leave his father, for if he should leave his father, his father would die.' You said to your servants: 'Unless your youngest brother comes down with you, you will not see my face again!'

83

"So when we came up to your servant, my father, we told him your words. And our father said: 'Go again, and buy us a little food.' We said: 'We cannot go. Only if our youngest brother is with us can we go, for we may not see the man's face if our youngest brother is not with us.'

"And your servant, my father, said to us: 'You know that my wife bore me two sons. One I lost and surely he was torn to pieces. I have not seen him since. If you take this one from me too, and any harm befalls him, you will bring down my grey hairs with sorrow to the grave.'

"Now, therefore, when I come to your servant, my father, and he sees the lad is not with us, his life being bound up with the lad's life, he shall surely die, and your servants will have brought down their father to the grave with sorrow.

"For your servant took upon him responsibility for the lad, saying, 'If I do not bring him back to you, then I shall bear the blame forever.'

"Now therefore, I beg of you, let your servant stay instead of the lad, a slave to my lord. And let the lad go home with his brothers. For how shall I go up to my father if the lad is not with me, and see the grief that would come upon my father?"

JOSEPH REVEALS WHO HE IS

Then Joseph could not restrain himself before all of them that stood around him. He cried:

"Let everyone leave me!" So the Egyptians departed, and Joseph made himself known to his brothers. But he wept aloud, and the Egyptians and Pharaoh's household heard.

Joseph said to his brothers: "I am Joseph. Is my father still alive?"

His brothers could not answer him, for they were all overcome with fear.

Joseph said to his brothers:

"Come close to me, I beg you."

They came near, and he said: "I am Joseph, your brother, whom you sold into Egypt. Now do not grieve nor be angry with yourselves because you sold me here, for God sent me here ahead of you, to save your lives.

"For two years now the famine has been in the land, and there are five more years to come in which there shall be neither tilling nor harvest. God sent me here ahead of you to preserve your families on the earth and to save your lives. Therefore it was not really you that sent me here, but God, and he has made me an adviser to Pharaoh, and lord of his household, and a ruler throughout the land of Egypt.

"Hurry now, and go up to my father, and you will say to him: 'Your son Joseph says: God has made me lord of all Egypt. Come down to me without delay. You shall dwell in the land of Goshen, where you shall be near me, you, your children, and your children's children, your flocks and your herds, and all you own. And I will nourish you here, for there are still five years of famine to come, and you and your household would know poverty otherwise.'

"Now your eyes and the eyes of my brother, Benjamin, can see that it is really I who speak to you. You are to tell my father of all my glory in Egypt, and of all you have seen. Go and hurry, and bring my father down here."

He embraced Benjamin, his brother, and he wept, and Benjamin wept. Then he kissed all his brothers and wept with them, and after that his brothers talked with him.

PHARAOH'S INVITATION

EWS of the event was heard in Pharaoh's house. "Joseph's brothers have come." This pleased Pharaoh well, and his servants were pleased.

Pharaoh said to Joseph:

"Say to your brothers: 'Load your beasts, and go, hurry up to the land of Canaan. Get your father and your households and come to me, and I will give you the best of the land of Egypt, and you shall eat of the fat of the land.' And give these orders: 'Take wagons up from Egypt for your little ones and your wives, and bring your father and come back. Do not bring with you your goods, for the best of all the land of Egypt shall be yours.'"

Therefore Joseph gave his brothers wagons, and gave them provisions for the journey. To each of them he gave changes of clothes, but to Benjamin he gave three hundred pieces of silver and five changes of clothes. To his father he sent these gifts: ten asses loaded with the good things of Egypt, and ten she-asses loaded with corn and bread and meat for his provisions on the journey.

Then he sent his brothers away, and they left. He said to them, "See that you do not have any trouble on the way and do not quarrel."

They went up out of Egypt and

came to the land of Canaan to Jacob their father. They told him all, saying:

"Joseph is still alive! He is the governor over the land of Egypt."

Jacob's heart grew faint, for he could not believe it. But they told him every word Joseph had said to them, and when he saw the wagons which Joseph had sent to carry him, the spirit of Jacob revived. He said:

"It is enough that Joseph my son is still alive. I will go up and see him before I die."

JACOB'S DREAM

JACOB then left for Beer-sheba with everything he owned, and offered sacrifices to the God of his father Isaac.

God spoke to him at night in a dream, saying:

"Jacob, Jacob."

"Here I am," said Jacob.

God said:

"I am the God of your father. Do not fear to go down into Egypt, for I will establish you there as a great nation. I will go down with you into Egypt, and I will surely bring you up again. Joseph shall put his hand upon your eyes."

Jacob departed from Beer-sheba, and his sons carried their father, their little ones and their wives in the wagons which the Pharaoh had sent to carry them. They took their cattle and the goods which they had acquired in the land of Canaan. And so Jacob came into Egypt, and all his kindred with him: his sons and the sons of his sons, his daughters and his sons' daughters. All of them he brought with him into Egypt.

JACOB IN EGYPT

JACOB came into the land of Goshen. And Joseph made ready his chariot and went up to meet his father. He presented himself to him, and he fell on his neck, and he wept on his neck a good while. Jacob said to Joseph:

"Now I may die, since I have seen your face and know you are still alive."

Joseph took five of his brothers and presented them to Pharaoh. And Pharaoh spoke to them saying:

"What is your occupation?" And they answered, "We are shepherds We pray you, on account of the famine in Canaan, to let us dwell in Goshen." Then Pharaoh turned to Joseph and said: "Your father and your brothers have come to you. The land of Egypt is before you. Have your father and your brothers dwell in the best part of the land of Goshen. If you know any men of great value among them, make them overseers of the cattle that belong to me."

Then Joseph brought in Jacob, his father, and set him before Pharaoh. And Jacob blessed Pharaoh.

THE FAMINE

 JOSEPH placed his father and his brothers in the best of the land, in the land of Rameses, as Pharaoh had ordered. Joseph provided his father, his brothers and all his father's household with bread, according to the size of the families.

Now the famine was everywhere very great. Both Egypt and the land of Canaan were exhausted by it. So Joseph gathered from the people all the money that was in the land of Egypt and in the land of Canaan in exchange for the grain that he sold them. Joseph brought the money into Pharaoh's house.

When the money failed in the land of Egypt and in the land of Canaan, all the Egyptians came to Joseph, saying:

"Give us bread! Must we die before your eyes because the money has lost its value?"

Joseph said: "Give your cattle, and I will give you bread for your cattle."

So they brought their cattle and Joseph gave them bread in exchange for horses, flocks and herds, and for asses.

During that year, he fed them with bread in exchange for their cattle. When the year was ended, they came to him the second year, saying to him:

"We will not hide from my lord that, since our money is gone and my lord has our herds of cattle, there is nothing left in the sight of my lord, except our bodies and our land. Why should we die before your eyes, both we and our land?

"Buy us and our land for bread, and we may live and not die and that our land may not be barren."

So Joseph bought all the land of Egypt for Pharaoh. Every Egyptian sold his field, for the famine prevailed over them, and all the land became the

land. When the harvest time comes, you will give the fifth part of the harvest to Pharaoh, and four parts shall be your own for seed for the field and for your food and the food of your little ones."

"You have saved our lives," they said.

"Let us find grace in the sight of my lord, and we will be the servants of Pharaoh."

Joseph made it a law over the land of Egypt that Pharaoh should have the fifth part from the harvest of the land, except from the land of the priests.

property of Pharaoh. The people he removed to cities from one end of the border of Egypt to the other.

Only the priests kept their lands, for Pharaoh had assigned them a portion of food, and they lived on the portion Pharaoh had given them.

The priests therefore did not sell their lands.

And Joseph said to the people:

"Now, I have bought you and your land for Pharaoh. So, here is seed for you, and you shall sow the

Jacob lived in the land of Egypt for seventeen years, until he became a very old man. And when he was about to die, he called his son Joseph and said:

"If I have found grace in your sight, deal kindly and truly with me. Do not bury me in Egypt, I pray you. Let me lie with my fathers. Carry me out of Egypt and bury me in their burying place.

"Bury me where they buried Abraham and Sarah his wife, where they buried Isaac and Rebekah his wife, and where I buried Leah."

Joseph said:

"I will do as you have said."

"Swear to do as I wish," said Jacob.

Joseph swore to him, and Jacob bowed himself upon the bed's head. Then he said to Joseph:

"Behold, I will die soon! But God shall be with you and will bring you again to the land of your fathers."

Then Jacob called his twelve sons and said:

"Gather yourselves together, that I may tell you what will happen to you in the days to come. Gather, and hear me, sons of Jacob, and hear Israel your father."

Jacob, who was called Israel, told how the twelve tribes of Israel would descend from his twelve sons. And he spoke to each of the sons in turn: Reuben, Simeon, Levi, Judah, Issachar, Zebulun, Benjamin, Dan, Naphthali, Gad, Joseph and Asher. He foretold that Judah's tribe would be the one which all the others would praise, bowing down before it. And he blessed every son with a blessing.

Then Jacob gathered up his feet into the bed and yielded up the ghost and was united with his people.

Joseph fell upon his father's face, and wept upon him, and kissed him. Then he commanded his servants, the

physicians, to embalm his father.

The physicians embalmed Israel and then the Egyptians mourned for him threescore and ten days.

When the days of mourning were past, Joseph spoke to the house of Pharaoh, saying:

"If I have found grace in your eyes, speak, I pray you, in the ears of Pharaoh and say that my father made me swear to bury him in the grave he dug for himself in the land of Canaan. Therefore, may Pharaoh let me go up, I pray, and bury my father and then I will come again."

Pharaoh said:

"Go up and bury your father, according to his wishes."

JOSEPH BURIES HIS FATHER

So Joseph went up to bury his father, and with him went all the servants of Pharaoh, the elders of his house, and all the elders of the land of Egypt, all the household. Only the little ones, their flocks and their herds did they leave in the land of Goshen. Also chariots and horsemen went up with him. It was a very great caravan.

They came to the threshing-floor of Atad, which is beyond Jordan. There they mourned with great and sorrowing cries. For seven days Joseph mourned for his father.

Then Jacob's sons carried their father into the land of Canaan, as he had commanded. They buried him in the cave of the field of Machpelah.

After his father was buried, Joseph returned to Egypt, he and his brothers and all that went up with him to bury his father.

Now that their father was dead, Joseph's brothers said:

"If Joseph should ever hate us, he would surely make return for all the evil we did to him."

So they sent a messenger to Joseph, saying:

"Before his death, your father spoke to us, saying: 'You shall say to Joseph: Forgive the trespass of your brothers and the sin which they committed when they did evil to you.'"

Joseph wept when they spoke to him. And his brothers went to him and fell down before his face, and said:

"Behold, we are your servants!"

"Fear not," said Joseph. "Am I here in the place of God? You meant evil against me, but God meant to turn it to good and to bring to pass what is today: to keep many people alive.

"Therefore have no fear. I will nourish you, you and your little ones."

Then he comforted them and spoke kindly to them.

JOSEPH DIES

Thereafter, Joseph dwelt in Egypt, he and his father's house.

He lived to see Ephraim's and Manasseh's children and grandchildren. And when he was one hundred and ten years old, Joseph said to his brothers:

"God will surely visit you after my death, and bring you out of this land, into the land which he promised to Abraham, to Isaac, and to Jacob."

And Joseph exacted a promise from the children of Israel, saying: "God will surely visit you, and you shall carry my bones from here."

Joseph was an old man when he died, but less old than his father had been. He was embalmed and put in a coffin in Egypt.

THE
EXODUS
FROM
EGYPT

THE BIRTH OF MOSES

HE children of Israel were fruitful. They increased greatly in number and prospered, and the land of Egypt became filled with them.

But there arose a new king over Egypt who did not know Joseph and the great work he had done. This new Pharaoh said to his people:

"The children of Israel are more and mightier than we are. Let us deal wisely with them. For, if they continue growing in numbers, they may join our enemies and fight against us in time of war and go away from our land."

Therefore the Egyptians set taskmasters over the children of Israel and forced them to work for them. They built for Pharaoh the treasure cities of Pithom and Rameses. But the more the Egyptians oppressed them, the more the Israelites grew in strength and increased in number.

So the king of Egypt spoke to the Hebrew midwives, saying:

"When a Hebrew woman gives birth and you see that it is a son, then you shall kill him. But if it is a daughter, she shall live."

But the midwives feared God and did not do as the king of Egypt commanded them. Instead, they let the men children live. So the king called the midwives and said to them:

"Why have you done this thing? Why have you let the men children live?"

"Because," answered the midwives, "the Hebrew women give birth without our knowing of it before we come to them."

God was pleased with the midwives and dealt well with them. And the people continued to increase and grow stronger. So Pharaoh commanded his people, saying:

"Every Israelite son that is born you shall cast into the river, and every daughter you shall let live."

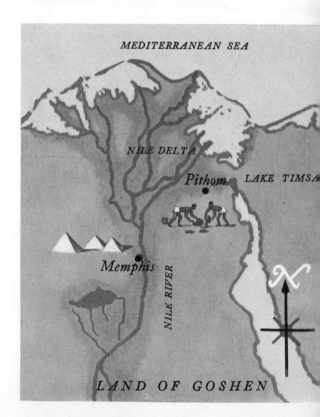

MOSES IN THE BULRUSHES

Now there was a man of the family of Levi whose wife bore him a son. And when she saw that he was a goodly child, she hid him for three months. Then, when she could no longer hide him, she took a basket made of bulrushes, daubed it with pitch and put the child into it. She took it and laid it in the reeds by the river's edge. And the baby's sister stood far away to watch what was done to him.

The daughter of Pharaoh came down to wash herself at the river, and her maids walked along by the river's side. When she saw the basket among the reeds, she sent her maids to fetch it.

When she opened the basket, she saw the child, and he was crying. So

she took pity on him and said, "This is one of the Hebrews' children."

The baby's sister came forward and said to Pharaoh's daughter:

"Shall I go and find a nurse from the Hebrew women to look after the child for you?"

"Go," said Pharaoh's daughter, and the girl went and called the child's mother. And Pharaoh's daughter said to the woman: "Take this child away and nurse it for me, and I will give you your wages."

So the mother took her child and nursed it. The child grew, and his mother brought him to Pharaoh's daughter, and he became her son. And she called him Moses (which means "drawn out") because, she said, "I drew him out of the water."

MOSES
IN MIDIAN

NE day, when Moses was grown up, he went out among his kinsmen and watched them labour. And he saw an Egyptian striking a Hebrew, one of his kinsmen. He looked this way and that way. When he saw that there was no one near, he killed the Egyptian and hid him in the sand.

When he went out the next day, he saw two Hebrew men fighting each other. He said to the one who was in the wrong:

"Why are you striking your own comrade?"

The man replied:

"Who made you a prince and judge over us? Do you intend to kill me as you killed the Egyptian?"

And Moses was afraid and said to himself, "What I have done must be known."

When Pharaoh heard of this, he tried to kill Moses, but Moses escaped from Pharaoh and went to live in the land of Midian.

There one day he sat down beside a well. Now the priest of Midian had seven daughters, and they came and drew water from the well, and filled the troughs to water their father's flock. Shepherds came and tried to drive them away, but Moses stood up and helped them, and watered their flock.

When they came home to their father, he said:

"How is it that you have come back so early today?"

And they answered:

"An Egyptian protected us from the shepherds, and also drew enough water for us, and watered the flock."

"Where is he?" their father asked. "Why have you left the man behind? Call him to eat with us."

Moses was happy to live with this man, and the man gave Moses his daughter Zipporah to be his wife.

Zipporah bore Moses a son, and he called him Gershom, which means "a stranger there", for he said, "I have been a stranger in a strange land."

And in due course it came to pass that the king of Egypt died. But the children of Israel were still oppressed and in slavery. In their suffering they cried out, and their cry carried up to God. He heard their groaning and remembered his promise to Abraham, to Isaac, and to Jacob.

And the Lord looked down upon the children of Israel and had pity on them.

GOD CALLS MOSES

At this time Moses was keeping the flock of his father-in-law, the priest of Midian, and he led the flock to the far side of the desert and came to the mountain of God, to Horeb. There the angel of the Lord appeared to him in a flame of fire out of the middle of a bush. Moses looked and saw that the bush burned with fire, but it was not destroyed.

And he said:

"I will stop here and see this great sight, and discover why the bush is not burnt."

When the Lord saw that he turned aside to see, he called out of the middle of the bush and said:

"Moses, Moses."

"Here am I," answered Moses.

"Do not come near," God said. "Take your shoes off your feet, for the place on which you are standing is holy ground."

And God said further:

"I am the God of your father, the God of Abraham, the God of Isaac, and the God of Jacob."

Moses hid his face, for he was afraid to look upon God.

And God said:

"I have seen the misery of my people who are in Egypt and I have heard their cries because of their task-masters. I realize their sorrows. So

I have come down to deliver them out of the hand of the Egyptians, and to bring them out of that land into a land good and large, into a land flowing with milk and honey.

"Come now therefore, and I will send you to Pharaoh, so that you may lead forth my people, the children of Israel, out of Egypt."

But Moses said to the Lord:

"Who am I, that I should go to Pharaoh, and that I should lead forth the children of Israel out of Egypt?"

And God said:

"Certainly I will be with you, and this shall be a token that I have sent you: When you have brought forth the people out of Egypt, you shall worship God upon this mountain."

Then Moses said to the Lord:

"When I come to the children of Israel and say to them, 'The God of your fathers has sent me to you' and they say to me, 'What is his name?' what shall I say to them?"

And God said:

"This you shall say to the children of Israel: 'The Lord God of your fathers, the God of Abraham, the God of Isaac, and the God of Jacob has sent me to you.

" 'Yahweh is my name for ever, and by this I will be remembered to all generations.'

"Go and gather the elders of Israel together, and tell them all that I have said to you. They shall listen to your voice, and you and the elders of Israel shall go to the king of Egypt and say to him, 'The Lord God of the Hebrews has met with us, and we beg you to let us go three days' journey into the wilderness, so that we may worship the Lord our God.'

"And I am sure that the king of Egypt will not let you go, but I will stretch out my hand and strike Egypt with all my wonders. And after that he will let you go."

THE MIRACULOUS SIGNS

Then Moses said:

"But they will not believe me nor listen to my voice. They will say, 'The Lord has not appeared to you.'"

And God said to him:

"What is that in your hand?"

"A rod," answered Moses.

"Cast it on the ground," said God. So Moses cast it on the ground, and it became a serpent, and he shrank away from it. God then said:

"Put forth your hand and take it by the tail." So Moses put forth his hand and caught the serpent,

and it became a rod in his hand. And God said:

"Thus the people may believe that the Lord God of their fathers, the God of Abraham, the God of Isaac, and the God of Jacob has appeared to you."

And God said furthermore to Moses:

"Now put your hand against your breast."

He put his hand against his breast, and when he took it away, he saw that his hand was white as snow and diseased as though with leprosy. The Lord said:

"Put your hand against your breast again."

He put his hand against his breast once more. When he took it away, he saw that it had become again like his other flesh. And God said:

"It shall come to pass, if they will not believe you nor listen to you because of the first sign, that they will believe the second sign. But if they will not believe either of these two signs, nor listen to your voice, you shall take water from the river and pour it upon the dry land. And the water which you take out of the river shall become blood upon the dry land."

But still Moses said to the Lord:

"O my Lord, I am not a good speaker. I was not before, and I am not since you have spoken to me, your servant. I am slow of speech and have a slow tongue."

Then the Lord said to him:

"Who has made man's mouth? Who makes the dumb, the deaf, the seeing, or the blind? Is it not I, the Lord? So go now, and I will be with your mouth, and I will teach you what you shall say."

But Moses said, "O my Lord, send, I beg you, someone else."

And God became angry with Moses, and he said:

"Is not Aaron the Levite your brother? I know that he can speak well.

Also I see that he is coming out to meet you, and when he sees you he will be glad in his heart. You shall speak to him and put words in his mouth. And I will be with your mouth and with his, and will teach you both what you shall do.

"He shall be your spokesman to the people. He shall take the place of a mouth for you, and you shall take the place of God for him. And you shall take this rod in your hand, to do signs with it."

MOSES RETURNS TO EGYPT

Moses went and returned to his father-in-law and said to him:

"Let me go, I beg you, and let me return to my kinsmen who are in Egypt, and see whether they are still alive."

"Go in peace," said he to Moses.

And God said to Moses in Midian:

"Go, return to Egypt, for all the men are dead who sought your life."

So Moses took his wife and his sons, and set them upon an ass, and he returned to the land of Egypt, taking the rod of God in his hand. And the Lord said to Moses: "When you return there, see that you do before Pharaoh all the wonders which I have put in your hand. But I will harden his heart so that he shall not let the people go."

And the Lord said to Aaron:

"Go into the wilderness to meet Moses."

Aaron went and met Moses at the mountain of God, and kissed him. And Moses told Aaron all that the Lord had said to him, and all the signs that he had told him to do.

Moses and Aaron went and gathered together all the elders of the children of Israel, and Aaron spoke all the words which the Lord had spoken to Moses, and did all the signs for the people to see.

The people believed. And when they heard that the Lord had visited the children of Israel, and that he had seen their suffering, they bowed their heads and worshipped.

PHARAOH AND THE ISRAELITES

MOSES and Aaron went before Pharaoh and spoke to him, saying: "These are the words of the God of Israel: 'Let my people go, so that they may hold a feast to me in the wilderness.'"

But Pharaoh said:

"Who is the Lord, that I should obey his voice and let Israel go? I do not know the Lord, nor will I let Israel go. Why do you, Moses and Aaron, interfere with the work of the people? Get back to your tasks. The people of the land are many now, and you make them rest from their labours."

The same day Pharaoh gave orders to the taskmasters of the people and their officers, saying:

"You shall no longer give the people straw to make bricks, as you have done in the past. Let them go and gather straw for themselves. But the number of bricks which they made before, you are still to demand of them. You shall require as much from them as before, for they are idle. That is

why they cry out saying, 'Let us go and sacrifice to our God.' Let the men be given more work, so that they may have no time to listen to empty talk."

The taskmasters and officers went out and spoke to the people, saying:

"Pharaoh says, 'I will not give you straw. Go out and get straw where you can find it, for you shall make no fewer bricks than before.'"

So the people were scattered throughout all the land of Egypt. And their taskmasters kept after them, saying, "Fulfil your works and your daily tasks, as when there was straw." And the officers of the children of Israel, whom Pharaoh's taskmasters had set over them, were beaten and asked, "Why have you not fulfilled your task of making bricks both yesterday and today, as many as you have made before?"

So the officers of the children of Israel came and cried out to Pharaoh, saying:

"Why do you deal with your servants in this way? No straw is given to us, and we are told, 'Make bricks.' We are beaten, but the fault is with your own people."

"You are idle," Pharaoh answered. "That is why you say, 'Let us go and sacrifice to the Lord.'

"So go now and work. There shall be no straw given to you. And still you shall have to make as many bricks as before."

The officers of the children of Israel, seeing that the number of bricks to be made was to be no less, went forth from Pharaoh. On their way, they met Moses and Aaron, and they said to them:

"May the Lord look upon you and judge you, because you have made us hateful in the eyes of Pharaoh and in the eyes of his servants, so that they want to kill us."

GOD SPEAKS TO MOSES

Then Moses returned to the Lord and said: "Lord, why have you treated these people so badly? Why have you sent me? For since I came to Pharaoh to speak in your name, he has done evil to these people, and you have done nothing to save them."

Then God said to Moses:

"Now you shall see what I will do to Pharaoh. For with a strong hand he shall let the people go. With a strong hand he will drive them out of his land.

"For I am the Lord. I appeared to Abraham, to Isaac, and to Jacob by the name of God Almighty. I made a promise to them, to give them the land of Canaan.

"Say to the children of Israel, 'I am the Lord, and I will free you from the burdens of the Egyptians, and I will take you out of slavery. I will make you my people, and I will be to you a God. I will bring you to the land I promised to give to Abraham, to Isaac, and to Jacob. And I will give it to you and your descendants.' "

Moses told the children of Israel all that the Lord had said. But they did not listen to Moses in their suffering and their misery. And God said to Moses:

"You shall say all that I have to tell you. And Aaron your brother shall speak to Pharaoh, telling him to send the children of Israel out of his land. But I will harden Pharaoh's heart and perform many signs and miracles in the land of Egypt. Still Pharaoh will not listen to you, so I will lay my hand on Egypt and bring forth my armies and my people out of Egypt by my great judgments.

"The Egyptians shall know that I am the Lord when I stretch forth my hand upon Egypt and bring the children of Israel out from among them."

THE TEN PLAGUES

OSES and Aaron did as the Lord commanded them. Moses was eighty years old and Aaron was eighty-three years old when they spoke to Pharaoh.

And God spoke to Moses and to Aaron, saying:

"When Pharaoh asks you to show him a miracle, then you shall say to Aaron, 'Take your rod and cast it before Pharaoh,' and it shall become a serpent."

So Moses and Aaron went before Pharaoh and they did as the Lord had told them. Aaron cast down the rod before Pharaoh and his servants, and it became a serpent.

Then Pharaoh called all the wise men and the sorcerers and the magicians of Egypt. In the same manner each man threw down his rod, and they all became serpents. But Aaron's rod swallowed up their rods.

THE PLAGUE UPON THE RIVER

Then the Lord hardened Pharaoh's heart, so that he did not listen to them, as the Lord had said. And God spoke to Moses, saying:

"Pharaoh's heart is hardened. He refuses to let the people go. So go to Pharaoh again in the morning. He is going out to the river. You shall stand by the river until he comes, and take

in your hand the rod which was turned into a serpent.

"You shall say to him, 'The Lord God of the Hebrews has sent me to you, saying, "Let my people go, so that they may worship me in the wilderness." Yet up to this time you would not listen. Now these are the words of the Lord: "In this way you shall know that I am the Lord." Behold, I will strike the rod that is in my hand upon the water in the river, and it shall be turned to blood. And the fish in the river shall die, and the river shall smell foul, and the Egyptians

shall not want to drink of the river.' "

Then God said further to Moses:
"Say to Aaron, 'Take your rod, and
stretch out your hand upon the waters
of Egypt, upon her streams, upon
her rivers, upon her ponds and all her
pools of water, so that they may become blood, so that there may be
blood throughout all the land of
Egypt, in all the pails of wood and
jugs of stone.' "

Moses and Aaron did everything as
the Lord commanded. Aaron lifted
up his rod and struck the water in the
river, in the sight of Pharaoh and his

servants, and all the water in the river
turned to blood. And the fish in the
river died, and the river smelled foul,
so that the Egyptians could not drink
the water of the river.

But the magicians of Egypt could do
the same with their enchantments, so
Pharaoh's heart was hardened. And he
did not listen to Moses and Aaron, as
the Lord had said.

Pharaoh turned and went into his
house, his heart unmoved by this, and
all the Egyptians dug round about the
river for water to drink, for they could
not drink of the water of the river.

THE PLAGUE OF FROGS

Seven days passed after the Lord had struck the waters. Then God said to Moses:

"Go to Pharaoh, and say to him, 'These are the words of the Lord: "Let my people go, so that they may worship me. If you refuse to let them go, then I will send a plague of frogs over all your country. The river shall bring forth quantities of frogs, which shall come up into your house, and into your bedroom and on to your bed, and into the houses of your servants and upon your people, and into your ovens and into your cooking bowls. And the frogs shall swarm over you and your people and over all your servants." ' "

And God commanded Moses, saying:

"Tell Aaron to stretch out his hand with your rod over the streams, over the rivers and over the ponds, and cause the frogs to come upon the land of Egypt."

Aaron stretched out his hand over the waters of Egypt, and the frogs came up and covered the land.

But the magicians did the same with their enchantments, and they brought up frogs upon the land of Egypt.

Then Pharaoh called for Moses and Aaron, and said:

"Pray to the Lord, and ask him to take the frogs away from me and from my people. And I will let the people go, in order that they may make sacrifices to the Lord:

Moses said to Pharaoh:

"When shall I pray for you, and for your servants and for your people, to have the frogs destroyed among you and your houses, so that they may remain only in the river?"

"Tomorrow," Pharaoh said. Then Moses said:

"It shall be as you ask, so that you may know that there is no one like the Lord our God. The frogs shall be taken from you and from your houses, and from your servants and from your people. They shall remain only in the river."

Moses and Aaron left Pharaoh, and Moses prayed to the Lord about the frogs which he had brought down upon Pharaoh. The Lord did according to the prayer of Moses. The frogs died out of the houses, out of the villages, and out of the fields. And they were gathered up in heaps, and the whole land smelled of them.

THE PLAGUE OF LICE

But when Pharaoh saw that they were gone, he hardened his heart and would not listen to Moses and Aaron, just as the Lord had said. So God said to Moses:

"Tell Aaron to stretch out his hand with his rod and strike the dust of the land, so that it may become lice throughout all the land of Egypt."

Moses did so. Aaron stretched out his hand with his rod and struck the dust of the earth. And it became lice on the men and on the beasts throughout all Egypt.

The magicians tried to do the same with their enchantments, but they could not. So they said to Pharaoh:

"This is the work of God."

THE PLAGUE OF FLIES

But Pharaoh's heart was hardened and he would not listen to them, as the Lord had said.

So God spoke to Moses, saying:

"Rise up early in the morning, and stand before Pharaoh as he comes down to the river, and say to him, "Go, sacrifice to your God here in Egypt."

But Moses said:

"We cannot worship our God before the eyes of the Egyptians because our sacrifices would seem vile to them. Our worship is an abomination to the Egyptians and if we made sacrifices to the Lord, would they not stone us?

'These are the words of the Lord: "If you will not let my people go, so that they may worship me, I will send swarms of flies upon you, upon your servants and upon your people, and into your houses. The houses of the Egyptians and all their land shall be full of swarms of flies. But on that day I will separate from this land the land of Goshen, in which my people dwell, so that no swarms of flies shall be there. From tomorrow I will put a division between my people and your people, so that you may know that I am the Lord over all the earth." ' "

And the Lord did so. There came a great swarm of flies into the house of Pharaoh, into his servants' houses and into all the land of Egypt. The land was ruined by the swarm of flies; they descended upon everything.

Pharaoh called for Moses and Aaron, and said to them:

We will go three days' journey into the wilderness and sacrifice to our God according to his command."

And Pharaoh said:

"I will let you go and sacrifice to the Lord your God in the wilderness. Only you shall not go very far away. Speak to your God for me."

"When I leave you," Moses answered, "I will pray to the Lord that the swarms of flies may leave Pharaoh, his servants and his people tomorrow. But Pharaoh must not deal dishonestly any more in not letting the people go to sacrifice to the Lord."

Moses left Pharaoh and prayed to the Lord, and the Lord did as Moses asked. He removed the swarms of flies from Pharaoh, from his servants and from his people. There remained not one.

But again Pharaoh hardened his heart and would not let the people go.

THE PLAGUE UPON THE CATTLE

Then God said to Moses:

"Go to Pharaoh and tell him that the Lord says, 'Let my people go, so that they may serve me. If you refuse, the hand of the Lord shall be upon your cattle, upon the horses, the asses, the camels, the oxen and the sheep. There shall be a terrible plague. But the Lord shall separate the cattle of Israel from the cattle of Egypt, and nothing shall die that belongs to the children of Israel.'"

And the Lord appointed a set time, saying, "Tomorrow I shall do this thing." And on the following day, all the cattle of Egypt died. But not one of the cattle of the children of Israel died.

Pharaoh sent his messengers to see, yet still his heart was hardened, and he did not let the people go.

THE PLAGUE OF SORES

So God said to Moses and to Aaron:

"Take handfuls of ashes from the furnace, and let Moses sprinkle them in the air in the sight of Pharaoh. They shall become fine dust throughout the land of Egypt, and they shall become sores upon man and upon beast throughout the land."

They took ashes from the furnace and stood before Pharaoh. And Moses sprinkled them in the air, and they caused sores to break out upon man and upon beast.

The magicians could not stand before Moses because of the sores, for they were on the magicians and on all the Egyptians.

But still Pharaoh's heart was hardened and he would not listen to them, as the Lord had said.

THE PLAGUE OF
HAIL AND FIRE

And God said to Moses:

"Rise up early in the morning and stand before Pharaoh and say to him, 'These are the words of the Lord God of the Hebrews: "I will send all my plagues on you, your servants and your people. You will know that there is none like me in all the earth. You still will not let my people go, so to-morrow about this time I will cause it to rain a terrible hail as has not been seen in Egypt since its foundation. Therefore gather your cattle now, and all that you have in your fields, for the hail shall come down upon every man and beast found in the fields and not brought home, and they shall die." ' "

Those of Pharaoh's people who feared the word of the Lord brought their servants and cattle to the houses, but those who did not believe the word of the Lord left their servants and their cattle in the field.

And in accordance with the Lord's command, Moses stretched out his rod towards the heavens, and the Lord sent thunder and hail. And fire ran upon the ground. Fire mixed with hail and nothing like it had been seen in the land since Egypt became a nation. The hail struck everything in the fields, man, beast and plant, and broke down every tree in the fields. Only in the land of Goshen, where the children of Israel were, was there no hail.

Pharaoh sent for Moses and Aaron, and said to them:

"I have sinned this time. The Lord is just and I and my people are wicked. Pray to the Lord that there may be no more thunder and hail, and I will let you go. You shall stay no longer."

Moses went from Pharaoh, out of the city, and spread his hands to the Lord, and the thunder and hail were stopped. But when Pharaoh saw this, he sinned even more and hardened his heart, and he would not let the children of Israel go.

THE PLAGUE OF LOCUSTS

God said to Moses:

"I have allowed all these things to take place so that you may tell your son, and your son's son, what things I have done in Egypt, and the signs that I have given so that you may know that I am the Lord."

Moses and Aaron came again before Pharaoh, and said to him:

"This is what the Lord God of the Hebrews says:

'How long will you refuse to humble yourself before me? If you will not let my people go, tomorrow I will bring locusts into your country. They shall cover the face of the earth so that it cannot be seen. They shall eat everything that has been left after the hail and every tree growing in the fields. They shall fill your house and the houses of all your servants, and the houses of all the Egyptians. Your fathers and your fathers' fathers have seen nothing like it in all their lives.' "

And they turned around and went out from Pharaoh.

And Pharaoh's servants said to him:

"How long shall this man bring suffering to us? Let the men go and worship their God. Do you not see that Egypt is destroyed?"

Moses and Aaron were brought again to Pharaoh, and he said to them:

"Go and worship the Lord your God. But who shall go with you?"

Moses answered: "We will go with our young and our old people, with our sons and with our daughters, with our flocks and our herds, for we must hold a feast to the Lord."

"Let the Lord be with you," said Pharaoh, "if I ever let you and your little ones go. But this shall not be, for you have an evil plan. Let only the men go and worship the Lord." And they were driven out from Pharaoh's presence.

Then Moses did as the Lord had commanded, and stretched out his rod over the land of Egypt.

And the Lord caused an east wind to blow over the land all that day and all that night. And when it was morning the east wind brought the locusts. The locusts went over all the land of Egypt. Never before or afterwards had anyone seen so many locusts. The whole land was darkened with them, and they ate every plant and all the fruit from the trees that the hail had left. Not one green thing re-mained throughout all the land of Egypt.

Pharaoh called quickly for Moses and Aaron and said:

"I have sinned against the Lord your God and against you. Forgive me, I beg of you, this once, and pray to the Lord your God that this plague may be taken from me."

Moses left Pharaoh and entreated the Lord.

The Lord then sent a very strong west wind, which took away the locusts and blew them into the Red Sea. Not one locust was left in the whole land of Egypt.

But still Pharaoh's heart was hardened and he would not let the children of Israel go.

THE PLAGUE OF DARKNESS

So God said to Moses:

"Stretch out your hand towards the heavens, so that there may be darkness over the land of Egypt, a darkness so thick that it may be felt."

Moses stretched forth his hand towards the heavens, and there was a thick darkness through-

out the land of Egypt for three days. The Egyptians could not see one another, and no one moved from his place for three days. But all the children of Israel had light where they lived.

Pharaoh called Moses and said:

"Go, worship the Lord. Only leave your flocks and herds behind. Your children may go with you."

"You must allow us sacrifices that we may offer to the Lord our God," Moses answered. "Our cattle must go with us. Not one animal shall be left behind, for we do not know how we must worship the Lord until we reach the place appointed."

But again Pharaoh's heart was hardened, and he would not let them go. And the Lord said to Moses:

"Yet one plague more will I bring upon Pharaoh and upon Egypt. Afterwards he will let you go. Indeed, he will drive you out altogether."

THE PLAGUE UPON THE FIRST-BORN

Moses came again before Pharaoh to tell him the words of the Lord: "'About midnight I will go out into Egypt, and all the first-born in the land of Egypt shall die, from the first-born child of Pharaoh upon his throne, to the first-born of the maidservant at the mill, and all the first-born of cattle. And there shall be a great cry throughout all the land of Egypt, such as was never heard before and shall never be again.

"But none of the children of Israel shall suffer in any way, neither they nor their animals. Thus you shall see how the Lord has put a difference between the Egyptians and Israel.'"

And Moses went out from Pharaoh in a great anger, but Pharaoh's heart was still hardened, and he would not let the children of Israel go.

THE NIGHT OF THE PASSOVER

**M**OSES called for all the elders of Israel and spoke to them, in accordance with the command of the Lord, saying:

"Take a lamb from your flocks, according to the size of your families, and kill it. Take a bunch of herbs and dip it in the blood that is in the basin, and strike with the blood the top and the two side posts of the doorways of your houses. And none of you shall go out of his house until morning.

"You shall roast the lamb and shall eat the meat with unleavened bread and with bitter herbs. When you eat it you shall be ready to depart, with your shoes on your feet and your staff in your hand. And you shall eat it in haste. It is the Lord's passover.

"For the Lord will pass through to strike the Egyptians, and when he sees the blood upon the doortop and on the two side posts, the Lord will pass over the door, and will not allow death to come into your houses to strike you.

"And you shall observe this thing as a covenant with God for you and for your sons forever. It shall come to pass, when you come to the land which the Lord will give to you, according to his promise, that you shall keep this service. And when your children

say, 'What do you mean by this service?' you shall say, 'It is the sacrifice of the Lord's passover, for he passed over the houses of the children of Israel in Egypt when he struck down the Egyptians, and he saved all our families.' "

The people bowed their heads and worshipped. Then the children of Israel went away and did as the Lord had commanded Moses and Aaron.

And it came to pass at midnight that the Lord struck down all the first-born in the land of Egypt, from the first-born child of Pharaoh on his throne to the first-born of the captive in the dungeon, and all the first-born of cattle.

Pharaoh rose up in the night, he and all his servants, and all the Egyptians. And there was a great cry in Egypt, for there was not a house where someone was not dead.

Pharaoh called for Moses and Aaron by night, and said:

"Rise up and get out from among my people, both you and all the children of Israel. And go worship the Lord as you have asked. And take your flocks and your herds, as you asked, and be gone."

And the Egyptians urged the people, and tried to send them out of the land in haste, for they said, "We are all dead men."

So the people took their dough before it was raised, and bound their kneading boards up in their clothes bundles on their shoulders. And the people of Israel departed and journeyed from Rameses to Succoth. There were about six hundred thousand of them on foot, not counting the children, and there also went with them many other people, and large flocks and herds of cattle.

The night they went out of Egypt, the children of Israel had been living in Egypt for four hundred and thirty years.

CROSSING THE RED SEA

 ONTINUING their journey from Succoth, the Israelites camped at Etham, at the edge of the wilderness. And the Lord went before them by day in a pillar of cloud to show them the way, and by night in a pillar of fire to give them light, so that they could travel by day and night. He did not take away from the people the pillar of cloud by day nor the pillar of fire by night.

It was told to the king of Egypt that the people had fled, and the hearts of Pharaoh and his servants were moved against the people, and they said:

"Why have we done this, and let Israel free from serving us?"

Then Pharaoh made ready his chariots and took his people with him. He took six hundred chariots chosen, of all the chariots of Egypt, and put captains over all of them.

The Lord hardened the heart of Pharaoh, king of Egypt, and Pharaoh pursued the children of Israel, for the children of Israel had gone out proudly.

The Egyptians came after them, all the horses and chariots of Pharaoh, his horsemen and his army, and overtook them camping beside the sea, near Pihahiroth, before Baalzephon.

When Pharaoh came near, the children of Israel looked up, and, seeing the Egyptians marching after them, they were very frightened. Then the children of Israel cried out to the Lord, and they said to Moses:

"Were there no graves in Egypt? Have you brought us away to die in the wilderness? Why have you treated us in this way, in bringing us out of Egypt? Did we not tell you in Egypt, 'Let us alone, so that we may serve the Egyptians?' For it would have been better for us to serve the Egyptians than to die in the wilderness."

"Do not be afraid," said Moses to the people. "Stand still and watch the power of the Lord to save you, as he will show you today, for the Egyptians whom you have seen today you shall never see again. The Lord will fight for you if you will be calm."

THE ISRAELITES PASS THROUGH SAFELY

And God said to Moses:

"Why do you cry to me? Tell the children of Israel to go forward. But you must lift up your rod and stretch out your hand over the sea, and divide it. And the children of Israel shall go on dry land through the middle of the sea.

"And you shall see that I will harden the hearts of the Egyptians, and they shall follow you. Then I will show my power over Pharaoh and over all his armies, his chariots and his horsemen. And the Egyptians shall know that I am the Lord, when I have shown my power."

Then the angel of God which went before the camp of Israel moved and went behind them. The pillar of cloud moved from in front of them and rose up behind them. It came between the camp of Israel and the camp of the Egyptians, but it gave light by night to Israel, so that the Egyptians did not come near Israel all that night.

Then Moses stretched out his hand over the sea, and the Lord caused the sea to go back by making a strong east wind blow all that night. It made the sea dry land, and the waters were divided.

The children of Israel walked into the middle of the sea upon the dry ground, and the waters were a wall on their right hand and on their left.

The Egyptians pursued them and went into the middle of the sea after them, all Pharaoh's horses, his chariots and his horsemen.

When morning came, the Lord looked down on the army of the Egyptians through the pillar of fire and the cloud, and troubled the forces of the Egyptians. He made the wheels fall off their chariots and made them drive heavily, so that the Egyptians said, "Let us flee from the children of Israel, for the Lord fights for them against the Egyptians."

THE EGYPTIANS
ARE DROWNED

Then God said to Moses:

"Stretch out your hand over the sea, so that the waters may come together again and cover the Egyptians, their chariots and their horsemen."

Moses stretched out his hand over the sea, and the sea returned to its bed when the morning appeared. The Egyptians fled before it, but the Lord overthrew the Egyptians in the middle of the sea. The waters returned and covered the chariots and the horsemen, and all the forces of Pharaoh that had followed him into the sea. Not one of them survived.

But the children of Israel had walked on dry land in the middle of the sea, and the waters had formed a wall for them on their right hand and on their left. Thus the Lord saved Israel that day from the hands of the Egyptians, and the Israelites saw the Egyptians dead upon the sea shore.

When Israel saw the great work the Lord did against the Egyptians, the people stood in awe of the Lord, and believed in him and his servant Moses.

Then Moses and the children of Israel sang this song to the Lord:

"I will sing to the Lord,
* for he has triumphed gloriously;*
The horse and his rider he has thrown into
* the sea.*
The Lord is my strength and song, and he has
* become my saviour;*
He is my God, and I will prepare him a
* house;*
He is my father's God, I will exalt him.
Who is like thee, O Lord of all the gods?
Who is like thee, glorious in holiness?
In thy mercy thou hast led forth the people
* thou hast saved;*
In thy strength thou hast guided them to thy
* holy dwelling."*

And Miriam the prophetess, the sister of Aaron, took a timbrel in her hand, and all the women followed her with timbrels and danced. And Miriam replied to them in song:

"Sing everyone to the Lord,
* for he has triumphed gloriously;*
The horse and his rider he has thrown into
* the sea."*

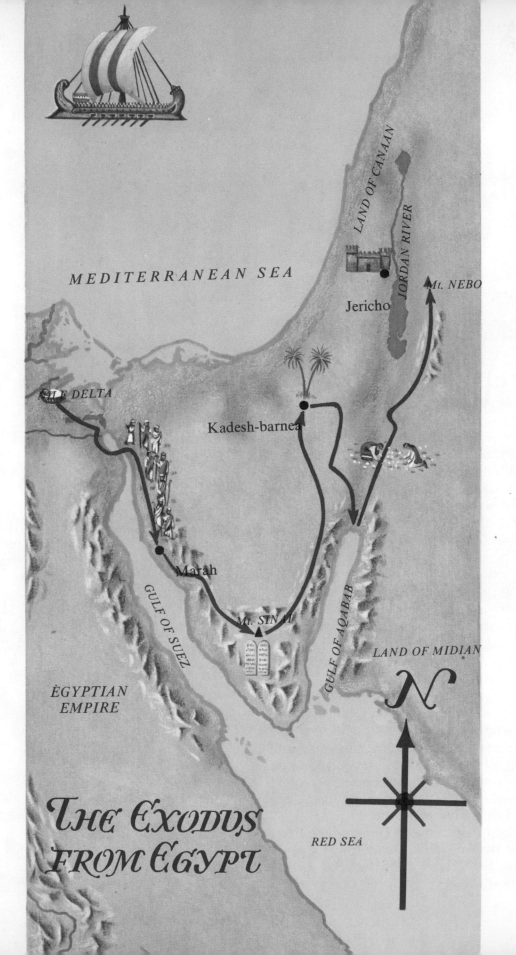

MEDITERRANEAN SEA

LAND OF CANAAN

JORDAN RIVER

Mt. NEBO

Jericho

NILE DELTA

Kadesh-barnea

Marah

GULF OF SUEZ

Mt. SINAI

GULF OF AQABAB

LAND OF MIDIAN

N

EGYPTIAN
EMPIRE

THE EXODUS
FROM EGYPT

RED SEA

THE BITTER WELL OF MARAH

 O Moses led the Israelites from the Red Sea into the wilderness of Shur. They went for three days in the wilderness and found no water.

When at last they came to Marah, they could not drink the water there, for it was bitter. For this reason it was given the name of Marah, meaning "bitterness".

The people murmured against Moses, saying:

"What shall we drink?"

Moses cried to the Lord, and the Lord showed him a tree which, when he cast it into the waters, made the waters sweet. And there the Lord laid down a law for them, saying:

"If you will listen carefully to the voice of the Lord your God, and will do what is right in his sight, and will give ear to his commandments, and keep all his laws, I will not bring upon you any of those diseases which I brought upon the Egyptians, for I am the Lord who heals you."

Then they came to Elim, where there were twelve wells of water and seventy palm trees, and they camped beside the waters.

MANNA FROM HEAVEN

 NWARD from Elim they journeyed, and all the children of Israel came to the wilderness of Sin, which is between Elim and Sinai, on the fifteenth day of the second month after their departure from Egypt. And the children of Israel murmured against Moses and Aaron in the wilderness, saying:

"It would have been better for us to die by the hand of the Lord in the land of Egypt, when we sat down to bowls of meat and ate our fill of bread. For you have brought us out into this wilderness to kill all of us with hunger."

THE BREAD IS GATHERED

Then God said to Moses:

"You shall see. I will rain bread down from heaven for you. The people shall go out and gather a certain amount every day, so that I may test them, to see whether they will obey my laws or not. And it shall be arranged that on the sixth day they shall prepare what they bring in, which shall be twice as much as they gather on other days."

Moses and Aaron said to all the children of Israel:

"When evening comes, you shall know that it is the Lord who brought you out of the land of Egypt. And when morning comes, you shall see the glory of the Lord. For he has heard your murmurings against him. Your murmurings are not against us—for what are we?—but against the Lord."

And while Aaron was speaking to the congregation of the children of Israel, they looked out over the wilderness, and there they saw the glory of the Lord appear in a cloud.

Then God spoke to Moses, saying:

had disappeared, they saw lying on the face of the wilderness small round things, as small as hoarfrost, on the ground. And Moses said to them:

"This is the bread which the Lord has given to you to eat. And this is the commandment of the Lord: You are to gather an omer (about a tenth of a bushel) for each man, depending on how many you have to feed. Each man is to gather for those in his tents."

So the children of Israel went out and gathered the bread. Some took more and some took less, but when they measured it with an omer, those who had gathered a great deal had

"I have heard the murmuring of the children of Israel. Speak to them and say. 'In the evening you shall eat meat, and in the morning you shall have your fill of bread, and so shall you know that I am the Lord your God.'"

And it came to pass that in the evening quails flew up all over the camp, and in the morning dew lay all around the people. And when the dew

nothing over, and those who had gathered little had enough. Each man had enough to feed his people.

"Do not leave any of it until the morning," Moses said.

Nevertheless they did not listen to Moses, and some of them left it until the next morning, and it bred worms and smelled foul. And Moses was angry with them.

So they gathered the bread every morning, each man according to those he had to feed, and when the sun grew hot, it melted.

When the sixth day came, they gathered twice as much bread, two omers for each man. And all the rulers of the congregation came to Moses for directions. And he said to them:

"This is what the Lord has said: 'Tomorrow is the day of rest, the Lord's sabbath. Bake what you want to bake today, and boil what you want to boil, and what is left you may save, to keep for tomorrow.'"

So they laid it away until the next

gather, and they found none. And the Lord said to Moses:

"How long will you refuse to keep my commandments and my laws? Because I have given you the sabbath, I give you the bread for two days on the sixth day. Let no man go out to seek food on the seventh day."

Now the house of Israel called the name of the food manna. It was white like coriander seeds, and the taste of it was like wafers made with honey.

And Moses spoke to the people, saying: "The Lord has commanded that an omer of manna shall be kept

morning, as Moses told them, and it did not smell bad, nor was there a single worm in it. And Moses said:

"Eat today, for today is the Lord's sabbath. Today you shall not find bread in the field. Six days you are to gather it, but on the seventh day, which is the sabbath, there shall be none." And so it was, for some of the people went out on the seventh day to

for your descendants, so that they may see the bread which was given to you in the wilderness, when you were brought from the land of Egypt."

And he commanded Aaron to take a pot and to put an omer of manna into it, to be kept for this purpose.

And the children of Israel ate manna for forty years, until they came to the borders of the land of Canaan.

WATER
FROM
THE ROCK

BUT it came to pass that when the children of Israel had left the wilderness of Sin, and had pitched their camp in Rephidim, they found that there was no water for them to drink.

Therefore they complained to Moses and said:

"Give us water that we may drink. Why did you bring us out of Egypt, to kill us and our children and our cattle with thirst?"

Moses cried to the Lord, saying:

"What shall I do to these people? They are almost ready to stone me."

God said:

"Go on before the people, and take with you the elders of Israel. Take in your hand the rod which you used to strike the river, and go. I will stand before you there upon the rock in Horeb. And you shall strike the rock, and water shall come out of it so that the people may drink."

And this Moses did, while the elders of Israel looked on.

Moses gave to this place the name of Massah, meaning "temptation", because the children of Israel tempted the Lord and tried to test him, saying, "Is the Lord with us, or not?"

THE DEFEAT OF AMALEK

 MALEK came with his army and attacked the people of Israel as they camped in Rephidim. And Moses said to Joshua:

"Choose men and go out and fight with Amalek. Tomorrow I will stand on the top of the hill with the rod of God in my hand."

So Joshua did as Moses had said to him, and fought with Amalek. And Moses, Aaron and Hur went up to the top of the hill. And it came to pass that when Moses held up his hand, Israel was victorious, and when he let down his hand, Amalek was victorious.

But Moses' hands became weary, so they took a stone and put it under him, and he sat on it. And Aaron and Hur held up his hands, the one on the one side and the other on the other.

Thus Moses' hands were steady until the going down of the sun. And Joshua defeated Amalek and his people.

JETHRO ADVISES MOSES

WHEN Jethro, the priest of Midian, Moses' father-in-law, heard of all that God had done for Moses and for Israel his people, he came to see Moses in the wilderness.

Moses went out to meet his father-in-law and told him all that the Lord had done to Pharaoh and to the Egyptians for Israel's sake. And Jethro said:

"Blessed be the Lord. Now I know that he is greater than all gods."

And it came to pass on the next day that Moses sat to judge the people, and the people stood by Moses from the morning to the evening. And when Jethro saw this, he said:

"What is this thing that you do with the people? Why do you sit by yourself alone, and why do all the people stand by you from morning to evening?"

And Moses said to his father-in-law: "The people come to me to inquire of God. When they have a matter, they come to me, and I make them know the statutes of God, and his laws."

And Moses' father-in-law said to him: "The thing that you do is not good. You will surely wear away, both you and this people who are with you. For this thing is too heavy for you. You are not able to perform it by yourself alone. Listen now to my voice. I will give you advice.

"You should choose from the people able men, men who fear God, men of truth and honesty. Place them over the people, to be rulers of thousands, and rulers of hundreds, rulers of fifties and rulers of tens. And let them judge the people at all times. Every great matter they shall bring to you, but every small matter they shall judge themselves. Thus shall it be easier for you, and they shall share the

burden with you. If you shall do this thing, and God so commands you, then you shall be able to endure, and all this people also shall go to their place in peace."

Moses listened to the voice of his father-in-law, and did all that he said. He chose able men from all Israel and made them rulers of thousands, rulers of hundreds, rulers of fifties, and rulers of tens. And they judged the people at all times. The difficult cases they brought to Moses, but every small matter they judged themselves.

And Moses let his father-in-law depart. And he went his way into his own land.

THE TEN COMMANDMENTS

IN the third month after the children of Israel had left Egypt, they came into the desert of Sinai. They pitched their tents in the wilderness and camped there before the mountain.

Moses went up to talk to the Lord, and God called to him from the mountain, saying:

"Say to the children of Israel, 'You have seen what I did to the Egyptians, and how I carried you on eagles' wings and brought you to myself. Now if you will obey my voice and keep your agreement with me, then you shall be a special treasure to me, more than any other people. You shall be a kingdom of priests to me, and a holy nation.' These are the words you shall speak to the children of Israel."

Moses came down and called for the elders of the people, and laid before them all the words of the Lord. And the people answered together and said:

"All that the Lord has spoken, we will do."

Then Moses told the Lord what the people had said. And God was pleased and spoke to Moses, saying:

"Lo, I will come to you in a thick cloud, so that the people may hear when I speak to you, and believe you forever.

"Now go to the people and bless them today and tomorrow. Have them wash their clothes and be ready for the third day. For the third day the Lord will come down in the sight of all the people upon Mount Sinai. You shall set bounds for the people, and warn them to take care not to go up on the mountain or touch the side of it, for whoever touches the mountain shall surely be put to death. Anyone who does touch it shall be stoned or shot, whether it be beast or man. When the trumpet sounds a long blast, they shall come up to the mountain."

Moses went down from the mountain to the people, and he blessed them, and they washed their clothes. And he said to them:

"Be ready for the third day."

When the third day came, in the morning there was thunder and lightning, and a thick cloud lay upon the mountain. Then the voice of a trumpet sounded so loud that all the people in the camp trembled.

And Moses led the people out of the camp to meet with God, and they stood at the foot of the mountain.

Mount Sinai was covered with smoke, because the Lord descended on it in fire. The smoke rose up like the smoke of a furnace, and the whole mountain trembled and shook.

When the voice of the trumpet sounded long blasts, and grew louder and louder, Moses spoke, and God answered him by a voice. Then the Lord came down upon the top of Mount Sinai, and he called Moses up to the top of the mountain, and Moses went up.

And God spoke all these words, saying:

"I am the Lord your God, who

brought you out of the land of Egypt, out of the house of slavery.

"You shall have no gods other than me.

"You shall not make any sculptured image or any likeness of anything that is in heaven above, or on the earth beneath, or in the water under the earth. You shall not bow down to them nor worship them. For I, the Lord your God, am a jealous God, punishing the offspring of those who hate me, and showing mercy to thousands of those that love me and keep my commandments.

"You shall not use the name of the Lord your God carelessly.

"Remember the sabbath day, to keep it holy. Six days you shall labour and do all your work, but the seventh day is the sabbath of the Lord your God. In it you shall do no work, you, nor any member of your family and household, nor any person living with you. For in six days the Lord made heaven and earth, the sea and all that is in them, and rested the seventh day. Therefore the Lord blessed the seventh day and made it holy.

"Respect your father and your mother, so that your days may be many in the land the Lord your God gives to you.

"You shall not kill.

"You shall not commit adultery.

"You shall not steal.

"You shall not wrongly accuse your neighbour.

"You shall not envy your neighbour, nor desire to have his house, his wife, his servants, his animals, nor anything that is his."

All the people saw the thunder and lightning and heard the noise of the trumpet and saw the mountain smoke. And when they did so, they moved back and stood at a distance. And they said to Moses:

"Speak to us, and we will listen.

But do not let God speak to us, for fear that we may die."

And Moses said to the people:

"Do not fear, for God has come to test you, so that you may learn to have respect for him, so that you may do no wrong."

The people stood far off while Moses drew near to the thick darkness where the Lord was.

LAWS FOR GOVERNING THE TRIBES

And God spoke to Moses and gave him laws to govern the tribes of Israel in all their acts. And among the laws that were given were the following:

"Anyone who strikes another man and kills him must himself be put to death.

"Anyone who strikes his father or his mother shall be put to death.

"Anyone who kidnaps another, and sells him or keeps him as a slave shall be put to death.

"Anyone who curses his father or his mother shall be put to death.

"Life shall be given for life, an eye for an eye, a tooth for a tooth, burning for burning, wound for wound.

"But if a thief is killed by a person who attacks him in the act of stealing, that person shall not be punished for murder.

"If an ox gores a man or woman, and they die, then the ox shall be stoned and he shall not be eaten, but the owner of the ox shall not be charged. But if the ox was accustomed to push with his horn in time past and it has been made known to his owner and he has not kept him in, the ox shall be stoned and the owner also shall be put to death.

"If a man steals an ox or a sheep and kills it or sells it, he shall restore five oxen for an ox and four sheep for a sheep. If the animal is found in his hand alive, whether it is ox or ass or sheep, he shall restore double.

"Any man who worships any god other than the Lord shall be destroyed.

"You shall deal kindly with strangers, for you were strangers in the land of Egypt.

"You shall care for the widow and the fatherless child. If you hurt them, and they cry to the Lord, their cry shall be heard. The Lord's anger shall be great, and he will cause your own death, so that your wives shall be widows and your children fatherless.

"If you lend money to any of my people who are poor, you shall not take interest on the sum owed to you.

"You shall obey without complaint the ruler and the judges of the people."

THE ARK OF THE COVENANT

Moses came down and told the people all the words of the Lord and all his laws, and the people said:

"Everything the Lord has said, we will do."

Moses wrote down all the words of the Lord, and he arose early in the morning and built an altar to the Lord, with twelve pillars for the twelve tribes of Israel, and he sacrificed to the Lord.

Then Moses and Aaron and seventy of the elders of Israel rose up, and they saw the Lord of Israel. And God said to Moses:

"Come up to me in the mountain, and I will give you tablets of stone with the law and the commandments which I have written, so that you may teach them."

Moses and his minister Joshua rose up and before he went into the mountain of God, Moses said to the elders:

"Wait here for us. Aaron and Hur are with you: if any man has any

dispute to settle, let him go to them."

When Moses went to the mountain, a cloud covered it. The glory of the Lord was over Mount Sinai, and the cloud covered it for six days. On the seventh day God called to Moses from the cloud, and the sight of the glory of the Lord was like a raging fire on the top of the mountain, to the eyes of the children of Israel.

Moses went into the cloud and up the mountain, and he was on the mountain for forty days and forty nights.

And God spoke to Moses, saying:

"Tell the people of Israel to bring me offerings. From every man who gives willingly with his heart you shall take the offering. And this is what you will receive from them: gold, silver and brass, cloths of blue, purple and scarlet, fine linen, goats' hair, rams' skins dyed red, badgers' skins and acacia wood, oil for lighting, spices for anointing and for sweet incense, onyx stones and other jewels.

"And let them make me a sanctuary so that I may live among them. They shall make it according to all that I tell you.

"They shall make me an ark of acacia wood. It shall be a chest four feet long, two feet wide and two feet high. It is to be covered with gold

inside and out, and it shall have a gold band around it. At each corner it shall have a gold ring, and through these rings shall be passed gold-covered rods of acacia wood, so that the ark may be carried.

"These rods shall remain in the rings of the ark and shall not be taken from it. And they shall put in the ark the laws I shall give you.

"They shall make also a mercy seat, a throne of pure gold, four feet long and two feet wide. At each end of the mercy seat there shall be the figure of an angel in beaten gold. And the angels shall stretch their wings upward, covering the mercy seat with them. Their faces shall look to one another and shall be inclined slightly downwards. And the mercy seat shall be put upon the ark, and in the ark shall be put the law and the commandments that I shall give you.

"And there I will meet with you, and speak to you from above the mercy seat, from between the two angels upon the ark.

"And they shall make a table of acacia wood, and cover it with gold, and put a gold band around it with gold rings at each corner. And gold-covered rods of acacia wood shall be passed through the rings, so that the table may be carried.

"And they shall make a candlestick of pure gold. Of beaten work shall the candlestick be made. Its shaft and its branches, its bowls and its flowers shall be of the same. And six branches shall come out of the sides of it, three branches out of one side, and three out of the other side. It shall all be one beaten work of pure gold. And there shall be seven lamps like this. And the tongs and the snuffers thereof shall be of pure gold. See that they are made after the pattern showed on the mountain.

"And they shall make a tabernacle, a tent lined with fine linen and with blue, purple and scarlet cloth, and covered with goats' hair cloth, rams' skins dyed red and badgers' skins.

"And the ark of the testimony, with the mercy seat upon it, shall be kept in the tabernacle and covered with a veil, a curtain of blue, purple and scarlet cloth. In front of the veil shall be kept the table. On the table shall be set showbread, twelve loaves of sacred bread shall be set there every sabbath, to be eaten by the priests.

"And the people of Israel shall

ments to consecrate him. And these are the garments which they shall make: a breastplate, an ephod, a robe, an embroidered coat, a turban and a girdle.

"And they shall make the ephod of gold, of blue, of purple, of scarlet and fine twined linen, with skilful work. And they shall make for the breastplate chains of pure gold. And Aaron shall bear the names of the children of Israel on the breastplate of judgment upon his heart when he goes into the holy place, as a memorial before the Lord.

"And they shall make the robe all

make an altar, and set it up before the tabernacle.

"Take Aaron your brother and his sons with him from among the children of Israel, that he may minister to me in the priest's office. And you shall make holy garments for Aaron your brother, for glory and for beauty. You shall speak to all that are wisehearted, whom I have filled with the spirit of wisdom, that they make Aaron's gar-

of blue, and beneath, on the hem of it, you shall make pomegranates of blue, and of purple and of scarlet, with bells of gold between them. Aaron shall wear these garments when he ministers so that his sound may be heard both when he goes in to worship before the Lord, and when he comes out. And you shall make a plate of pure gold, and engrave upon it in the manner of a signet, HOLINESS TO THE LORD. You shall put it on the front of the turban and it shall be attached with a lace of blue.

"This plate shall be at all times upon Aaron's forehead as a token of his ministry in order that the holy offerings of the people of Israel may be acceptable before the Lord.

"Aaron and his sons shall be anointed with oil and shall be made priests, so that they may make sacrifices to me for the people.

"And for the sacrifice you shall take one young bullock and two lambs without blemish, unleavened bread, unleavened cakes tempered with oil, and unleavened wafers anointed with oil. You shall make them of wheat flour, and place them in a basket, bringing it with the bullock and the two rams.

"Then you shall bring Aaron and his sons to the door of the tabernacle of the congregation and wash them with water.

"All these things shall be possible because I have given you men of skill and intelligence, whom I have filled with the spirit of God. These men are craftsmen of great experience and understanding. They are able to work in gold, silver and brass, to cut and set stones and to carve timber. They have the talent to make all that I have commanded, whether the tabernacle of the congregation, the ark of the testimony or the mercy seat upon it.

"Speak to the people of Israel and say: 'You shall keep my sabbaths as a sign between me and you through all generations. Six days may work be done but the seventh is a day of rest, holy to the Lord, for having made heaven and earth in six days, the Lord rested on the seventh.' "

And when God had finished speaking to Moses upon Mount Sinai, he gave him two tablets of stone, the tablets of the law and commandments, written by the hand of the Lord.

THE MAKING OF THE GOLDEN CALF

WHEN the people saw that Moses was not coming down from the mountain at once, they gathered round Aaron and said to him: "Make us gods to go before us, for we do not know what has become of Moses, who brought us out of the land of Egypt."

So Aaron said to them:

"Break off the golden ear-rings which your wives and sons and daughters wear in their ears, and bring them to me."

So all the people broke off the golden ear-rings in their ears and brought them to Aaron. He took them from their hands and melted the gold and fashioned it with a tool into the shape of a calf.

"Let this be your god, O Israel, which brought you up out of the land of Egypt," they said.

When Aaron saw it, he built an altar before it. Then he made a proclamation, saying:

"Tomorrow is a feast to the Lord."

They rose up early the next morning and offered burnt offerings and brought peace offerings, and the people sat down to eat and to drink and rose up to play.

Then God said to Moses:

"Go down. For your people whom you have brought out of the land of Egypt have corrupted themselves. They have turned aside from the way I commanded them to go. They have made themselves a golden calf and worshipped it. They have made sacrifices to it and have said, 'This is your god, O Israel, which brought you out of the land of Egypt.'"

And God said to Moses:

"I have watched this people, and they are a stubborn people. Now

therefore leave me alone, for my anger has grown hot against them, and I will destroy them and make a great nation of you alone."

But Moses pleaded with the Lord his God, saying:

"Lord, why are you angry against your people whom you have brought out of the land of Egypt by great power and with a mighty hand? Are the Egyptians to say, 'He led them out as a trick to slay them in the mountains, and to destroy them from the face of the earth?' Turn from your fierce anger against your people. Remember Abraham, Isaac, and Israel, your servants, to whom you swore by your own name that you would multiply their offspring like the stars of the heaven, and give all this land you have spoken of to their children, and that they would inherit it for ever."

So the Lord repented of the evil which he planned to do to his people.

MOSES' ANGER

Then Moses turned and went down from the mountain, with the two tablets of the laws in his hand. The tablets were covered with writing on both sides and were the work of God, and the writing was the writing of God engraved upon the tablets.

When Joshua heard the noise of the people as they shouted, he said to Moses:

"There is noise of war in the camp."

"It is not the voice of those who shout for victory," Moses said, "nor those who cry in defeat, but the noise of those who sing that I hear."

As soon as he came close to the camp, he saw the calf and the dancing, and Moses' anger grew hot, and he hurled down the tablets from his hands, and they broke at the foot of the mountain.

He took the calf which they had made and burned it in the fire, and ground it to powder and sprinkled it upon the water, and made the people of Israel drink it.

And Moses said to Aaron:

"What did the people do to you that made you lead them into such great wrongdoing?"

"Do not be angry," Aaron said. "You know the people, and how they are set on mischief. They said to me, 'Make us gods which shall go before us, for we do not know what has become of Moses who led us out of the land of Egypt.' And I said to them, 'Let those who have gold break it off.' So they gave it to me. Then I cast it into the fire, and there came out this calf."

And on the following day Moses said to the people:

"You have sinned a great sin. And now I will go up to the Lord. Perhaps I can obtain forgiveness from him for the sin you have committed."

And Moses returned to the Lord and said:

"Oh, this people have sinned a great sin, and have made gods of gold. Yet, will you forgive their sin? If not, I beg you to blot me entirely out of your book."

"Whoever has sinned against me, him I blot out of my book," the Lord answered. "So go now, lead the people to the place I have told you of. My angel shall go before you. The time shall come when I shall punish the people for their sin."

THE LORD'S PUNISHMENT

And the Lord punished the people with a plague, because they had made the calf with Aaron.

And God spoke to Moses, saying:

"Depart, you and the people you have led up out of the land of Egypt, and go to the land which I promised to Abraham, to Isaac, and to Jacob for their children. I will send an angel before you to a land flowing with milk and honey. But I will not go with you myself, because you are a stubborn people."

When the people heard these words, they mourned. And not a man of them wore his ornaments.

And Moses took the holy tent and pitched it outside the camp, some way off, and called it the Tabernacle of the congregation. And whenever Moses went out into the tabernacle, all the people rose up and stood at their tent doors and followed Moses with their eyes until he was gone inside. Then the cloudy pillar descended and stood at the tabernacle door.

The Lord spoke to Moses face to face, as a man speaks to his friend. And when Moses returned to the camp, his servant Joshua remained each time in the tabernacle.

RENEWAL OF THE COVENANT

ND God said unto Moses: "Take two tablets of stone like the first, and I will write upon these tablets the words that were on the first tablets which you broke.

"And be ready in the morning, and come up in the morning to Mount Sinai, and stand there before me at the top of the mountain. No man shall come up with you, nor must any man be seen anywhere on the mountain, nor must the flocks or herds feed anywhere near it."

So Moses cut two tablets of stone like the first. And he rose up early in the morning and went up Mount Sinai, as the Lord had commanded, taking in his hand the two tablets of stone.

And God came down in the cloud and stood with him there and said:

"I am the Lord, the Lord God, merciful and gracious, patient and with great goodness and truth. I show mercy to thousands, forgiving evil, wrongdoing and sin, but I punish the guilty even in their children and their children's children, to the third and to the fourth generation."

Moses bowed his head to the earth and worshipped, saying:

"If now I have found grace in your sight, O Lord, I pray you to come among us. We are a stubborn people, but forgive our wrongdoing and our sin, and take us to be your people."

GOD'S PROMISE TO THE ISRAELITES

And God said:

"Behold, I will make a promise: I will do wonders for all your people such as have not been done anywhere in any nation. And all your people shall see the work of the Lord, for it is a wonderful thing that I will do.

"I will drive out before you the Amorites, the Canaanites, the Hittites, the Perizzites, the Hivites and the Jebusites. Not only must you make no agreement with the people living in the land to which you are going, but you shall destroy their altars and break their images. And you shall worship no god other than the Lord.

"You must keep all my commandments and worship me according to my laws."

Moses was with the Lord forty days and forty nights. During this time he did not eat or drink, and he wrote upon the tablets the words of the law and the ten commandments.

And when Moses came down from Mount Sinai with the two tablets in his hand, he did not know that the skin of his face shone after his encounter with God. And when Aaron and the children of Israel saw Moses, they were afraid to come near him because his face shone. Moses called to them, and Aaron and all the rulers of the congregation came to him, and Moses talked with them.

Afterwards, all the children of Israel came, and Moses told them all that the

Lord had said to him on Mount Sinai.

Moses put a veil over his face until he had finished speaking to them. But when he went to speak to the Lord, he took the veil off. And all the children of Israel saw that the skin of Moses' face shone.

According to the commandment God had given to Moses, the children of Israel made the tabernacle. In it they placed the ark containing the tablets of stone on which were written the ten commandments and the law.

And God commanded that the tabernacle should be raised up, and he covered it with a cloud. When the cloud was taken up from over the tabernacle, the children of Israel continued their journeys. But if the cloud covered the tabernacle, they did not journey until the day that it was taken up. For the cloud of the Lord was upon the tabernacle by day, and fire was on it by night, so that all the house of Israel could see it during all their journeys.

THE DEPARTURE FROM SINAI

IT came to pass on the twentieth day of the second month of the second year after the children of Israel had left Egypt that the cloud was taken up from over the tabernacle.

So the children of Israel journeyed out of the wilderness of Sinai. The ark of the covenant of the Lord went before them, to show them where they should stop. And the cloud came to rest in the wilderness of Paran, three days' journey from Mount Sinai.

THE PEOPLE CRY OUT FOR FOOD

There the children of Israel complained again and said:

"Who shall give us food to eat? We remember the fish which we did eat freely in Egypt. We remember the cucumbers and the melons, the leeks, the onions and the garlic. But now there is nothing but this manna for us to eat."

Moses heard the people's cries, and the anger of the Lord was greatly kindled. Moses also was displeased, and he said to the Lord:

"Why have you laid the burden of this people upon me, to bring them to the land which you promised to their fathers? Where will I find food to give to all of them? For they are weeping and saying to me, 'Give us food to eat.' I cannot bear this burden alone. I pray you to kill me and save me from my misery."

And God said:

"Gather seventy men of the elders of Israel, and bring them to the tabernacle to stand there with you. I will come down and talk with you there, and I will make them share the burden of the people, so that you no longer bear it alone.

"And say to the people, 'You shall eat meat, not for one day, nor two

days, nor five days, nor ten days, nor twenty days, but for a whole month, until you are bursting with it and begin to hate it.' "

Moses answered the Lord, saying:

"The people number six hundred thousand, and you have said you will give them meat to eat for a whole month. Shall the flocks be slaughtered or shall all the fish of the sea be gathered so as to be enough for them?"

And God said:

"Has the Lord's power decreased at all? You shall see now whether my word shall be carried out or not."

Moses went out and told the people the words of the Lord and gathered the seventy men of the elders. And the Lord sent forth a wind, and brought quails from the sea. He let them fall by the camp, about a day's journey on the one side and about a day's journey on the other side, all around the camp. The people went out and gathered the quails all that day and all that night and all the next day. The least that anyone gathered was about a bushel.

But even while they were eating the quails, the Lord struck the people with a terrible plague. Many of them died and were buried in that place.

THE ISRAELITES PREPARE TO ENTER CANAAN

THE Lord spoke to Moses in the wilderness of Paran saying: "Send out men to look over the land of Canaan, which I have promised to the children of Israel. Send a man from every tribe, each one to be a ruler among his people."

Moses chose twelve men, one from each of the tribes of Israel. He sent them to spy out the land of Canaan, saying to them:

"Go up into the mountains and look over the land. See what it is like, whether the people who dwell there are strong or weak, few or many. See what the land itself is like that they dwell in, whether it is good or bad. See what their cities are like, whether they live in tents or in strong buildings. See whether the land is rich or poor, whether it has wood or not, and bring back some of the fruit of the land."

Now it was the time for the first ripe grapes. So the men went out and searched the land. They came to a brook, and there they cut down a branch with a cluster of grapes on it. They carried it between them slung on a staff and they brought also some pomegranates and figs. They gave the place the name of Eschcol, meaning "a cluster of grapes", because of the grapes they had cut down there.

They searched through the land for forty days. Then they returned to Moses and Aaron and all the congregation of the children of Israel, and brought word to them and showed them the fruit of the land.

THE PEOPLE MURMUR AGAINST MOSES

And when the men returned, they said to Moses:

"We came to the land to which you sent us. It is indeed flowing with milk and honey, and this is the fruit of it. Yet the people are strong who dwell in the land, and the cities are walled and very large. We saw the children of Anak there. The Amalekites inhabit the south. The Hittites, the Jebusites and the Amorites live in the mountains, and the Canaanites have the land by the sea and along the River Jordan."

Caleb, who had been among the men sent to spy out the land, silenced the people and said:

"Let us go at once and take possession of the land, for we are strong enough to overcome it."

But the others who had gone out with him said:

"We are not able to fight those people, for they are stronger than we."

And they gave an evil report to the children of Israel concerning the land they had searched out, saying:

"The land which we went to look over is a land that eats up its inhabitants. All the people we saw in it are men of great height. We saw there giants, the sons of Anak who was descended from giants. We looked like grasshoppers by the side of them."

Then all the congregation lifted up their voices and cried. All the people wept that night. And the children of Israel murmured against Moses and Aaron, saying to them:

"Would to God that we had died in the land of Egypt, or that we had died in the wilderness! Why has the Lord brought us to this land to be killed in battle, so that our wives and children may be captured? Would it not be better for us to return to Egypt?"

And the people said to one another:

"Let us choose a captain, and let us return to Egypt."

Then Caleb and Joshua, who had also been with those who had searched

then he will bring us into this land and give it to us, a land flowing with milk and honey. But do not rebel against the Lord, and do not fear the people of the land, for they have no defence. The Lord is with us. So do not fear them."

But the people threatened to stone them. And the glory of the Lord appeared in the tabernacle before all the children of Israel, and God said to Moses:

"How long will this people provoke me? How long will it be before they believe me, for all the signs which I have shown them? I will strike them with a plague. I will disinherit them and make a great nation of you alone."

MOSES ASKS GOD'S FORGIVENESS

Moses answered the Lord, saying:

"Then the Egyptians shall hear of it and they will tell the inhabitants of this land, who have heard that you are the Lord of this people. They have heard that you are seen by them face to face, that your cloud stands over them, and that you go before them by daytime in a pillar of cloud and in a pillar of fire by night. If now you kill all this people, the nations which have heard of your fame will say, 'Because the Lord was not able to bring this people into the land which he promised them, he has destroyed them in the wilderness.'

"Now I beg of you, let the Lord's power be great, even as you have spoken saying: 'The Lord is patient, and of great mercy, forgiving sin and wrongdoing.' Forgive, I beg of you, the sin of this people, according to the greatness of your mercy, as you have forgiven them from Egypt even until now."

the land, spoke to all the company of the children of Israel, saying:

"The land which we passed through to look over is an exceedingly good land. If the Lord is pleased with us,

THE MURMURERS
ARE PUNISHED

And God said to Moses:

"Because all those men who have seen my glory, and the miracles I did in Egypt and in the wilderness have not listened to my voice, they indeed shall not see the land which I promised to their fathers.

"Say to the children of Israel, 'You who have murmured against me shall die in the wilderness, but your children which you said would be captured, them will I bring to that land which you have despised. But as for you, you shall fall in this wilderness. And your children shall wander in the wilderness for forty years, one year for each of the days spent in searching out the land. For forty years I shall withhold my promise.'"

And of the men whom Moses sent to search out the land and who returned and made the congregation murmur against him by giving an evil report on the land, all except Caleb and Joshua died of a plague sent by the Lord.

Then the people rose up early in the morning and went to the top of the mountain saying:

"We are here, and will go to the place the Lord has promised, for we have sinned."

But Moses said to them:

"You must not go up the mountain. Because you turned away from the Lord, the Lord will not be with you."

Yet some of them continued and went without Moses and the ark of the covenant of the Lord, and they were struck down by the Amalekites and the Canaanites.

THE WANDERING CONTINUES

before the rock, and Moses said to them:

"Hear now, you rebels. Must we fetch water out of this rock?"

And Moses raised his hand, and struck the rock twice with his rod. The water came flowing out, and the congregation drank and their cattle drank.

But God said to Moses and Aaron:

"Because you did not believe in me, to show my power in the eyes of the children of Israel, you shall not bring this assembly to the land that I have given them."

HE children of Israel continued their wandering into the desert of Sin. They stopped at Kadesh, where Miriam, the sister of Aaron, died and was buried.

Once again there was no water for the people, and they gathered themselves together against Moses and Aaron, saying:

"Would to God that we had died when our brothers died. Why have you brought the congregation of the Lord into this wilderness so that we and our cattle should die here? Why did you make us come out of Egypt to bring us to this evil place? It is no place of plenty, of figs, of vines or of pomegranates. Nor is there any water to drink."

And God said to Moses:

"Take the rod and gather the people together, you and Aaron. Speak to the rock while they look on. It shall send forth water, enough for all the people and their cattle to drink."

Moses took the rod. He and Aaron gathered the congregation together

161

PASSAGE THROUGH EDOM IS REFUSED

Moses sent messengers from Kadesh to the king of Edom, where the descendants of Esau lived, saying:

"We come from your kinsmen of Israel. You know all the hardship we have suffered, how the Egyptians illtreated us and our fathers. And when we cried to the Lord, he heard us and brought us out of the land of Egypt. Now we are in Kadesh, a city on your border, and we beg you to let us pass through your country.

"We will not go through the fields or the vineyards, and we will not drink the water from your wells. We will go by the king's highway. We will not turn to the right hand or to the left until we have passed your borders."

But the king of Edom answered:

"You shall not pass through for we will come out against you with swords."

The children of Israel said to him:

"We will go by the highway, and if our cattle drink your water, then we will pay for it."

"You shall not pass through," Edom said again. And the Edomites came out against the Israelites with many people and refused to give the Israelites passage through their country.

AARON DIES

So the children of Israel turned away from Edom, and they came to Mount Hor. And the Lord spoke to Moses and Aaron on Mount Hor, saying:

"Aaron shall be gathered to his people. He shall not enter the land I have given to the children of Israel, because you rebelled against my word at the water of Meribah. Take Aaron and Eleazar his son and bring them up Mount Hor. And take from Aaron his priestly robes, and put them on Eleazar his son. Aaron shall be gathered to his people and shall die there."

Moses did as the Lord commanded. They went up on to Mount Hor while all the congregation looked on. And Moses took from Aaron his priestly robes and put them on Eleazar his son. Aaron died there at the top of the mountain, and Moses and Eleazar came down from the mountain. And all the congregation mourned for Aaron thirty days.

THE PEOPLE AGAIN REBEL

Now when the Israelites entered Canaan, they were attacked and some were taken prisoners. But later they were victorious and overcame their attackers.

In order to go round the land of Edom, the Israelites journeyed from Mount Hor by way of the Red Sea. The people were much discouraged by the land and they spoke against the Lord and against Moses, saying:

"Why have you brought us out of Egypt to die in the wilderness? For there is no bread and no water, and we hate the light bread we eat."

And the Lord sent fierce serpents among the people to bite them. And many of the people of Israel died.

So they came to Moses and said:

"We have sinned, for we have spoken against the Lord and against you. Pray to the Lord that he take the serpents away from us."

Moses prayed for the people, and God said to him:

"Make a serpent of brass and put it on a pole. And it shall be that everyone who is bitten shall live if he looks at it."

So Moses made a serpent of brass and put it on a pole. And it came to pass that if a serpent had bitten any man, when he looked at the serpent of brass, he lived.

THE AMORITES ARE DEFEATED

The wanderings of the children of Israel continued, west of Edom and along by the western edge of the land of the Moabites, until they reached the country of the Amorites. They pitched their tents in the plains of Moab, near Jericho.

And they sent messengers to Sihon, king of the Amorites, saying:

"Let us pass through your land. We will not turn into the fields or into the vineyards. We will not drink the water of the wells. But we will go by the king's highway until we pass your borders."

But Sihon would not let the people pass through his country. He gathered all his people together and went out into the wilderness against Israel. He came to Jahaz and fought against Israel.

The Israelites defeated the Amorites and took all their land and dwelt in their cities and villages.

Then they turned and went by way of Bashan. And Og, the king of Bashan, went out against them, he and all his people.

And God said to Moses:

"Fear him not. For I have put him in your hands, and all his people and his land. And you shall do to him as you did to Sihon, the king of the Amorites." So the Israelites killed Og, the king of Bashan, and his sons and all his people and possessed his land.

BALAAM AND THE KING OF MOAB

BALAK, the son of Zippor, was king of the Moabites at that time, and he feared the children of Israel. For he knew of all that they had done to the Amorites. So he sent messengers to Balaam at Pethor, in the north, saying:

"There is a people come out from Egypt. They cover the whole land and are close to my country. Come therefore, I beg you, and curse this people for me, so that I may conquer them and drive them out of the land. For I know that he whom you bless is blessed, and he whom you curse is cursed."

The elders of Moab and the elders of Midian came to Balaam with Balak's message. And Balaam said to them:

"Stay here this night, and I will answer you tomorrow when the Lord has spoken to me."

The elders of Moab stayed with Balaam. And God came to Balaam and said:

"What men are these with you?"

"Balak the son of Zippor, king of Moab, has sent them to me," Balaam answered, "so that I may help him to drive out a people come from Egypt."

And God said to Balaam:

"You shall not go with them. You shall not curse the people, for they are blessed."

Balaam rose up in the morning and said to the messengers of Balak:

"Go back to your land. The Lord refuses to let me go with you."

And the elders of Moab rose and went back to Balak and told him that Balaam refused to come with them. So Balak sent other messengers, a greater number and more honourable than the first. They came to Balaam and said to him:

"We bring a message from Balak the son of Zippor: 'Let nothing prevent you from coming to me, I beg of

you. For I will give you very great honours. I will do whatever you tell me. I beg you then to come and curse this people for me.' "

Balaam answered the servants of Balak, saying: "If Balak were to give me his house full of silver and gold, I cannot go beyond the word of the Lord, to do less or more. So I ask you also to stay here this night, so that I may know what the Lord will say further to me."

And God came to Balaam at night and said to him:

"If the men come to call you, rise up and go with them. But you shall do as I shall tell you."

167

BALAAM AND THE ANGEL

And Balaam rose up in the morning and saddled his ass, and went with the princes of Moab. And God was angry because he went. So the angel of the Lord stood in the way to oppose him.

Now Balaam was riding upon his ass, and his two servants were with him, and the ass saw the angel of the Lord standing in the way with his sword drawn in his hand. So the ass turned aside out of the way and went into the field.

Balaam beat the ass, to turn her back on to the path. But the angel of the Lord stood in a path of the vineyards, a wall being on both sides. When the ass saw the angel of the Lord, she pushed herself against a wall and crushed Balaam's foot against the wall. So Balaam beat the ass again.

The angel of the Lord went further and stood in a narrow place where there was no way to turn either to the right or to the left. And when the ass saw the angel of the Lord, she fell down under Balaam. Balaam was still more angry, and he beat the ass with a staff.

Then the Lord opened the mouth of the ass, and she said to Balaam:

"What have I done to you that you have beaten me these three times?"

Balaam said to the ass:

"Because you have mocked me. I wish there were a sword in my hand, for now I would kill you."

Then the ass said to Balaam: "Am I not your ass, upon which you have ridden ever since I became yours? Have I ever treated you so before?"

"No," said Balaam. So God opened Balaam's eyes and he saw the angel of the Lord standing in the way, with his sword drawn in his hand. And he bowed his head and fell flat on his face. And the angel of the Lord said to him:

"Why have you beaten your ass these three times? I went out to oppose you because your way is against me. The ass saw me and turned from me these three times. If she had not turned from me, I would surely have killed you, and saved her life."

Balaam said to the angel of the Lord:

"I have sinned, for I did not know that you were standing in the way against me. So now, if it displeases you, I will not go on."

But the angel of the Lord said to Balaam:

"Go with the men, but you shall speak only the words that I tell you."

BALAAM IS BROUGHT TO BALAK

So Balaam went with the princes of Balak. And when Balak heard that Balaam had come, he went out to meet him in a city on the farthest border of Moab, and he said to Balaam:

"Did I not urgently send for you? Why did you not come to me? Am I not able to give you great honours?"

And Balaam answered:

"You see that I have come to you, but have I now power at all to say anything? I shall speak the words that God puts into my mouth."

The next day, Balak brought Balaam up into the high places, so that he could see all the camps of the people of Israel. Then Balaam said to Balak:

"Build here seven altars and prepare seven oxen and seven rams."

Balak did as Balaam said, and together they offered on every altar a bullock and a ram. Then Balaam said to Balak:

"Stand by your burnt offering and I will go and see whether the Lord will come to me. Whatever he commands me, I will tell you."

Balaam went to the top of a hill, and God met him and said to him:

"Return to Balak, and you shall speak the words I give you."

Balaam returned to Balak, who was standing by the burnt sacrifice with all the princes of Moab, and Balaam spoke. But the words that he spoke were blessings upon Israel, and not curses.

Three times the sacrifices were offered, and each time the words God gave to Balaam were words of blessing:

"How goodly are your tents, O Jacob,
And your tabernacles, O Israel!
As the valleys they are spread forth,
As the gardens by the river's side,
As the sweet aloe trees
  which the Lord has planted,
And as the cedar trees beside the waters.
God brought you forth out of Egypt,
He shall eat up the nations your enemies,
And shall break their bones.
And pierce them through
  with his arrows.
Blessed is he who blesses you,
And cursed is he who curses you.

Then Balak was very angry with Balaam, and he said:

"I called you to curse my enemies, but now you have blessed them these three times. Flee then to your own country: I thought I was to give you

great honour, but the Lord has kept you back from honour."

Balaam answered:

"Did I not say to the messengers you sent to me, 'If Balak were to give me his house full of silver and gold, I cannot go beyond the commandment of the Lord, to do either good or bad; but I will speak as the Lord tells me?' And now I go back to my people, but before I go I will tell you what this nation shall do to your nation in time to come."

And Balaam made this prophecy:

"*There shall come a star out of Jacob,*
And a sceptre shall rise out of Israel,
And shall strike the land of Moab,
And destroy all the children of
*   Sheth.*
Edom shall be conquered,
And Israel shall do valiantly.
Out of Jacob shall come a man
*   of great power,*
And he shall destroy all that remains
*   of the city.*"

Then Balaam rose and returned to his own country, and Balak also went his way.

MOSES' LAST WORDS TO HIS PEOPLE

THE forty years of wandering were coming to an end and Moses spoke to the people of Israel, saying:

"Now these are the commandments, the statutes, and the judgments which the Lord your God commanded me to teach you, so that you might do them in the land which you go to possess. Hear, therefore, O Israel, and be sure to do it, that all may be well with you and that you may increase mightily, as the Lord God of your fathers promised you, in the land flowing with milk and honey.

"The Lord our God is one Lord, and you shall love the Lord your God with all your heart and with all your soul and with all your might.

"And these words which I command you this day shall be in your heart, and you shall teach them carefully to your children. You shall talk of them when you sit in your house, and when you walk along the road, and when you lie down, and when you rise up.

"You shall bind them as a sign on your hand, and they shall be as frontlets between your eyes. And you shall write them upon the posts of your house, and on your gates.

"You shall fear the Lord your God, and serve him, and shall swear by his name. You shall not go after other gods, the gods of the people who are round about you, lest the anger of the Lord your God be kindled against you and destroy you from the face of the earth.

"And it shall come to pass when your son asks you in time to come, 'What do the testimonies and the statutes and the judgments mean?' that you shall say to your son, 'We were Pharaoh's servants in

Egypt, and the Lord brought us out of Egypt with a mighty hand, and the Lord showed signs and wonders, great and grievous, against Egypt, against Pharaoh, and against all his household, before our eyes.

" 'And he brought us out from there that he might bring us into and give us the land which he promised to our fathers. And the Lord commanded us to obey all these statutes: to fear the Lord our God, for our good always, that he might preserve us alive as it is this day. And it shall be our righteousness if we observe all these commandments before the Lord our God, as he has commanded us.'

"All these commandments I have given you, so that you may live, and multiply, and go in to possess the land which the Lord promised to your fathers. And you shall remember all the way which the Lord your God led you for these forty years in the wilderness, to humble you and to test you, to know what was in your hearts, whether you would keep his commandments or not. And he humbled you, and caused you to go hungry, and fed you with manna, which neither you nor your fathers had ever seen before, so that he might make you know that man does not live by bread only, but by every word that comes from the mouth of God.

"You shall also remember that as a father punishes his son, so the Lord your God punishes you. Therefore you shall keep the commandments of the Lord your God, to walk in his ways and to stand in awe of him.

"For the Lord your God is bringing you to a good land, a land of brooks and water, of fountains and wells that spring out of valleys and hills; a land of wheat and barley, of vines, fig trees and pomegranates; a land of oil-olives and honey; a land where you shall have plenty of bread to eat, where you shall not lack any thing; a land whose stones are iron and out of whose hills you may dig brass.

"When you have eaten and are full, then you shall bless the Lord your God, and give him thanks for the good land he has given you.

"Beware that you forget not the Lord your God; that you keep his commandments, his judgments and his laws which I have given you.

"Take care that when you have eaten and are full, and have built fine houses to live in, and when your herds and flocks multiply, and your silver and gold and all that you have has increased, that you do not become proud and forget the Lord your God who brought you forth out of the land of Egypt, from the house of slavery; who led you through that great and terrible wilderness, where there were fierce serpents, and scorpions, and drought, and not a drop of water. Do not forget the Lord who brought you water out of the rock of flint, who fed you in the wilderness with manna so that he might humble you and test you. Take care that you do not say in your hearts, 'My power and the strength of my hand have got me these riches.'

"But you shall remember the Lord your God, for it is he who makes you able to get riches, so that he may keep the promise which he made to your fathers, as he does today.

"And it shall be, if you ever forget the Lord your God, and follow other gods and worship them, you shall indeed perish. You shall perish as the nations which the Lord has destroyed before your eyes, because you would not obey the voice of the Lord your God."

THE LORD IS GOING BEFORE YOU

And Moses continued, saying:

"Hear, O Israel: You are to pass over Jordan, to go in to possess nations greater and stronger than you. Understand therefore that the Lord your God is going over before, that he shall destroy them as a raging fire, and he shall bring them down before you. So you shall drive them out and destroy them quickly, as the Lord has said.

"Do not say in your heart, after the Lord your God has driven them before you, 'It is because of my own goodness that the Lord has brought me to possess this land.' It is because of the wickedness of these nations that the Lord is driving them out before you. It is not because of your own goodness, or the upright-

ness of your heart, but because of their wickedness, and so that the Lord your God may keep the promise which he made to your fathers, Abraham, Isaac, and Jacob.

"Therefore, as I have said, you shall keep these words of mine in your heart and in your soul, and you shall teach them to your children, speaking of them at all times: when you are in your houses, and when you are making a journey, when you lie down to sleep, and when you rise in the morning. You shall write them on the doorways of your houses and on your gates, so that you may live long, and so that your children may live long, in the land which the Lord promised your fathers.

"And it shall come to pass, if you listen diligently to the voice of the Lord your God and observe and do all his commandments, that the Lord your God will set you on high above all the nations of the earth. And all these blessings shall come to you, if you listen to the voice of the Lord your God.

"Blessed you shall be in the city,
* and blessed shall you be in the field.*
Blessed shall be the fruit of your body,
* and the fruit of your ground,*
* and the fruit of your cattle,*
* and the flocks of your sheep.*
Blessed you shall be when you come in
* and blessed shall you be when you go out.*

"But it shall come to pass, if you will not listen to the voice of the Lord your God and observe and do all his

commandments, that all these curses shall come upon you:

"Cursed you shall be in the city,
* and cursed shall you be in the field.*
Cursed shall be the fruit of your body,
* and the fruit of your land,*
* and the flocks of your sheep.*
Cursed you shall be when you come in,
* and cursed shall you be when you go out.*

"The Lord shall strike you with a burning fever, and with the sword and with mildew, and these shall plague you until you perish. The Lord shall make the rain of your land powder and dust. From heaven it shall come down upon you until you are destroyed.

"The Lord shall bring a nation against you from afar, from the end of the earth, as swift as the eagle flies, a nation whose tongue you shall not understand, a nation of fierce appearance which shall show no favour to the old or young. It shall besiege you at all your gates, until your high walls which you trusted come down. And it shall besiege you throughout all the land which the Lord your God has given you.

"If you will not do all the words of this law that are written in this book, the Lord shall scatter you among all people, from one end of the earth to the other. And there you shall serve other gods which neither you nor your fathers have known, gods of wood and stone. And among these nations you shall find no ease, nor shall the sole of your foot have rest, but the Lord shall give you there a trembling heart, and failing of eyes and sorrow of mind.

"Your life shall hang in doubt before you and you shall fear day and night and shall have no assurance for your life. In the morning you shall say, 'Would to God it were evening!' And at evening you shall say, 'Would to God it were morning!' And the Lord shall bring you back into Egypt in ships, and there you shall be offered for sale as slaves, but no man shall buy you.

"And it shall come to pass when all these things have happened to you, the blessing and the curse, you shall return to the Lord your God and shall obey his voice according to all that I command you this day, you and your children with all your heart and with all your soul. Then the Lord your God will have compassion upon you and will return and gather you from all nations where he has scattered you. And the Lord will bring you into the land which your fathers possessed, and you shall possess it. And he will do you good and multiply you more than your fathers.

"See, I have set before you this day life and good, and death and evil. I call heaven and earth to record this day against you, that I have set before you life and death, blessing and cursing. Therefore choose life so both you and your offspring may live and love the Lord your God."

THE DEATH OF MOSES

ND Moses went and spoke these words to all Israel. Then he said to them:

"I am a hundred and twenty years old this day. I can no longer go out and come in. Also the Lord has said to me, 'You shall not go over the Jordan.' Joshua, he shall go over before you, as the Lord has said."

And Moses called Joshua and said to him in the sight of all Israel:

"Be strong and of good courage. For you must go with this people into the land which the Lord has promised their fathers. And you shall cause them to inherit it."

Then God said to Moses:

"Behold, you shall sleep with your fathers, and this people will rise up and will forsake me and break the agreement which I have made with them. Take down therefore this song and teach it to the people of Israel that they may learn it by heart. It shall be a witness for me against them. Then I will hide my face from them, when they have turned to other gods. Many evils and troubles shall plague them."

So Moses spoke in the ears of all the congregation of Israel the words of this song:

"Give ear, O you heavens, and I will speak;
and hear, O earth, the words of my mouth.

My doctrine shall drop as the rain,
my speech shall distill as the dew,

as the small rain upon the tender herb,
and as the showers upon the grass.

For I will proclaim the name of the Lord.

He is the Rock, his work is perfect,
for all his ways are just.

A God of truth and without iniquity,
just and right is he.

Remember the days of old,
consider the years of many generations.

Ask your father and he will show you,
your elders, and they will tell you.

For the Lord's portion is his people,
  Jacob is his inheritance.

He found him in a desert land,
  and in the waste of the howling wilderness.

He led him about, he instructed him,
  he kept him as the apple of his eye.

As an eagle stirs up her nest,
  flutters over her young,
  spreads out her wings, takes them,
  carries them on her wings.

So the Lord alone did lead him,
  and there was no strange god with him.

He made him ride on the high places
  of the earth, that he might eat
  the increase of the fields,

and he made him suck honey out of the rock,
  and oil out of the flinty rock.

Of the Rock that begot you
  you are unmindful,
  and have forgotten God who formed you.

The Lord saw it, and spurned them,
  because of the provocation
  of his children.

And he said, I will hide my face from them,
  I will see what their end shall be.

For they are a very wayward generation,
  children in whom there is no faith.

For they are a nation void of counsel,
  nor is there any understanding in them.

O that they were wise and understood this,
  and would see their ending!"

And after Moses came and spoke all the words of this song in the ears of the people, God spoke to him, the same day, saying:

"Go up on to Mount Nebo, in the land of Moab near Jericho. And look at the land of Canaan which I am giving to the children of Israel. And die on the mount and be gathered to your people, as Aaron your brother died on Mount Hor and was gathered to his people. You shall see the land before you, but you shall not go into this land which I have promised to the children of Israel."

So Moses went up from the plains of Moab into the mountain of Nebo, to the peak of Pisgah, by Jericho. And the Lord showed him all the land he was giving to each of the tribes of Israel. And the Lord spoke to him, saying:

"This is the land which I promised to Abraham, to Isaac, and to Jacob, saying I would give it to their children. I have allowed you to see it with your own eyes, but you shall not go over there."

So Moses the servant of the Lord died there in the land of Moab, according to the word of the Lord. He was buried in a valley in the land of Moab, near Bethpeor, but no man knows to this day where his grave lies.

And Moses was a hundred and twenty years old when he died. But his eye was not dimmed, and his strength had not failed him.

The children of Israel wept for Moses in the plains of Moab for thirty days. Then the days of weeping and mourning for Moses were over.

And Joshua, the son of Nun, was full of the spirit of wisdom, for Moses had laid his hands on him and blessed him. And the children of Israel listened to him and did as the Lord commanded.

Never again in Israel was there a prophet like Moses, whom the Lord knew face to face, and who did all the signs and wonders which the Lord sent him to do to Pharaoh in the land of Egypt. Such was the wondrous power which Moses showed in the sight of all Israel.

THE
RISE OF
ISRAEL

THE INVASION OF CANAAN

FTER the death of Moses, the Lord put Joshua in command of the children of Israel. "Be strong and full of courage," said the Lord. "Do not be afraid, and do not be dismayed; for the Lord your God is with you wherever you go."

Joshua commanded the officers of the people: "Go among the people and tell them to prepare food, for within three days we shall cross the River Jordan to enter the land which the Lord has given us."

He said this to all the people and they agreed to obey him as they had obeyed Moses.

JOSHUA SENDS SPIES

Joshua sent two men to spy on Jericho. They went there and came to the house of a woman named Rahab and took a room there.

But the king of Jericho was warned of their arrival and sent word to Rahab: "Bring out the men who came to you and are now in your house, for they have come to spy in our country."

But the woman took the two men and hid them, and when questioned, she replied: "There were two men who came here, but I did not know where they had come from. And the men left about the time it was getting dark. Where they were going I do not know, but if you pursue them quickly you will overtake them."

The woman had taken the spies up

on to the roof of her house and had hidden them under stalks of flax which she had laid out on the roof.

And the men searched for them all the way to the River Jordan.

Before the men on the roof had lain down for the night Rahab came up to them and said: "I know that the Lord has given you this land, and that all its inhabitants are afraid of you. For we have heard how the Lord dried up the waters of the Red Sea for you when you came out of Egypt, and as soon as we heard that, our hearts melted, and not a man had any courage left, all because of you. For the Lord your God is God in heaven above and in the earth beneath. Therefore I pray you, swear to me by the Lord, that since I have shown you kindness you will show kindness to me and my family. Promise to save the lives of my father and my mother and my brothers and sisters, and all their possessions, and make sure that we are not killed."

THE SPIES MAKE
A PROMISE

The men said: "We will save your lives in exchange for our own, on the condition that you do not utter a word about us to the king. And when the Lord has given us this land, we will deal kindly and honestly with you."

Rahab's house was built upon the town wall, so she tied a rope to the parapet and the men climbed down it. As they went she said: "Go to the mountains and hide there for three days until your pursuers have come back here; and after that you may go on your way."

anyone goes out from your house into the street, whatever happens to him will be his own fault, and we shall not be guilty; but we will be responsible for whomsoever stays with you in the house, and we will see that no one touches him. But if you say a word about our business here, then we will not keep our promise."

"It shall be just as you say," she said. Then she sent them away, and after they had left she tied the piece of scarlet cord in the window.

The two men went into the mountains and stayed there for three days while the pursuers searched unsuccessfully for them, and finally gave up the hunt and went back to the city.

And the men said: "We shall keep this oath which you have made us swear. When the children of Israel come into the land, you must tie a piece of scarlet cord in the window, and bring your father and mother and your brothers and all your father's household into your house. Then if

Then the two men came back down the mountain and crossed the river and came back to Joshua. They told him all the things that had happened to them. And they said to Joshua: "Truly the Lord has delivered all the country into our hands, for all the people of Jericho faint with fear of us."

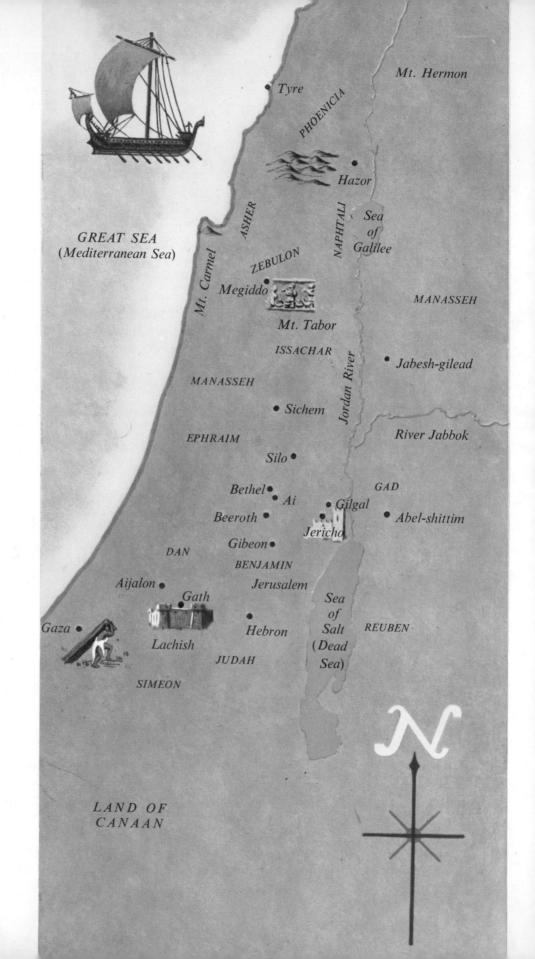

GREAT SEA
(Mediterranean Sea)

Tyre

PHOENICIA

Mt. Hermon

Hazor

ASHER

NAPHTALI

Sea
of
Galilee

MANASSEH

Mt. Carmel

ZEBULON

Megiddo

Mt. Tabor

ISSACHAR

Jordan River

Jabesh-gilead

MANASSEH

Sichem

River Jabbok

EPHRAIM

Silo

Bethel

Ai

Gilgal

GAD

Abel-shittim

Beeroth

Jericho

Gibeon

DAN

BENJAMIN

Jerusalem

Aijalon

Gath

Sea
of
Salt
(Dead
Sea)

REUBEN

Gaza

Hebron

Lachish

JUDAH

SIMEON

LAND OF
CANAAN

N

184

THE FALL OF JERICHO

ERICHO, that great city, was tightly shut up, because of the children of Israel; no one went out of the city, and no one came in.

Then the Lord told Joshua how he and the children of Israel could capture the city. Joshua called the priests and the people and gave them their orders.

To the priests he said: "Take up the ark of the covenant and let seven priests carrying seven trumpets of rams' horns march before the ark of the Lord." And to the people he said: "Surround the city, and let those that are armed march before the ark of the Lord."

When Joshua had spoken to the people, the seven priests bearing seven trumpets of rams' horns went forward before the ark of the Lord and blew on their trumpets. The armed men went before the priests and the rear guard followed after the ark of the Lord.

Joshua had commanded the people: "You shall not shout nor make any noise nor shall any word come out of your mouths until the day when I bid you shout. Then you shall shout."

So the ark of the Lord circled the city, going about it once. Then everyone came back to the camp and stayed there.

Next day Joshua rose early in the morning, and the priests took up the ark of the Lord. Again seven priests, bearing seven trumpets of rams' horns, went steadily ahead, blowing on their trumpets. The armed guard went before them, and the rear guard came after the ark of the Lord.

The second day they circled the city once and returned to the camp. This they did for six days.

On the seventh day they rose early, at the dawning of the day, and circled the city in the same way seven times.

At the seventh time, while the priests blew on their trumpets, Joshua said to the people: "Shout, for the Lord has given you the city. And the city and everyone in it shall be accursed, except for Rahab, who shall live, she and all that are with her in the house, because she hid the messengers that we sent."

So the people shouted while the priests blew on their trumpets. When the people heard the sound of the trumpet and shouted with a great shout, the wall of Jericho fell down flat. The people of Israel went into the city, each man walking straight ahead, and they took the city and put all its inhabitants to the sword.

RAHAB IS SPARED

But Joshua had said to the two men who had spied for him: "Go into Rahab's house and bring out the woman and all her family, as you promised her."

And the young men who had served as spies went in and brought out Rahab and her father and her mother and her brothers and all their possessions. They brought out all her family and left them outside the city at the camp of the Israelites.

Then they burned the city and all that was in it, except for the silver and gold and the vessels of brass and iron, which they put into the treasury of the house of the Lord.

And Joshua saved Rahab's life and her father's household and all that she had, and she went to live in Israel. He did this because she had hidden the messengers he had sent to spy on the city of Jericho.

JOSHUA AND THE HIVITES

 ND God said to Joshua: "Fear not, and be not dismayed. Take all the people of war with you and go up to the city of Ai. I have given to you the king of Ai and his people and his city and his land, and you shall do to Ai and her king as you did to Jericho and her king."

So Joshua did as the Lord had told him. He ambushed the city of Ai and destroyed it utterly. And the possessions and the cattle of the people of Ai were given as booty to the children of Israel.

All the cities of Jordan were afraid of Joshua when they heard what had happened to Jericho and Ai. And they gathered themselves together with one accord to fight with Joshua and Israel.

The people of Gibeon, who were

rich and wily, wanted to make a treaty with him. They sent messengers, dressed in tattered clothing, with mouldy bread in their packs and with patched and leaking wineskins. These messengers came to Joshua in his camp at Gilgal, saying that they had come from a far country.

And Joshua said: "Who are you? And where do you come from?"

The men of Gibeon answered: "We have come from a very distant country. This bread of ours was taken hot and fresh from the oven when we started out, and now, behold, it is dry and mouldy. These skins which we filled with wine were then new, and, behold, they are split. And our garments and shoes have become old because of the length of our journey."

The men of Israel looked at the food and the wineskins and the clothes and did not ask counsel from the mouth of the Lord. Joshua drew up a peace treaty and swore a solemn oath that the Israelites would keep it.

But three days later they learned that these were their neighbours, the Hivites. The children of Israel reached the rich city of Gibeon, but they could not fight, because of the solemn peace treaty.

Then Joshua sent for the Hivites and asked: "Why have you cheated us, saying you live very far from us, when you dwell among us? Now you are cursed, and none of you shall be freed from being bondsmen and hewers of wood and drawers of water for the house of God."

And the people of Gibeon said: "We were told that the Lord your God commanded his servant Moses to give you all the land and to destroy all the inhabitants of the land. Therefore we were afraid of our lives, because of you, and that is why we did this thing. But now we are in your hands and we shall do as you say."

THE SUN AND MOON OBEY JOSHUA

When the king of Jerusalem heard that Joshua had made peace with the Hivites he was afraid, because Gibeon was a rich and royal city and its men were famous for their might. So he conspired with four other kings and they set forth to lay siege to Gibeon.

The Gibeonites sent a message to Joshua, who was in his camp at Gilgal, saying: "Come quickly and save us, for all the kings of the Amorites that dwell in the mountains have joined together against us."

And God said unto Joshua: "Fear them not, for I have delivered them into your hands. Not a man of them shall stand before thee."

So Joshua and his army left Gilgal and took the Amorites by surprise and killed many of them and put the others to flight. As they fled, the Lord cast hailstones from heaven upon them, and more Amorites died from these hailstones than were killed by the children of Israel.

Then Joshua spoke: "Sun, stand still above Gibeon, and moon, stay above the valley of Ajalon."

And the sun stood still and the moon stayed, until the Israelites had avenged themselves upon their enemies. And never before had there been a day like this, when the Lord obeyed the voice of a man; for the Lord fought for Israel.

So Joshua struck all the country of the hills and of the vale and of the springs, and all their kings. He left none remaining, but utterly destroyed all that breathed, as the Lord God of Israel commanded. All these kings and their land did Joshua take, because the Lord God of Israel fought for Israel.

Joshua made war a long time. There was not a city that made peace with the children of Israel, except the Hivites,

the inhabitants of Gibeon. All others they took in battle. So Joshua took the whole land, according to all that the Lord said to Moses, and Joshua gave it for an inheritance to Israel, according to their division by tribes. And the land rested from war.

THE AGED JOSHUA SPEAKS TO THE PEOPLE

And it came to pass, a long time after the Lord had given Israel rest from all their enemies round about, that Joshua waxed old and stricken in age.

So he called for all Israel, and for their elders, and for their heads, and for their judges, and for their officers, and said to them:

"I am old and stricken in age. And you have seen all that the Lord your

God has done to these nations because of you. Behold, I have divided among you by lot these nations that remain, to be an inheritance for your tribes. And the Lord your God, he shall expel them from before you and drive them from out of your sight, and you shall possess their land, as the Lord your God has promised you.

"Be you therefore very courageous and do all that is written in the book of the law of Moses, and turn not aside, either to the right or the left. Of these nations that remain among you, neither make mention of the name of their gods nor swear by them nor serve them nor bow down to them. Take care that you love the Lord your God. Otherwise, if you do associate with the survivors of these nations, know for a certainty that the Lord will no longer drive out any nations from before you, but they shall be snares and traps to you, and scourges in your sides, and thorns in your eyes; until you perish from this good land which the Lord has given you.

"And, behold, this day I am going to die. And you know in your hearts and in your souls that not one thing has failed of all the good things which the Lord your God spoke concerning you. All have come to pass, and not one thing has failed."

So Joshua let the people depart, every man to his inheritance. And it came to pass after these things that Joshua, the son of Nun, the servant of the Lord, died, being a hundred and ten years old. And they buried him in the borders of his inheritance, in Timnath-serah which is on the mount of Ephraim, on the north side of the hill of Gaash.

THE SLAYING OF SISERA

BECAUSE the children of Israel did evil in the sight of the Lord, the Lord made them the captives of Jabin, king of Canaan. Jabin's army was commanded by a great captain called Sisera. He had nine hundred chariots, and for twenty years he oppressed the children of Israel.

One of the judges in Israel was a woman called Deborah, and she sent for a man called Barak and said: "Go to Mount Tabor with ten thousand men and I will deliver Sisera with all his soldiers and his chariots into your hands."

Barak said: "I will go if you accompany me, but not otherwise."

So Deborah agreed to go with him, but she warned him that he would gain no honour from the expedition, for the Lord would sell Sisera into the hands of a woman.

The armies of Barak and Sisera met on the slopes of Mount Tabor and the Lord defeated Sisera and his chariots, and Barak slew all his men. Sisera himself alighted from his chariot and fled on foot. When he reached Kedesh he stopped at the tent of Heber the Kenite, who was one of his king's allies. Heber's wife, Jael, came out to meet him, saying: "Come in, do not be afraid."

Sisera went into the tent, and Jael made him lie down and covered him with a cloak.

He said: "I am thirsty, give me some water to drink."

She gave him milk to quench his thirst and made him comfortable. He said: "Stand in the door of the tent, and if anybody comes and asks any questions, say that there is nobody here." Then Sisera fell asleep, for he was very tired, and while he slept Jael killed him.

Presently Barak appeared in pursuit of Sisera, and Jael went up to him and said: "Come and I will show you the man for whom you are looking."

So the children of Israel conquered Jabin, king of Canaan, and the land was at peace for forty years.

SONG OF REJOICING

Then Deborah and Barak the son of Abinoam sang on that day these words:

Praise ye the Lord
* for the avenging of Israel,*
When the people willingly offered themselves.
Hear, O ye kings; give ear, O ye princes.
I, even I, will sing unto the Lord;
I will sing praise to the Lord God of Israel.
Lord, when thou wentest out of Seir,
When thou marchedst
* out of the field of Edom.*
The earth trembled, and the heavens dropped,
The clouds also dropped water.
The mountains melted from before the Lord,
Even that Sinai
* from before the Lord God of Israel.*
Blessed above women shall Jael
* the wife of Heber the Kenite be;*
Blessed shall she be above women in the tent.
He asked water, and she gave him milk.
She brought forth butter in a lordly dish.
She put her hand to the nail,
And her right hand to the workman's hammer,
And with the hammer she smote Sisera,
* she smote off his head,*
When she had pierced
* and stricken through his temples*
At her feet he bowed, he fell, he lay down.
Where he bowed, there he fell down dead.
So let all your enemies perish, O Lord.

GIDEON AND THE MIDIANITES

IN time the children of Israel went back to their evil ways. Because of this the Lord delivered them into the power of the Midianites for seven years. The Midianites ravaged the land, and the children of Israel were obliged to live in dens in the mountains and in caves and fortified places.

When the seven years were up, an angel of the Lord came and sat under an oak in Ophrah which belonged to Joash the Abiezerite. His son Gideon was threshing wheat to hide from the Midianites.

AN ANGEL APPEARS TO GIDEON

The angel of the Lord appeared to Gideon and said to him: "The Lord is with you, you mighty man of valour."

Gideon said to him: "O my Lord, if the Lord is with us, why has all this happened to us? Where are all his miracles, of which our fathers told us? Did not the Lord bring us up from Egypt? The Lord has forsaken us now, and has given us up to the Midianites."

The angel looked at him and said: "Go out in your strength and you shall save Israel from the Midianites. Have I not sent you?"

"If I have found favour in your sight," Gideon said to him, "show me a sign that it it is you who are talking with me. Stay here until I come back and bring a present and set it before you."

"I will wait here until you come again," the angel said.

So Gideon went in and prepared a young goat and some unleavened cakes. The meat he put in a basket and he put the broth in a pot and brought it out to the angel and presented it.

The angel of God said to him: "Take the meat and the unleavened cakes and lay them upon this rock and pour out the broth."

Gideon did as he was commanded.

Then the angel of the Lord stretched out the end of the staff that was in his hand and touched the meat and the unleavened cakes, and fire rose up out of the rock and consumed the meat and the unleavened cakes. And the angel of the Lord disappeared from sight.

When Gideon saw that this was indeed an angel of the Lord, he said: "Alas! O Lord God! I am frightened because I have seen an angel of the Lord God face to face."

But God said to him: "Be at peace; do not be afraid, you shall not die."

Then Gideon built an altar to the Lord and called it Yahweh-Shalom, which means "The Lord is Peace".

GOD ADDRESSES GIDEON

That same night God spoke to him again and said: "Take a seven-year-old bull from your father's herd, and go to the altar which your father has set up to Baal. Throw down the altar and cut down the grove of trees that is by it. Then build an altar to the Lord God on the top of the rock, and kindle a fire from the wood of the grove, and sacrifice the bull to the Lord."

So Gideon took ten of his servants and did as the Lord had commanded him to do. He dared not do it in the daytime, for fear of the villagers and the rest of his father's household, so he did it under cover of night.

The next morning the villagers saw what had happened. When they discovered that Gideon was responsible for the pulling down of Baal's altar, they went to Joash and said: "Bring out your son, for he must die."

But Joash defended Gideon and said: "Do you have to plead for Baal, who is a god? If any of you dare to, let him be put to death at once. Let Baal speak for himself."

Then the Midianites and the Amalekites banded together and camped in the valley of Jezreel, but the spirit of the Lord came upon Gideon and he blew a trumpet and all the men flocked to his side.

Gideon spoke to the Lord saying: "If you will save Israel by my hand, give me a token. Behold, I shall put a fleece of wool on the floor and if the dew is on the fleece only and all the earth beside it is dry, I shall know that you mean me to save Israel."

The next morning he rose early and wrung a bowlful of water out of the fleece.

But still he doubted and said: "Do not be angry with me, but grant me one more sign. Let the fleece be dry and upon all the ground let there be dew." And the Lord did so that night; for only the fleece was dry, and there was dew on all the ground.

GIDEON PICKS HIS MEN

Then Gideon assembled an army of the men of Israel behind him. They pitched their tents beside the well of Harod, so that the ranks of the Midianites were off to the north of them by the hill of Moreh, in the valley.

And God said to Gideon: "The people with you are too many for me to give them a victory over the Midianites, for then Israel might boast of its own power, saying, 'Our own hands have saved us.' Go to the people, therefore, and tell everyone who is fearful and afraid, to go back, and leave Mount Gilead."

Twenty-two thousand of the people returned, and ten thousand stayed.

Then God spoke to Gideon, saying: "There are still too many people. Bring them down to the water, and I will test them for you. If I say, 'This one shall go with you,' he shall go with you, and if I say, 'This one shall not go with you,' he shall not go."

So Gideon brought the people down to the water, and God said to Gideon: "Set apart those who lap the water with their tongues, as a dog laps, and those who kneel down to drink."

The number of those who lapped, putting their hands to their mouths, was three hundred men. All the rest of the people bowed down upon their knees to drink the water.

Then God said to Gideon: "By the three hundred men who lapped, I will save you and will deliver the Midianites into your hands. Let all the other people go to their homes."

So the chosen people took food in

their hands, and their trumpets, and Gideon sent all the rest of the Israelites to their tents and kept only those three hundred men. And the army of Midian was beneath, in the valley.

THEY SPY ON THE MIDIANITES

The same night God spoke to Gideon, saying:

"Arise, go down to the camp, for I have given it into your hands. But if you are afraid to go down, take your servant Phurah down with you to the camp. You will hear what the Midianites are saying, and afterward your hands will be strengthened for the battle."

Gideon went down with Phurah to the outermost of the armed men that

were in the camp. There the Midianites and the Amalekites and all the children of the east lay along the valley, like grasshoppers in their numbers, and their camels were countless, as many as the sands by the seaside.

When Gideon came near, a man was telling a dream to his companion, and he said:

"I have dreamed a dream, and in it a cake of barley bread tumbled into the camp of Midian. It came to a tent and struck it so that the tent fell and overturned, and lay upon the ground."

His companion answered and said: "This is nothing else than the sword of Gideon, the son of Joash, a man of Israel. For God is giving him a victory over Midian and all the army."

When Gideon heard the telling of the dream and the interpretation of it, he worshipped God. Then he returned to the army of Israel and said: "Arise, for the Lord has given into your hands the army of Midian."

He divided the three hundred men into three companies, and he put a trumpet into every man's hand, and gave them empty pitchers with lights inside them.

"Watch me and do likewise," he said to them. "And see that when I come to the outskirts of the camp, you do whatever I do. When I and those who are with me blow on our trumpets, then you blow on your trumpets too, on every side of the whole camp, and shout: 'The sword of the Lord and of Gideon!'"

THE ISRAELITES ATTACK

So Gideon and the hundred men who were with him came to the outskirts of the camp in the beginning of the middle watch, when a new watch had just been posted. Then they blew on their trumpets and broke the pitchers that they held in their hands. And the three companies all blew on their trumpets and broke the pitchers and held the lights in their left hands and the trumpets in their right hands. And they cried: "The sword of the Lord and of Gideon!"

They stood, every man in his place, round about the camp, and all the army of Midian awoke and cried out.

The three hundred blew on their trumpets and through the whole army of the Midianites the Lord made men turn their swords against one another, and they fled in confusion. The men of Israel pursued them beyond Jordan, killing their leaders Oreb and Zeeb.

Then the men of Israel said to Gideon: "Be our ruler, you and your son and your son's son, for you have delivered us from the hand of Midian."

But Gideon said: "I will not rule over you, neither shall my son rule over you. The Lord shall rule over you. But I have one request to make of you. Will you all give me the gold earrings that you took from your prey?"

For the Midianites were Ishmaelites and wore gold rings in their ears.

The men of Israel said: "We give them willingly."

They spread a cloak on the ground and every man cast in the earrings that he had taken from his victims. The weight of the earrings amounted to seventeen hundred shekels of gold, and there were also ornaments and collars and purple raiment from the kings of Midian, and the chains which had been round their camels' necks. And

Gideon took all these and put them in his city of Ophrah.

Thus was Midian utterly conquered by the children of Israel, and the country lived in peace for forty years, during the life of Gideon.

JOTHAM AND ABIMELECH

GIDEON'S wives were many, and when he died he left seventy sons. One of these, Abimelech, went to his mother's people in Shechem and said to them: "Do you want all those seventy sons of Gideon to reign over you? Would you not rather it were I alone, who am your near relation?"

They agreed that they would rather have him as ruler, and they gave him seventy pieces of silver with which he hired mercenaries who followed him to Ophrah. There Abimelech slew all his brothers except Jotham, the youngest, who hid himself.

Then all the men of Shechem gathered together and hailed Abimelech as king.

Jotham heard of this and he went and stood on the top of Mount Gerizim, and lifted up his voice. And he cried: "Listen to me, you men of Shechem, that the Lord may give ear to you.

"The trees went forth once upon a time to choose a king, and they said to the olive tree, 'Rule over us.'

"But the olive tree said to them, 'Should I leave my rich oil, by means of which both men and gods are honoured, and go to be king over the trees?'

"Then the trees said to the fig tree, 'You come and rule over us.'

"But the fig tree said to them, 'Should I forsake my sweetness and my good fruit, and go to be king over the trees?'

"Then the trees said to the vine, 'You come and rule over us.'

"And the vine said to them, 'Should I leave my wine which cheers gods and men, and go to be king over the trees?'

"Then all the trees said to the bramble, 'You come and rule over us.'

"And the bramble said: 'If you really appoint me king over you, then come and put your trust in my shadow, and if not, let fire come out of the bramble, and devour the cedars of Lebanon.'"

Jotham went on: "My father fought for you and risked his life and delivered you out of the hand of Midian. Today you have risen against my father's house and have slain his sons, and made Abimelech, the son of his maidservant, king, because he is your relation. If you consider that you dealt justly with Gideon, rejoice in Abimelech, and he in you, but if not, let Shechem destroy Abimelech, and let Abimelech devour Shechem."

Then Jotham ran away and he went to live in Beer, for fear of his brother Abimelech.

After three years Abimelech quarrelled with the men of Shechem who had raised him to power, and Abimelech destroyed them. But as he was besieging a tower within the city of Thebez, a woman cast a millstone down on his head.

Then Abimelech called his armourbearer and said to him:

"Draw your sword and kill me, so that nobody can say that I was slain by a woman."

Thus was Jotham's parable fulfilled.

JEPHTHAH'S VOW

EPHTHAH, the son of Gilead, was a mighty man of valour. He was a soldier of fortune who had been cast off by his brothers and therefore lived apart from them in the land of Tob. When the Ammonites made war against Israel, the people turned to Jephthah and asked him to be their captain and lead their armies.

This Jephthah agreed to do, but before going into battle he made a vow to the Lord. He said: "O God, if without fail you will deliver the children of Ammon into my hand, then when I return in peace to my own home, I swear that I shall offer up to the Lord as a burnt offering whatsoever shall first come out of the door of my house to greet me."

Then Jephthah went forth to battle and the Lord delivered the Ammonites into his power. He smote them from Aroer to Minnith and the plain of the vineyards, and destroyed them utterly.

After the battle he went back to Mizpah and as he approached his house, his daughter came out to meet him with timbrels and dances. She was his only child and he loved her more than all things of the world.

When he saw her Jephthah rent his

garments and cried out in despair: "Alas, my daughter, what have you done to me? For I have pledged my word to the Lord and I cannot go back on it."

And he told her what he had done. His daughter answered:

"No, Father, you cannot break your

oath, since the Lord has given you the victory over the Ammonites. You must do unto me as you promised. But grant me one favour, let me live for two months, that I may go with my maids and weep over my youth and mourn for the children that will never be mine."

"Go," said her father.

So Jephthah's daughter and her maidens went into the mountains, and all together they bewailed her sad fate.

But when the two months were up she came back to her father's house and he fulfilled his oath and offered her up as a sacrifice to the Lord.

SAMSON AND THE PHILISTINES

So Samson went to Timnath with his parents. As he came to the vineyards a young lion tried to attack him, and he killed it with his bare hands, but he did not tell his father and mother what he had done. He met the Philistine girl and spoke to her and she pleased him very much. When he returned again to see her, he turned aside to look for the carcass of the lion which he had killed, and found it with a swarm of bees and honey inside. He took out a handful of the honey and ate it, and gave some to his parents, but he did not tell them from where it came.

SAMSON'S RIDDLE

Later on, the marriage was arranged and a wedding feast was prepared. Thirty young Philistine men were present, and Samson said to them: "Here is a riddle for you, and if you can solve it for me within seven days of the feast, then I shall give you thirty sheets and thirty suits of clothes, but if you fail to find the answer, you must give me thirty sheets and thirty changes of clothing."

So they said: "Tell us your riddle."

Samson said: "Out of the eater came forth meat, and out of the strong came forth sweetness."

Three days passed and the Philistines had found no answer to the riddle.

On the seventh day they said to Samson's wife: "Coax your husband and persuade him to tell us the solution. Otherwise we shall set fire to your father's house and burn you alive."

Samson's wife wept and said to him: "You must hate me instead of loving me, for you have given my people a riddle to solve, and you have not told me the answer to it."

He said: "I have told neither my father nor my mother. Why should I tell you?"

FOR forty years the people of Israel were enslaved by the Philistines because of their evil ways in the sight of the Lord.

There was a man called Manoah of the family of the Danites, and he had no children. The angel of the Lord appeared to his wife and told her that she was to have a son.

The angel said: "Be cautious and drink no wine nor any strong drink, and do not eat any unclean thing. You will have a son and no razor shall come near his head, for he is dedicated to God from birth, and he shall begin to deliver Israel from the Philistines."

Later the angel appeared to Manoah also, and in due course he and his wife had a son whom they called Samson.

Samson grew up tall and strong, and when he was a grown man he went down to Timnath and saw a daughter of the Philistines and wanted to make her his wife. At first his parents withheld their accord, for they wished him to marry one of his own people. They did not know that this marriage was part of the Lord's plans to destroy the Philistines, but when Samson insisted, they abided by his wishes.

She went on weeping for seven days all the time that their feast was going on. At last, on the seventh day, Samson could bear it no longer and he told her the answer and she passed it on to her countrymen.

Before sunset on the seventh day, the men of the city said to Samson: "What is sweeter than honey? And what is stronger than a lion?"

Samson saw what had happened and he said:

"You would never have found the answer to my riddle if you had not threatened my wife."

He went down to Ashkelon and there he killed thirty men and took their belongings. From these he took thirty suits of clothes, which he gave to the men who had answered the riddle. Then he went back to his father's house. He was exceedingly angry at the Philistines and with the woman whom he had married.

SAMSON ANGERS
THE PHILISTINES

He caught three hundred foxes and
tied them tail to tail, and fixed torches
between their tails. Then he set fire to
the torches and let the foxes go to run
among the cornfields of the Philistines.
The shocks and the standing corn, the
vineyards, and the olives all caught fire
and were burned up.

After this the Philistines went up and
pitched their camp in Judah at Lehi,
and the men of Judah asked them why
they had come.

The Philistines said: "We have come
to capture and punish Samson."

Then three thousand men of Judah
went up to the top of the rock Etam and
said to Samson: "Do you not know
that the Philistines are our overlords?
We are going to bind you and give you
into their hands."

Samson said: "Promise me that you
will not yourselves attack me."

They said: "No, but we will bind you
fast and hand you over to them. But we
promise not to kill you."

So they bound him with two new
cords and brought him up from the
rock.

When he came to Lehi, where the
Philistines were encamped, they
shouted with triumph. But the spirit of
the Lord descended upon Samson and
the cords on his arms became as soft
as scorched flax, and the fetters fell
from his hands. He looked around and
saw the clean white jawbone of an ass,
and he picked it up, and with it he slew
a thousand men.

Then he threw away the jawbone and
called the place Remathlehi in memory
of his victory. But now he was parched
with thirst, and he called on the Lord
and said: "Lord, you have granted me
this great victory, but must I now die
of thirst and fall into the hands of the
enemy?"

God touched a hollow place in the rock, and water gushed out of it, so that Samson could drink his fill until his strength returned to him.

After that he became a judge in Israel under the Philistines and he judged the people for twenty years.

SAMSON'S MIGHTY STRENGTH

Samson loved a woman whose name was Delilah. The leaders of the Philistines came to her and said: "Coax him and learn what gives him his great strength, and by what means we may triumph over him, so that we may bind him and humble him. For this we will give you, each of us, eleven hundred pieces of silver."

So Delilah said to Samson: "Tell me, I beg you, what gives you your great strength, and how you could be bound to be made helpless."

"If anyone bound me with seven green willow stems that had never been dried, I should be as weak as any other man," Samson said to her.

Then the leaders of the Philistines brought to her seven green willow stems which had not been dried, and she bound him with them.

Now there were men lying in wait, waiting with her in the room. And she said to Samson: "The Philistines are upon you, Samson!"

But Samson broke the stems as a strand of hemp is broken when it touches the fire. So the secret of his strength was not known.

Delilah said to Samson: "See, you have mocked me and told me lies. Now tell me, I beg you, with what could you be securely bound?"

And he said to her: "If they bind me fast with new ropes that have never been used, then I shall be as weak as any other man."

Delilah therefore took new ropes and bound him with them and said to him: "The Philistines are upon you, Samson!"

And again there were men lying in wait in the room. But Samson broke the ropes from his arms like a thread.

Delilah said again to Samson: "Up to now you have mocked me and told me lies. Tell me now with what you could really be bound."

And he said to her: "Weave the seven locks of my hair with the web of cloth on your loom."

She did so while he slept, and fastened it with the pin of the loom. Then she said to him: "The Philistines are upon you, Samson!"

But he waked out of his sleep and carried away the pin of the loom and the web of cloth.

SAMSON TELLS HIS SECRET

Then she said to him: "How can you say 'I love you' when you do not trust me in your heart? Three times now you have mocked me and have not told me what the secret of your great strength is."

She continued entreating him every day, and when she had urged him, so that his soul was vexed unto death, he told her all that was in his heart.

"A razor has never touched my head," he said to her, "for I have been consecrated to God, since before I was born. If I were shaved, my strength would go from me, and I would become weak and be like any other man."

When Delilah saw that he had told her the secret of his heart, she called again for the lords of the Philistines, saying: "Come up once more, for he has told me the secret of his heart." Then the lords of the Philistines came up to her, bringing the money in their hands.

Delilah made Samson go to sleep with his head on her knees. Then she

called for a man and had him shave off the seven locks of Samson's hair. By that she humbled him, for his strength went from him.

Then she said: "The Philistines are upon you, Samson!"

He awoke from his sleep and said: "I will go out, as I did the other times,

and shake myself." For he did not know that the power of the Lord was gone from him.

The Philistines quickly took him, and put out his eyes, and took him down to Gaza. There they bound him with fetters of brass and made him grind in the prison house.

SAMSON'S REVENGE

Gradually the hair of his head began to grow again. But the Philistines did not notice.

They gathered together to offer a great sacrifice to Dagon, their god, and to rejoice. They said: "Our god

has delivered Samson our enemy into our hands."

When they saw Samson they praised their god, for they said: "Our god has delivered into our hands our enemy and the destroyer of our country, who has slain many of us."

It happened that, while the hearts of the people were merry, they said: "Call Samson out, so that he can entertain us." So they brought Samson up out of the prison house and mocked him.

When they stood him up between two pillars, Samson said to the boy who held him by the hand:

"Let me feel the pillars which support the house, so that I may lean upon them."

Now the house was full of men and women, and all the leaders of the Philistines were there. There were about three thousand men and women on the roof, watching while Samson was being mocked.

Then Samson called out to the Lord and said:

"O Lord God, remember me, I pray you, and strengthen me, I pray you, only this once, O God, that I may take revenge on the Philistines for my two eyes."

Then Samson took hold of the two middle pillars upon which the house stood, and which held it up. He held one with his right hand, and the other with his left.

Samson said: "Let me die with the Philistines." And he bowed himself with all his might, and the house fell upon all the people who were inside. The number he killed at his death was greater than he killed in his life.

Then his brothers, and all the household of his father, came down and took his body. And they took him home, and buried him between Zorah and Eshtaol, in the burying place of Manoah his father.

RUTH THE FAITHFUL DAUGHTER-IN-LAW

IT happened, in the old days when the judges ruled Israel, that there was a famine in the land. And a certain man of Bethlehem of Judah went to stay in the country of Moab, he and his wife and his two sons. The name of the man was Elimelech, and the name of his wife was Naomi, and his two sons were Mahlon and Chilion. They came into the country of Moab and stayed there.

Elimelech, Naomi's husband, died, and she was left with her two sons. They took wives of the women of Moab. The name of the one was Orpah, and the name of the other, Ruth. They lived there for about ten years.

Then Mahlon and Chilion both died, and their mother was left without husband or sons. She arose with her daughters-in-law, to return home from the country of Moab, for she had heard in the country of Moab that the Lord had visited his people and given them food again. Therefore she left the place where she was, with her two daughters-in-law, and they started to go back to the land of Judah.

But Naomi said to her two daughters-in-law: "Go, return each of you to her mother's house. May the Lord be as kind to you as you have been to the dead and to me."

They lifted up their voices and wept. Orpah kissed her mother-in-law, but Ruth clung to her.

And Naomi said to Ruth: "See, your sister-in-law has gone back to her people and to her gods. You go after your sister-in-law."

But Ruth said: "Do not ask me to leave you or to go back instead of following after you. For where you go, I will go; and where you stop, I will stop. Your people shall be my people, and your God my God. Where you die, I shall die, and there will I be buried. The Lord punish me if anything but death part me from you!"

When Naomi saw that Ruth was determined to go with her, she agreed. So the two travelled on until they came to Bethlehem. They reached Bethlehem at the beginning of the barley harvest.

Now Naomi had a kinsman of her husband's, a mighty man of great wealth, of the family of Elimelech. His name was Boaz.

Ruth said to Naomi: "Let me go now to the fields and glean ears of grain after whoever gives me his permission to do so."

And Naomi said to her: "Go, my daughter."

So Ruth came to the field and gleaned after the reapers. It was her fortune to light on a part of the field belonging to Boaz.

RUTH PLEASES BOAZ

It happened that Boaz came from Bethlehem and said to the reapers: "The Lord be with you."

And they answered him: "The Lord bless you."

Then Boaz said to the servant who was in charge of the reapers: "Whose girl is that?"

The servant in charge of the reapers answered and said: "It is the Moabitish girl who came back with Naomi from the country of Moab. She asked permission to gather and glean after the reapers among the sheaves, so she came and has worked since morning, until just now when she rested a little in the shelter."

Then Boaz said to Ruth: "Do you hear me, my daughter? Do not go to glean in another field, nor go away from here, but stay close by my maidservants. Watch the field where they reap and follow them. I have ordered the servants not to touch you. And when you are thirsty, go to the water jars and drink from the water which the young men have drawn."

Then she fell on her face and bowed herself to the ground and said to him: "Why should I have found favour in your eyes, that you should take notice of me, seeing that I am a stranger?"

Boaz answered and said to her: "I have heard all that you have done for your mother-in-law since the death of your husband, and how you have left your father and mother and the land of your birth, and have come to a people you had never known before. May the Lord repay your good deeds, and may a full reward be given you by the Lord God of Israel under whose wings you have come to rest."

Then she said: "Let me find favour in your sight, my lord; for you have comforted me by speaking friendly words to your handmaid, when I am not in truth a handmaid of yours."

And Boaz said to her: "At mealtime come here and eat of the bread and dip your piece into the sauce."

So she sat beside the reapers, and he passed her parched grain, and she ate until she had had enough, and then left.

When she arose to glean again, Boaz gave orders to his young men, saying: "Let her glean even among the sheaves, and do not reproach her. And also let fall some handfuls on purpose for her, and leave them so that she may glean them, and do not stop her."

So she gleaned in the field until evening, and threshed out what she had gleaned.

She gathered it up and went into the city and showed her mother-in-law what she had gleaned.

Her mother-in-law said to her: "Where did you glean today? Where did you work? Blessed be he that took notice of you."

She told her mother-in-law with whom she had worked, saying: "The man with whom I worked today is named Boaz."

Then Naomi said to her daughter-in-law: "May the Lord bless him, for the Lord has not stopped showing kindness to the living and the dead." And she added: "The man is near of kin to us, one of our next kinsmen."

Ruth said: "He told me, too, to stay near his young men until they have finished his harvest."

And Naomi said to Ruth: "It is good that you go out with his maidservants, so that you do not go into any other field.

So Ruth stayed close to the maidens of Boaz to glean until the end of the barley harvest and of the wheat harvest; and she lived with her mother-in-law.

NAOMI INSTRUCTS RUTH

Then Naomi said to Ruth: "My daughter, I must seek peace that all may be well with you. Boaz, with whose maidens you have been working, is our kinsman and can help you. Tonight he is winnowing barley on the threshing floor. Wash and anoint yourself and put on your best robe and go down to the threshing floor and wait until he has finished eating and drinking. Then tell him you are there, and he will tell you what to do."

Ruth did all that her mother-in-law told her, and at midnight, after he had eaten and drunk, Boaz realized that she was there, and he said: "Who is it?"

She answered: "I am Ruth, your handmaid. Help me, for you are my near kinsman."

Boaz said: "The Lord bless you, my daughter, for you have proved yourself to be a virtuous woman, and I will do whatever you want. It is true that I am a near kinsman, but there is another who is even more closely related than I. Wait until tomorrow morning, and we shall see if he will perform his duty as your kinsman. If not, I swear before the Lord that I shall do it in his place. And now lie down until the morning."

So Ruth lay down on the threshing floor and the next morning Boaz said to her: "Bring your veil to me and hold it out."

When she did so he measured out six measures of barley into the veil, and she went back to the city and to her mother-in-law.

Ruth told Naomi all that Boaz had said and showed her the six measures

215

of barley, and Naomi said: "Wait quietly, my daughter, until you know what is to result from this. This man will not rest until he has provided for you this very day."

In the meantime Boaz went up to the gate and there he met Ruth's kinsman and called him to stop and take counsel with him and with ten elders of the city.

Boaz said to the kinsman: "Naomi has returned from the land of Moab and is selling a piece of land which belonged to our brother Elimelech. I have thought to tell you of this in advance, so that you could buy it before the inhabitants and the elders of my people. If you wish to redeem it, do so. If not, tell me, so that I may know, for after you no man has the right to do so."

The kinsman said: "I will do so."

Then Boaz told him: "If you buy the land from Naomi, you must also marry Ruth the Moabitess, to raise up the name of the dead upon his inheritance."

When the kinsman heard this, he said: "I cannot redeem it for myself, for fear of risking my own inher-

itance. Will you take over my rights?"

It was the custom in Israel that if a man made over his rights, he took off his shoe and gave it to his neighbour. When the kinsman said to Boaz: "Buy it for yourself", he drew off his shoe. Boaz said to the elders and to all the people: "You are witnesses that I have bought from Naomi all that belonged to Elimelech, and to Chilion and Mahlon. And I have purchased Ruth the Moabitess, the wife of Mahlon, to be my wife, to raise up the name of the dead upon his inheritance. You are all witnesses."

And the elders and all the people agreed and said: "We are witnesses. And may the Lord bless your house and make it famous in Bethlehem."

So Boaz took Ruth as his wife and Ruth bore him a son. And the women said to Naomi: "Blessed be the name of the Lord, who has not left you without a kinsman, and may his name be famous in Israel. To you he shall be a restorer of your life and a support in your old age, for he is the child of your daughter-in-law who loves you and is better to you than seven sons."

So Naomi took the child and became his nurse.

And the women her neighbours said: "It is as though he were Naomi's own son."

And the child was called Obed. He became the father of Jesse, who was the father of David.

SAMUEL CHILD OF THE LORD

When she had weaned him, she took him up with her, with a young bull of three years and one measure of flour and a bottle of wine. She brought him to the house of the Lord in Shiloh, when the child was still very young.

And so the young bull was slain and the child was brought to Eli the priest. And Hannah said: "O my lord, I am the woman who stood in the temple here, praying to the Lord. I prayed for this child, and the Lord has given me what I asked of him. Therefore

ONCE there was a woman named Hannah who was bitter in her soul because she had no sons or daughters. She prayed to the Lord and wept sadly. And she vowed a vow:

"O Lord of hosts, if you will look down upon the sadness of your handmaiden and remember me, and will give to your handmaiden a man child, then I will give him to the Lord all the days of his life, and no razor shall touch his head."

It came to pass in due time that Hannah bore a son, and she called him Samuel, "Because," she said, "I asked him of the Lord."

Her husband Elkanah, and all his household, went up to offer to the Lord the yearly sacrifice. But Hannah did not go, for she said to her husband: "I will not go up until the child is weaned, and then I will take him so that he may appear before the Lord and stay there for ever."

Elkanah her husband said to her: "Do what seems to you best. Wait until you have weaned him; only keep your word to the Lord." So the woman stayed at home and nursed her son until he was old enough to wean.

I have lent him to the Lord. As long as he lives he shall be lent to the Lord."

Then they worshipped the Lord there. And when Elkanah and his household went home, Samuel stayed, and was taught by Eli the priest.

Each year Samuel's mother made him a little coat and brought it to him when she came up with her husband to offer the yearly sacrifice.

And the child Samuel grew, and was in favour both with the Lord and with men. And he ministered to the Lord before Eli.

GOD CALLS SAMUEL

Eli's eyes began to grow dim, so that he could not see. Once, when Eli was lying down in his place, before the lamp of God was put out in the temple where the ark of the Lord was kept, and before Samuel had lain down to sleep, God called Samuel, and he answered: "Here I am."

And Samuel ran to Eli and said: "Here I am; you called me."

Eli said: "I did not call. Lie down and sleep."

He went and lay down, and again God called: "Samuel."

Samuel arose and went to Eli and said: "Here I am, for you called me."

And Eli answered: "I did not call, my son; lie down again."

Now Samuel did not yet recognize the Lord, nor had the voice of the Lord been made known to him.

And God called Samuel again a third time, and he arose and went to Eli and said: "Here I am, for you called me."

Then Eli understood that the Lord had called the child. So Eli said to Samuel: "Go and lie down, and if he calls you, you are to say: 'Speak, Lord, for your servant is listening.'"

So Samuel went and lay down in his place.

And God came and stood there, and called as at the other times: "Samuel, Samuel."

Then Samuel answered: "Speak, for your servant is listening."

And then God said to Samuel: "Behold, I am going to do something in Israel at which the ears of everyone who hears it shall tingle. On an appointed day I will perform against Eli all the things I have spoken of concerning his household" (for Eli's sons were very wicked) "and when I begin I shall finish it. For I have told him that I will judge his house for

you, and more, if you hide anything from me of the things he said to you."

So Samuel told him everything, and hid nothing from him.

Eli said: "It is the Lord: let him do whatever seems good to him."

Samuel grew, and the Lord was with him. And all Israel, from Dan to Beersheba, knew that Samuel was to be a prophet of the Lord.

THE PHILISTINES
CAPTURE THE ARK

Now Israel went out to battle against the Philistines. After a bloody day's reverses, the elders of Israel said: "Why has the Lord struck us today before the Philistines? Let us fetch the ark of the covenant of the Lord from Shiloh, so that when it comes among us it may save us from the hand of our enemies."

So the people sent to Shiloh, and when the ark of the covenant of the Lord came into the camp, all Israel shouted with a great shout, so that the earth rang out.

And when the Philistines heard the noise of the shout, they said: "What does this mean, the noise of this great shout in the camp of the Hebrews?"

They learned that the ark of the Lord had come into the camp, and they were afraid, for they said: "God has come into the camp. Woe unto us! This is the god that struck the Egyptians with all the plagues in the wilderness."

But their leaders said: "Be strong and act like men, O Philistines, so that you do not become servants to the Hebrews as they have been to you. Quit yourselves like men and fight."

And the Philistines fought and Israel was defeated. There was a very great slaughter. Thirty thousand of Israel's footmen fell, and the ark of God was taken.

ever for the wickedness of which he knows, because his sons became evil, and he did not restrain them. Therefor I have sworn to the house of Eli that their wickedness shall not be cleansed with sacrifices nor offerings for ever."

Samuel lay until morning. Then he opened the doors of the house of the Lord, but he feared to tell Eli of the vision. Then Eli called Samuel and said: "Samuel, my son."

And he answered: "Here I am."

And Eli said: "What was it that the Lord said to you? I beg you not to hide it from me. May God punish

SAMUEL
AND
SAUL

AMUEL judged Israel all the days of his life. He went from year to year on circuit to Bethel and Gilgal and Mizpeh and judged Israel in all these places. But his home was in Ramah and there he judged Israel and built an altar unto the Lord.

When Samuel was old he made his sons Joel and Abiah judges over Israel. But they did not walk in his ways, for they took bribes and delivered false judgments.

THE PEOPLE ASK FOR A KING

Then all the elders of Israel gathered themselves together and came to Samuel in Ramah and said to him: "Behold, you are old and your sons do not walk in your ways. Give us a king to judge us, like all the other nations."

Their words displeased Samuel. He prayed to the Lord and God answered, saying: "Listen to the voice of all the people, for it is not you that they have rejected, but me, that I may not reign over them. And as they have forsaken me and served false gods ever since the day that I brought them up out of Egypt, even so do they unto

you. So listen to their voice. Nevertheless, make a solemn protest, and show them what kind of a king is going to reign over them."

So Samuel told the people what God had said to him. And he said: "This is the kind of king who will reign over you. He will take your sons to be his charioteers and his horsemen, and to run before his chariots, to till his ground and reap his harvests and to manufacture his weapons and his chariots. He will take your daughters to be his cooks and bakers; your fields will he take and your best vineyards, and olive groves, and give them to his servants. And he will take a tenth part of your grain and of your vintage, and give it to his officers and his servants. He will take your menservants and your maidservants, your best young men and your asses, and put them to work for him. And you will complain and mourn because of this king whom you have chosen, but the Lord will not listen to you."

However, the people refused to obey the voice of Samuel. They said: "No, we want a king like all the other nations, a king to judge us and fight our battles."

Samuel listened and repeated what they had said to the Lord.

And God said to him: "Give them their way and find them a king."

So Samuel said to the men of Israel: "All of you, go back to your own city."

Now there was a Benjamite called Kish, a man of power and standing, and he had a son whose name was Saul. Saul was the most handsome man of Israel, and he stood head and shoulders above all others.

Kish had lost some of his asses, so he said to his son Saul: "Take one of the servants with you, and go and look for my asses."

So Saul travelled across the Mount

Ephraim and through the land of Sha-
lisha and the land of Shalim and the
land of the Benjamites, but he found
no trace of his father's asses.

When they came to the land of Zuph,
Saul said to his servant: "Come, let
us go home, or my father will cease to
think about his asses and begin to
wonder about our own fate. But in this
city there is a man of God, and he is

an honourable man. Let us go to see
him, and perhaps he can show us which
path to follow. Only, if we do consult
him, what shall we bring as a present?
For we have nothing left that is fit for
a man of God."

Saul's servant said: "See, I have the
fourth part of a shekel of silver. We can
give that to the man of God and he will
tell us which way to go."

SAUL MEETS SAMUEL

They went into the city and the maidens at the well told them that Samuel was going to bless a sacrifice that day on the high place, so they went on to the high place and met Samuel on his way there.

The Lord had warned Samuel the day before that a Benjamite was coming to meet him, and that this was the man whom he should anoint king of Israel. When Samuel saw Saul, the Lord said: "Here is the man of whom I spoke, the one who shall reign over my people."

So Samuel spoke to Saul and told him to set his mind no longer upon the lost asses for they had been found. He said: "To whom does Israel look? Is it not to you and all your father's house?"

Saul said: "I am a Benjamite, a member of the smallest of all the tribes of Israel, and my family is the least important in the tribe of Ben-

jamin. Why do you speak to me in this manner?"

Samuel took Saul and his servant and brought them into the parlour and made them sit at the head of the table, above all the other guests, of whom there were about thirty. And Samuel told the cook to serve Saul with the special portion of meat which had been reserved for the guest of honour.

The next day Samuel took a vial of oil, and poured it upon Saul's head and kissed him and said: "Is it not because the Lord has anointed you to be captain of his people?"

Saul went back to his own country, and the Spirit of God came upon him and he prophesied, so that those who knew him before were amazed and said: "What has happened to the son of Kish? Is Saul also one of the prophets?" Saul told his family that he had met a man of God who had told him that the lost asses were found, but, in telling them, he made no mention of his anointing or of the kingdom.

SAUL IS PROCLAIMED KING

Now Samuel called the people together at Mizpeh and said to them: "Thus says the Lord God of Israel, 'I brought Israel out of Egypt and delivered you out of the hand of the Egyptians and out of the hand of all kingdoms and those that oppressed you.' But you have this day rejected your God who himself saved you from your adversities and your tribulations, and you have said to him: 'Nay, but set a king over us.'

"Now therefore present yourselves before the Lord by your tribes and by your thousands." And when Samuel had caused all the tribes of Israel to come near, the tribe of Benjamin was indicated by lot. When he had caused the tribe of Benjamin to come near by families, the family of Matri was indicated, and Saul, the son of Kish, was indicated. But when they sought him, he could not at first be found.

And when they did find him, he was among the baggage. He was brought into the crowd, and when he stood among them he was higher than any of them from his shoulders upward.

And Samuel said: "Look, there is the man whom the Lord has chosen, and there is nobody like him among all the people."

And all the people shouted and said: "God save the king."

Saul became a great king and a mighty man of valour, and he led the children of Israel into many battles against their enemies the Philistines, but after a while he disobeyed the laws of the Lord.

Samuel warned him, saying: "You have been very foolish in not keeping the commandment of the Lord your God, for had you done so, the Lord would have established your kingdom upon Israel for ever. But now your kingdom will not continue."

JONATHAN BREAKS THE OATH

Saul had a son name Jonathan and it came to pass one day in the course of a battle that Saul said to the people: "Cursed be the man that eats any food until evening, that I may be avenged of my enemies." So none of the people tasted any food.

And all they of the land came to a wood and there was honey on the ground. But no man put his hand to his mouth, for the people feared the curse.

But Jonathan did not hear when his father charged the people with the oath. Therefore, he put the end of the rod that was in his hand and dipped it in a honeycomb and put his hand to his mouth.

Then one of the people said, 'Your father ordered the people with an oath, saying: 'Cursed be the man that eats any food this day.' " But Jonathan said: "My father has troubled the land."

After a battle with the Philistines, Saul said: "Let us go down after them again by night and fight them until the morning light, and let us not leave a man alive among them."

Saul asked counsel of God: "Shall I go down after the Philistines? Will you deliver them into the hand of Israel?"

But the Lord did not answer him that day. So Saul said: "Draw together all chiefs of the people, and let us see what sin has been done this day. For, as the Lord lives that saves Israel, even if the sin be Jonathan my son's, he shall surely die."

Therefore lots were chosen, first between Saul and Jonathan on one side and the people on the other, and then between Saul and Jonathan. And Jonathan was indicated. Then Saul said to Jonathan, "Tell me what you have done." And Jonathan told him: "I did but taste a little honey with the

end of the rod that was in my hand, and lo, I must die."

And Saul answered: "You shall surely die, Jonathan."

THE PEOPLE RESCUE JONATHAN

Then the people said to Saul: "Shall Jonathan die who has wrought this great salvation in Israel? God forbid. As the Lord lives, there shall not one hair of his head fall to the ground, for he has worked with God this day."

So the people rescued Jonathan and he did not die.

Then Saul went up from following the Philistines, and the Philistines went to their own place.

SAUL DISOBEYS THE LORD

Samuel said to Saul: "The Lord sent me to anoint you to be king over his people, over Israel. Now therefore listen to the voice of the words of the Lord. Thus says the Lord of hosts: 'I remember what Amalek did to Israel, how he laid in wait for him on the road when he came from Egypt. Now go and attack Amalek and utterly destroy all that they have, and do not spare them. But slay both man and woman, child and baby, ox and sheep, camel and ass.' "

Saul struck the Amalekites from Havilah to Shur, near Egypt. He took Agag the king of the Amalekites alive, and utterly destroyed all the people with the edge of the sword. But Saul and the people spared the best of the sheep and of the oxen and of the fatlings, and the lambs and all that was good, and would not destroy them.

But everything that was vile they destroyed utterly.

Then the word of the Lord came to Samuel, saying: "I regret that I have set up Saul to be king. For he has turned back from following me, and has not performed my commandments." And it grieved Samuel, and he cried to the Lord all night.

And Samuel came to Saul, and Saul said to him: "Blessed be you of the Lord. I have performed the commandment of the Lord."

Samuel said: "What means then this bleating of sheep and the lowing of oxen which I hear?"

And Saul said: "They have brought them from the Amalekites, for the people spared the best of the sheep and of the oxen to sacrifice to the Lord your God. And the rest we have destroyed utterly."

Then Samuel said to Saul: "The Lord sent you on a journey and said, 'Go and utterly destroy the sinners, the Amalekites.' Why then did you not obey the voice of the Lord?

"Has the Lord as great delight in burnt offerings and sacrifices as in obeying the voice of the Lord? Behold, to obey is better than to sacrifice, and to listen than the fat of rams. For rebellion is like the sin of witchcraft, and stubbornness is like iniquity and idolatry. Because you have rejected the word of the Lord, he has also rejected you from being king."

Saul said: "I have sinned, for I have disobeyed the commandments of the Lord, because I feared the people and obeyed their voice. Nevertheless, pardon my sin, I pray you, and come back with me, so that I may worship the Lord."

But Samuel answered: "I will not go back with you, for you have rejected the word of the Lord, and the Lord has rejected you from being king over Israel."

Samuel turned to go away, but Saul took hold of the skirt of his mantle and the skirt tore.

Samuel said to him: "The Lord has torn the kingdom of Israel from you today, and has given it to a neighbour of yours who is better than you. The strength of Israel will not lie or repent; for he is not a man if he must repent."

Saul said: "I have done wrong, but I pray you to honour me now, before the elders of my people and before Israel, and go back with me, that I may worship the Lord your God."

Samuel relented and went back with Saul; and Saul worshipped the Lord.

Then Samuel returned to Ramah, and Saul went to his house.

As long as he lived Samuel never saw Saul again, but he mourned for him. And the Lord regretted that he had made Saul king over Israel.

DAVID THE LORD'S CHOSEN ONE

THE Lord God said to Samuel: "How long will you mourn for Saul, seeing I have rejected him from reigning over Israel? Fill your horn with oil and go. I will send you to Jesse of Bethlehem, for I have chosen a king from among his sons."

Samuel did as the Lord told him and came to Bethlehem. The elders of the town trembled at his coming and said: "Do you come peaceably?"

"Peaceably," he said, "I have come to sacrifice to the Lord. Make yourselves ready and come with me to the sacrifice."

He blessed Jesse and his sons and called them to the sacrifice.

When they came, he looked at Eliab and said: "Surely the Lord's chosen one is before him now."

But God answered, saying: "Do not look at his face or the height of him, because I have refused him. For the Lord does not see as man sees. Man looks on the outward appearance, but the Lord looks at the heart."

Then Jesse called Abinadab and made him pass before Samuel; but Samuel said: "The Lord has not chosen this one either."

Then Jesse made Shammah pass by, and Samuel said: "Neither has the Lord chosen this one."

One after the other, Jesse made seven of his sons pass before Samuel. And Samuel said to Jesse: "The Lord has not chosen these." Then he asked: "Are all your children here?"

And Jesse said: "There is still the youngest, David. He is keeping the sheep."

Samuel said to Jesse: "Send and fetch him here, for we will not sit down until he comes."

David was sent for, and soon appeared. He was a fine, healthy boy, and handsome.

Then God said to Samuel: "Arise, anoint him, for this is he."

Then Samuel took the horn of oil and anointed David in the midst of his brothers. And the Spirit of the Lord was with David from that day on.

DAVID MEETS SAUL THE KING

And the spirit of the Lord departed from Saul, and an evil spirit troubled him.

Then Saul's servants said to him: "You see, an evil spirit from God is sent to trouble you. Now if you will command your servants, who are here before you, to find a man who is a cunning player on the harp, then when the evil spirit comes from God, he will play upon the strings, and you will be well."

"Find me a man who can play well," said Saul to his servants, "and bring him to me."

Then one of the servants answered and said: "I have seen a son of Jesse the Bethlehemite, who is clever at playing, an exceedingly courageous man, a man of war, prudent in all things, a handsome person and the Lord is with him."

Therefore Saul sent messengers to

Jesse, and said: "Send me your son David, who is tending the sheep."

Jesse took an ass loaded with food, and a bottle of wine, and a kid, and sent them by David his son to Saul. And David came to Saul and stood before him, and served him.

Saul loved David very much and he was made the king's armour-bearer.

Then Saul sent word to Jesse, saying: "Let David stay with me, for he pleases me very much."

And it was true that when the evil spirit from God came upon Saul, David took a harp and played upon the strings, and Saul was refreshed and felt well again. The evil spirit departed from him at the sound of the music.

DAVID AND GOLIATH

GOLIATH CHALLENGES THE ISRAELITES

Goliath stood and cried out to the armies of Israel: "Why have you come out to set up your armies in battle array? Am I not a Philistine, and you servants of Saul? Choose a man to represent you and let him come down to me. If he can fight me and kill me, then we will be your servants, but if I win over him and kill him, then you shall be our servants and serve us." And he added: "I defy the armies of Israel this day; send me a man that we may fight together."

When Saul and all the Israelites heard those words of the Philistine, they were dismayed and very much frightened. And every morning and evening for forty days the Philistine drew near and challenged the Israelites.

David at this time left the court of Saul to go home and feed his father's sheep at Bethlehem. His three eldest brothers were in the army of Saul.

Now Jesse said to David his son: "Take a measure of this parched grain and these ten loaves for your brothers and run to your brothers' camp. Take these ten cheeses to the captain of their group, and see how your brothers are faring."

David rose early in the morning and left the sheep with a keeper, and departed as Jesse had commanded him. He came to the battle line just as the army was going out to fight, shouting their battle cry. For Israel and the Philistines had put the army in battle array, army against army.

David left his baggage in the hands of the keeper of the baggage, and ran among the army. He came up to his brothers and saluted them.

As he talked with them, there appeared the champion Goliath, out of the armies of the Philistines, and he made his challenge, and David heard it.

OW the Philistines gathered their forces for battle. They gathered at Shochoh, and they camped in Ephes-dammim.

Saul and the men of Israel were gathered together and camped in the valley of Elah, lined up in battle array against the Philistines.

The Philistines stood on a mountain on one side, and Israel stood on a mountain on the other side, and there was a valley between them.

Out from the camp of the Philistines came a champion named Goliath of Gath, whose height was nine feet and nine inches. He had a helmet of brass upon his head, and he was armed with a coat of mail, and the weight of the coat was five thousand shekels of brass. He had plates of brass upon his legs, and a shield of brass between his shoulders. The staff of his spear was like a weaver's beam, and his spear's head weighed six hundred shekels of iron. A shield bearer walked before him.

All the men of Israel, when they saw the man, fled from him and were very much afraid. "Have you seen this man who came up?" the men of Israel said. "He has come up to challenge Israel, and to the man who can kill him the king will give great riches, and he will give him his daughter in marriage, and will make his father's house free in Israel."

And David spoke to the men who stood near him, saying: "Who is this heathen Philistine, that he should chal-

and the wickedness of your heart, for you have come down just so that you might see the battle."

David said: "What have I now done? Is there not a reason?" He turned from him towards another man and spoke to him in the same way, and the people spoke again of the reward.

And when the people heard the words which David spoke, they repeated them before Saul, and he sent for the boy.

lenge the armies of the living God?"

Eliab, his eldest brother, heard him speak to the men, and Eliab's anger was kindled against David, and he said: "Why did you come down here? With whom did you leave those few sheep in the wilderness? I know your pride

DAVID OFFERS TO FIGHT

And David said to Saul: "Let no man's heart be troubled because of Goliath. I, your servant, will go and fight with this Philistine."

Saul said: "You are not able to go

out to fight with this Philistine, for you are but a boy, and he has been a man of war since his youth."

David said to Saul: "Your servant kept his father's sheep, and a lion came, and a bear, and took a lamb out of the flock. I gave chase, and struck the lion down, and rescued it out of his mouth, and when he arose against me, I caught him by his beard and struck him and killed him. Your servant killed both the lion and the bear, and this heathen Philistine will be as one

Then Saul said to David: "Go, and the Lord be with you."

Saul armed David with his armour, and he put a helmet of brass on his head, and clothed him in a coat of mail. David fastened Saul's sword upon his armour and tried to walk, in order to test the armour, but finding he could not, he said to Saul: "I cannot fight with these, for I am not used to them." Saul's pieces of armour were too heavy and cumbersome so he undid them and took them off.

of them, seeing that he has challenged the armies of the living God."

Moreover, David said: "The Lord who saved me from the paw of the lion and from the paw of the bear, he will save me from the hand of this Philistine."

He took his staff in his hand, and bending down chose five smooth stones out of the brook, and put them in a shepherd's bag which he carried with him. With his sling in his hand he drew near to the giant Philistine, who waited.

TRIUMPH WITH A SLING

The Philistine came on and drew near to David, and the shield bearer went before him. But when the Philistine looked and saw David, he despised him, for he was but a boy, fine and fair of face.

The Philistine said to David: "Am I a dog, that you come to fight me with sticks?" And the Philistine cursed David by his gods.

And the Philistine said to David: "Come to me, and I will give your flesh to the fowls of the air, and to the beasts of the field."

Then David said to the Philistine: "You come to me with a sword and with a spear and with a shield, but I come to you in the name of the Lord of hosts, the God of the army of Israel, whom you have challenged. This day the Lord will put you into my hands, and I will strike you down and take your head from you, and I will give the bodies of the army of the Philistines to the birds of the air and to the wild beasts of the earth, so that all the earth may know that there is a God in Israel. And everyone gathered here will know that the Lord saves not with sword and spear, but the battle is the Lord's and he will give you into our hands."

Then, as the Philistine rose up and came nearer to meet David, David hurried and ran towards the army to meet the Philistine. And he put his hand into his bag, and took out a stone, and slung it, and hit the Philistine in his forehead, so that the stone sank into his forehead and he fell upon his face on the earth.

So David triumphed over the Philistine with a sling and with a stone, and struck down the Philistine and killed him; but there was no sword in David's hand.

Therefore David ran and stood upon the Philistine and taking Goliath's sword cut off his head and killed him.

When the Philistines saw that their champion was dead, they fled. And the men of Israel arose, shouting, and pursued the Philistines all the way to the valley, to the gates of Ekron.

The Philistines who were wounded fell down by the road to Shaaraim, as far as Gath and Ekron. Then the children of Israel came back from chasing the Philistines and pillaged their tents. And David took the head of the Philistine and brought it to Jerusalem; but he put the armour in his own tent.

And when Saul had seen David going forth against Goliath, he had said to Abner, his general: "Abner, whose son is this youth?"

Abner said: "Upon my word, O king, I do not know."

The king said: "Find out who is this stripling's father."

And as David returned from the slaughter of the Philistine, Abner took him and brought him before Saul with Goliath's head in his hand.

And Saul said: "Whose son are you, young man?"

David said: "I am the son of your servant, Jesse the Bethlehemite."

SAUL'S JEALOUSY

AUL took David home that day, and would not let him go back to his father's house. He set him over all his men of war, and the people and the palace servants accepted him. Jonathan, Saul's son, came to love David as his own brother, and they made a covenant of friendship.

But as David was returning from the slaughter of the Philistines, the women came out of the cities of Israel, singing and dancing, to meet king Saul, with tabrets and other musical instruments. And the women sang to each other as they played, and said:

"Saul has slain his thousands,
And David his ten thousands."

This much displeased Saul, and he said: "If they reckon that David is ten times better than I, he will soon want to have the kingdom for himself."

And from this time forward Saul eyed David with suspicion.

The next day, David was playing his harp as before, and an evil spirit came upon Saul and he picked up a javelin and threw it at David, saying: "I will pin David to the wall with it."

David avoided the point of the javelin, and Saul was more than ever afraid of him, for he knew that the Lord was with David, and no longer with him.

But David behaved very wisely in all his ways and all Israel loved and trusted him.

Then Saul said to David: "Here is my elder daughter Merab. I will give her to you as your wife, if you will fight my battles for me." For Saul did not want to kill David with his own hand, and he hoped that he would fall in battle with the Philistines.

David said: "Who am I, and what is my family, that I should be the king's son-in-law?"

But at the time that Merab should have been given to David, instead Saul married her to Adriel the Meholathite.

But it happened that Michal, Saul's younger daughter, also loved David, and when Saul was told of this, he was very pleased, thinking that through her love he might ensnare and destroy David.

So he sent for David and told him: "Today you will be my son-in-law, and marry the other of my daughters."

To his servants he said: "Take David aside and tell him privately that the king delights in him, and that all the people love him, and so it is fitting that he should be the king's son-in-law."

DAVID MARRIES SAUL'S DAUGHTER

But when he heard this, David said: "I am too poor and insignificant to marry a king's daughter."

The servants reported this to Saul and he said: "Tell David that the king does not wish for any dowry, only the death of a hundred Philistines, to be avenged of the king's enemies."

When David heard this he was pleased, for he wanted very much to be the king's son-in-law, so he went forth with his men and slew two hundred Philistines, and Saul gave him Michal as his wife.

But Saul saw and knew that the Lord was with David, and that Michal loved him, and he was still more afraid of David, and still more his enemy.

And Saul spoke to Jonathan his son and to all his servants and ordered them to kill David. But Jonathan went to his friend and said: "My father Saul is trying to kill you, so I beg of you to go and hide yourself. Tomorrow morning I shall go out and stand beside my father in the field where you are, and I will talk to him about you, and whatever I learn I shall tell you."

The next day Jonathan talked to Saul as he had promised, and told him what a great and good man David was, and urged his father not to stain his hands with innocent blood.

Saul listened to Jonathan's words and promised that David should not be slain.

So Jonathan called David from his hiding place and brought him before Saul and for a time all was well, and when the Philistines went to war again, David fought against them and slew many of them.

But again Saul was possessed by an evil spirit, and sat with his javelin in his hand while David played the harp. Again he tried to kill David, and again

David slipped out of the path of the javelin and escaped from the palace.

Saul sent messengers to his house to watch and slay him in the morning, and Michal, David's wife, said to her husband: "If you do not get away tonight, tomorrow you will be killed."

So Michal let David down through a window, and then she made up the bed to look as though David were lying asleep in it.

And when Saul sent his messengers to take David, she said: "He is ill."

But Saul sent the messengers back to see David, saying: "Bring him up to me in his bed and I shall slay him."

When the messengers came in, they saw that there was no one in the bed.

Saul said to Michal: "Why have you deceived me and helped my enemy to escape."

Michal answered: "He said to me, 'Let me escape; otherwise I shall kill you.'"

When David fled he took refuge with Samuel at Naioth in Ramah.

DAVID AND JONATHAN

AVID left Naioth and came to Jonathan and said to him: "What have I done that your father should try to kill me?"

Jonathan said: "I will do all in my power to try to save you. I know that my father will do nothing without consulting me, so I shall speak to him about your fate and tell you what he says. If he is ill disposed towards you, I shall warn you so that you may flee, but whatever passes, we shall remain friends for ever and ever."

So they made a solemn covenant of friendship, for Jonathan loved David as he loved his own soul.

Then Jonathan said to David: "Tomorrow is the feast of the new moon, and you will be missed, because your seat will be empty. When you have stayed away three days, come down quickly and wait by the stone Ezel. I will shoot three arrows beside the stone, as if I shot at a target. And watch, I will send a boy, saying: 'Go, find the arrows.' If I expressly say to the boy, 'See the arrows are on this side of you, pick them up,' then you come out, for there will be peace and no harm will be done to you, as the Lord lives. But if I say to the young man, 'See, the arrows are beyond you,' go your way, for the Lord will have sent you away. And

concerning friendship of which we have spoken, may the Lord be between you and me for ever."

So David hid himself in the field.

When the moon had come, the king sat down to the feast. The king sat upon his seat, as always, a seat along the wall, and Jonathan and Abner sat beside Saul, but David's place was empty.

Still Saul did not say anything that day.

But it happened on the next day, which was the second day of the month, that David's place was empty again, and Saul said to Jonathan: "Why did the son of Jesse not come to dinner either yesterday or today?"

And Jonathan answered: "David earnestly asked permission of me to go to Bethlehem, for he said his family was to have a sacrifice there, and his brother had bidden him to come, and he desired to see all his brothers. That is why he did not come to the king's table."

Then Saul's anger was kindled against Jonathan, and he said to him: "You son of a perverse, rebellious woman, do I not know that you have chosen the son of Jesse to your own downfall? For as long as he lives, you shall not be established in the kingdom. Now send and fetch him to me, for he must die."

But Jonathan answered Saul his father, and said to him: "Why should he be slain? What has he done?"

Then Saul threw a javelin at him to strike him, and by that Jonathan knew that his father was determined to kill David. So Jonathan arose from the table in fierce anger, and ate not at all the second day of the month, for he grieved for David.

In the morning Jonathan went out into the field at the time he had set with David, taking a little boy with him.

He said to the lad: "Run and hunt for the arrows which I am going to shoot." And as the lad ran, he shot an arrow beyond him.

When the lad had come to the place where the arrow fell, Jonathan cried out to the lad and said: "Is not the arrow beyond you?" And again he cried: "Make haste, do not delay!"

Jonathan's lad took up the fallen arrow and came to his master, but the lad did not understand the meaning.

Only Jonathan and David knew of the matter.

Then Jonathan gave his weapons to the lad, and said to him: "Go, carry them down to the city." And as soon as the lad was gone, David rose up from a place toward the south and fell on his face on the ground, and bowed himself three times.

They kissed each other and wept with each other, and Jonathan said to David: "Go in peace, for we have both sworn in the name of the Lord, saying, 'May the Lord be between you and me, and between your children and my children for ever.'"

David arose and departed, and Jonathan went back to the city.

SAUL'S WRATH

AVID came to Ahimelech, the priest of Nob. He asked for food and Ahimelech gave him some of the hallowed bread. Because he had no weapons, Ahimelech brought out the sword of Goliath which lay wrapped in a cloth, and said: "If you want this sword, it is yours, for it is the only one here."

So David took the sword of Goliath, the Philistine whom he had slain, but as he was afraid of the wrath of Saul, he went and hid in the cave of Adullam. When his brothers and all his father's house heard that he was there, they came to him. And everyone that was in distress, and everyone that was in debt, and everyone that was discontented, gathered themselves unto him. He became a captain over them and there were about four hundred men with him.

One of the foremost herdsmen of Saul, Doeg the Edomite, was at Nob when David visited the priest Ahimelech. He came to Saul and told him how the priest gave unto David food and a sword. When he heard this, Saul sent to Nob and commanded Ahimelech and all his family to come before him.

When they came to him, Saul said: "Why have you conspired against me with the son of Jesse, and given him bread and a sword? And why did you intercede with the Lord for him and against me?"

Ahimelech answered: "You have no more faithful subject than David. Is he not your son-in-law, obedient to your bidding and honoured in your house? Did I intercede with the Lord for him? Never. Let not the king impute such a thing to his servant nor to all the house of my father, for your servant knew nothing about this matter and pleads his innocence."

The king said: "You shall surely die, Ahimelech, you and all your father's house." And he said to the soldiers who stood beside him: "Kill the priests of the Lord, for they are friends of David, and they knew when he fled and did not tell me."

But the servants of the king would not slay the priests of the Lord.

So the king said to Doeg the Edomite: "Fall upon the priests of the Lord. They are enemies to me."

Doeg the Edomite turned and fell upon the priests, and on that day he slew eighty-five of them. And he attacked the city of Nob and killed everything inside it.

Only one of the sons of Ahimelech,

named Abiathar, escaped and fled to David. He told David that Saul had killed the Lord's priests.

David said: "I knew it that day, that Doeg the Edomite would certainly tell Saul, so I am responsible for the death of all the members of your father's house. You must stay with me, and do not be afraid, for he who threatens my life, threatens your life, but with me you will be well guarded and protected."

DAVID AND ABIGAIL

 AMUEL died and all the Israelites were gathered together to lament him, and they buried him in his house at Ramah. And David arose and went down to the wilderness of Paran.

There was a man in Maon who owned land in Carmel. His name was Nabal, of the house of Caleb, and he was very rich. He had three thousand goats and a thousand sheep and his sheep were being shorn in Carmel. His wife was called Abigail and she was wise and beautiful, but Nabal was churlish and evil in his doings.

In the wilderness David heard that Nabal was shearing his sheep, so he called out ten of his young men and said to them: "Go to Carmel and greet Nabal from me, and say to him, 'Peace be to you and your house and all that you have. We have not harmed your shepherds while they were shearing near us in Carmel, nor have we stolen anything. So find favour with these young men, and pray give unto them, for themselves and for your son David.'"

The young men came and repeated this to Nabal, but he answered: "Who is David? And who is the son of Jesse? Many servants break away from their masters nowadays, and shall I take my bread and water, and the meat that I have killed for my shearers, and give it to these men of whom I know nothing?"

The young men went back to David, and told him how they had fared, and David said: "Gird on your swords." He also girded on his sword, and four hundred men went with David, leaving two hundred behind to look after their goods.

But one of Nabal's young men told Abigail about this, saying: "David sent messengers out of the wilderness to salute our master, but he insulted them. But they were very good to us, nothing was stolen and nobody was hurt, and they were like our defenders

during the time that we were together in the fields. What can we do now, for they are marching against our master, but he is such an evil man that nobody can speak to him."

Then Abigail made haste and took two hundred loaves and two bottles of wine and five sheep already cooked, and five measures of parched corn, and a hundred bunches of raisins and two hundred cakes of figs, and loaded them on asses. And she said to her servants: "Go on ahead of me and I shall follow." But she said nothing of this to her husband.

As she rode on the ass, she met David and his men and she alighted from her ass and fell at David's feet and bowed to the ground before him and said: "Listen, I beseech you, to the words of your handmaid. Pay no heed to this Nabal, this son of Belial, for he is a fool. I did not see the young men whom you sent, but I beg of you not to shed blood nor to avenge yourself upon your enemy. For the Lord will fight your battles even as you fight the battles of the Lord. And in the day of your triumph I implore you to remember your handmaid."

David said to Abigail: "Blessed be the Lord God of Israel for sending you here, and blessed be your counsel. Had you not come, I would surely have slain Nabal and all his household." Then he accepted her gifts and said: "Go in peace to your own house, for I will heed your advice."

247

Abigail went back to Nabal, who was holding a feast. He was drunk, so she told him nothing of what had happened. But the next morning, when he was sober, she told him, and Nabal's heart fainted within him, and he became as stone. And it came to pass that about ten days later, the Lord smote Nabal and he died.

When David heard that Nabal was dead, he praised God and sent for Abigail, intending to marry her, for Saul had given David's wife Michal in marriage to Phalti, the son of Laish.

When Abigail heard that David wished to marry her, she bowed her face to the ground and said: "Let me be a handmaid to wash the feet of the servants of my lord."

Then she mounted an ass, taking five young girls with her, and went with the messengers of David, and became his wife.

stole away, and no man saw him or knew that he was there or waked up, for they were all asleep. A deep sleep from the Lord had fallen upon them.

Then David went and stood on the top of a hill far off, a long distance from the camp.

David cried to the people, and to Abner, saying: "Are you not a courageous man? Who is like you in Israel? Why then have you not protected the lord your king? For one of the people came to destroy the king your lord. Look now for the king's spear and the jug of water that was beside his pillow."

Then Saul knew David's voice and said: "Is that your voice, my son David?"

And David said: "It is my voice, my lord, O king." And he added: "Why does my lord pursue his serv-

DAVID SPARES SAUL'S LIFE

David arose one night and came to where Saul had set up his tent. David saw the place where Saul lay, and Abner, the son of Ner, the captain of his army, lay beside him. Saul lay in the middle of the camp, and his men were encamped around him.

So David took the spear and the jug of water from beside Saul's pillow, and

ant this way? What have I done? What is the evil within me?"

Then Saul said: "I have sinned. Return to me, my son David, for I will never more do you any harm, because my life was precious to you this day. I see now that I have been foolish and very wrong."

Then Saul blessed David. And David went on his way, and Saul returned to the palace.

SAUL AND THE SPIRIT OF SAMUEL

NOW the Philistines gathered themselves together and came and pitched in Shunem. Then Saul gathered all Israel together and they pitched in Gilboa. And when Saul saw the army of the Philistines, he was afraid and his heart trembled greatly. But when Saul questioned the Lord, the Lord answered him not.

Then Saul said to his servants: "Seek me a woman that is a medium, that I may go to her and inquire of her." And his servants said: "There is a woman that is a medium at Endor." So Saul disguised himself and came to the woman by night. He said to her: "I pray you, bring forth the spirit whose name I shall give you."

Then the woman said: "Whom shall I bring up to you?" And he said: "Bring me up Samuel." And when the woman saw Samuel, she cried with a loud voice and spoke to Saul, saying: "Why have you deceived me? For you are Saul."

The king said to her: "Be not afraid. What did you see? What is he like?" She said: "An old man, and he is covered with a robe." And Saul knew that it was Samuel, and he stooped with his face to the ground, and bowed himself.

And Samuel said to Saul: "Why have you disturbed me?" Saul said: "I am greatly distressed, for the Philistines make war against me, and God has departed from me, and no longer answers me. Therefore I have called you, that you may make known to me what I shall do."

Then Samuel said: "Why do you ask me, seeing that the Lord has departed from you, and has become your enemy? The Lord has done to you as he spoke by me: he has broken up your kingdom and given it to your neighbour, to David. Moreover, the Lord will also deliver Israel with you into the hand of the Philistines,

and tomorrow you and your sons shall be with me."

Then Saul fell flat on the earth and was much afraid because of the words of Samuel, and there was no strength in him, for he had eaten no bread all day nor all night.

The woman saw that he was troubled and said to him: "Let me set a morsel of bread before you, and eat, that you may have strength when you go on your way." But he refused and said: "I will not eat."

Then his servants, together with the woman, compelled him to eat. He arose from the earth and sat upon a bed. Saul and his servants ate. Then they rose up, gathered their things, and went away in the night.

SAUL KILLS HIMSELF

Now the Philistines fought against Israel and the men of Israel fled from before the Philistines and were slain by them on Mount Gilboa. And the Philistines followed closely after Saul and his sons, and Saul himself was hard pressed in the battle and severely wounded by the Philistine archers.

Then Saul said to his armour-bearer: "Draw your sword and run me through with it, lest these heathen kill me and then dishonour my body."

But his armour-bearer dared not do such a thing.

Therefore Saul took a sword and fell upon it, and when the armour-bearer saw that Saul was dead, he also fell

upon his sword and died with his king.

So Saul perished with his three sons and his armour-bearer. and all his men, on that same day together.

And when the men of Israel, who were on the other side of the valley and the other side of Jordan, saw that Saul and his sons were dead and his army defeated, they forsook the cities and fled. And the Philistines came and dwelt in them.

Lest the daughters of the uncircumcised
*   triumph.*
Ye mountains of Gilboa, let there be no dew.
Neither let there be rain upon you,
*   nor fields of offerings;*
For there the shield of the mighty
*   is vilely cast away,*
The shield of Saul, as though he
*   had not been anointed with oil.*
From the blood of the slain,
*   from the fat of the mighty,*
The bow of Jonathan turned not back,
And the sword of Saul returned not empty.
Saul and Jonathan were lovely
*   and pleasant in their lives,*
And in their death they were not divided.
They were swifter than eagles,
They were stronger than lions.
Ye daughters of Israel, weep over Saul,
Who clothed you in scarlet,
*   with other delights,*
Who put on ornaments of gold upon your
*   apparel.*
How are the mighty fallen in the midst
*   of the battle!*
O Jonathan, thou wast slain
*   in thine high places.*
I am distressed for thee,
*   my brother Jonathan,*
Very pleasant hast thou been unto me.
Thy love to me was wonderful,
*   passing the love of women.*
How are the mighty fallen,
*   and the weapons of war perished!*

DAVID'S LAMENT FOR SAUL AND JONATHAN

When David learned of the death of Saul and Jonathan, he tore his clothes and fasted, and so did all the men who were with him. They mourned and wept and fasted until the evening, for Saul and for Israel; because they had fallen by the sword.

And David lamented with this lamentation over Saul and over Jonathan his son.

The beauty of Israel is slain upon
*   thy high places:*
How are the mighty fallen!
Tell it not in Gath,
Publish it not in the streets of Askelon,
Lest the daughters of the Philistines rejoice,

And it came to pass after this that the Lord told David to go up to Hebron. So he took his people, every man with his household and he led them across the plain and into the city. There they anointed him king over the house of Judah.

But Abner, the son of Ner, captain of Saul's army, took Ishbosheth, the son of Saul, and brought him to Mahanaim, and made him king over Gilead, and over the Ashurites, and over all Israel. Ishbosheth was forty years old when he began to reign over Israel, and reigned two years. But David and the house of Judah were stronger than they.

DAVID THE KING

THE HOUSE OF JUDAH SPREADS

After this it came to pass that David smote the Philistines and subdued them. And he smote Moab, and the Moabites became David's servants, and brought gifts. David smote also Hadadezer, the son of Rehob, king of Zobah, as he went to regain his border at the river Euphrates.

David took from him a thousand chariots and seven hundred horsemen and twenty thousand footmen. And when the Syrians of Damascus came to help Hadadezer, David slew twenty-two thousand of the Syrians. David put garrisons in Syria and the Syrians became David's servants and brought gifts. And the Lord preserved David wherever he went.

ND it came to pass that, after the death of Abner and Ishbosheth, all the tribes of Israel came to David in Hebron and spoke saying: "Behold, we are your bone and your flesh. Also, in time past, when Saul was king over us, you were our leader in Israel, and the Lord said to you: 'You shall feed my people Israel and you shall be a captain over Israel.'"

So king David made a league with them in Hebron before the Lord, and they anointed David king over Israel. David was thirty years old when he began to reign, and he reigned forty years. In Hebron he reigned over Judah seven years and six months, and in Jerusalem he reigned thirty and three years over all Israel and Judah.

DAVID CAPTURES JERUSALEM

David and his men went to Jerusalem, to the Jebusites, the inhabitants of the land, who spoke to him, saying: "Except that you take away the blind and the lame, you shall not come in here." Nevertheless, David encircled and overtook the stronghold of Zion.

He dwelt in the fort, and called it the city of David. And he built round about from Millo and inward. And David went on, and grew great, and the Lord God of hosts was with him.

DAVID FINDS JONATHAN'S SON

But after all his victories David said, "Is there any that is left of the house of Saul, that I may show him kindness for Jonathan's sake?" A servant of the house of Saul whose name was Ziba was called unto David. And the king asked him, "Is there not any still of the house of Saul that I may show kindness unto him?" And Ziba said unto the king, "Jonathan has a son who is lame on his feet." So the king gave orders to fetch the son.

Now when the son of Jonathan, whose name was Mephibosheth, had come unto David, he fell on his face and did reverence. And David said, "Mephibosheth!" And he answered, "Behold your servant!" David said unto him, "Fear not: for I will show you kindness for Jonathan, your father's sake and I will restore to you all the lands of Saul your grandfather; and you shall eat with me at my table continually." And Mephibosheth said, "Why should you be so kind unto such a dead dog as I am?"

Then the king called to Ziba, and said unto him, "I have given to your master's grandson all that belonged to Saul. You and your sons, and your servants, shall till the land for him, and shall bring in fruits that your master's son may have food to eat: but Mephibosheth your master's son shall eat bread always at my table." So Mephibosheth dwelt in Jerusalem and dined always at David's table and was lame on both his feet.

DAVID AND BATHSHEBA

T was the time when kings go forth to battle, and David sent Joab, his general, and his servants with him, and they destroyed the children of Ammon and besieged Rabbah. But David remained in Jerusalem.

One evening he rose from his bed and walked on the roof of his palace. He saw a very beautiful woman and sent to ask who she was. He was told: "She is Bathsheba, the daughter of Eliam, the wife of Uriah the Hittite."

David fell in love with Bathsheba, and he sent to Joab, saying: "Send me Uriah the Hittite."

So Joab sent Uriah to David, and when he came the king asked how Joab and the army were, and how the war prospered. Then he gave Uriah food and told him he could go to his own home. But Uriah slept at the door of the king's house with all the servants of his lord.

The next morning David asked him why he had not gone to his own home, and Uriah answered: "The ark and Israel and Judah live in tents, and my lord Joab and the servants of my lord are encamped in the open fields. Shall I go home to my wife to eat and drink and sleep in comfort? As the Lord lives, and as your soul lives, I cannot do such a thing."

David said: "Wait until tomorrow and I shall let you go back."

Then David wrote a letter to Joab and sent it to him by the hand of Uriah. In it he said: "Set Uriah in the forefront of the hottest battle, and withdraw from him, so that he may be smitten and die."

When Joab was besieging the city, he assigned Uriah to a place where the bravest defenders were. The men of the city came out and fought with Joab, and some of his soldiers were killed, and among them was Uriah the Hittite.

When Bathsheba learned that Uriah was dead she wept for him. But when the days of her mourning were past, David sent and fetched her to his house, and she became his wife and bore him a son.

But the thing that David had done displeased the Lord. And the Lord sent Nathan to David.

DAVID JUDGES HIMSELF

Nathan came and said to him: "There were two men in one city, one rich and the other poor. The rich man had many flocks and herds, but the poor man had nothing except one little ewe lamb which he had bought and reared, so that it grew up with him and his children. It ate from his hand and drank from his cup, and he carried it in his arms, and it was like a daughter to him. And a traveller came to the rich man and asked for a meal. His host spared his own flocks and herds, but he took the poor man's lamb and killed and cooked it for the wayfarer."

When David heard this he was very angry, and he said to Nathan: "As the Lord lives, the man that has done this thing must surely die. And he must refund the value of the lamb four times over, because he did this thing and had no pity."

And Nathan said to David: "You are the man! The Lord God of Israel has given you so much, why have you disregarded the commandment of the Lord and done evil in his sight? You killed Uriah the Hittite with the sword of the children of Ammon and took his wife to be your wife."

David said to Nathan: "I have sinned before the Lord."

Nathan said: "The Lord has forgiven you your sin, and you shall not die. But because this deed has given rise to talk among the enemies of the Lord, the child that has been born to you will surely die."

Having said this, Nathan went back to his own home.

The child of Bathsheba and David fell sick, and David prayed to God, and fasted, and lay all night on the ground. He would neither eat nor drink, but on the seventh day the child died.

The servants of David were afraid to tell him that the child was dead, for they said: "While the child was still alive he would not listen when we spoke to him, so how will he be when we tell him that it is dead?"

But David saw that his servants were whispering together, and he knew that the child was dead. He asked them if it was so, and they said: "He is dead."

Then David arose and washed and anointed himself, and changed his clothes and came into the house of the Lord and worshipped. Then he went into his own house and when he required, they set bread before him and he sat down to eat.

His servants asked him: "How is it that you fasted and wept for the child while it was alive, and now that it is dead, you get up and eat again?"

He said: "While the child was still alive, I fasted and wept, for I thought 'Who can tell whether God will be gracious unto me, and allow the child to live?' But now that he is dead, why should I go on fasting? Can I bring him back again? I shall go to him, but he cannot return to me."

Then David consoled Bathsheba his wife, and in due course they had another son whom they called Solomon, and the Lord loved him.

DAVID AND ABSALOM

IN all Israel there was no handsomer man than Absalom, the king's favourite son. From the sole of his foot to the crown of his head, there was no blemish in him. He cut his hair every year when it became too heavy for his head, and his hair weighed two hundred shekels on the king's scales.

And king David loved Absalom very dearly.

Absalom had chariots and horses and fifty men to attend him. He would rise early in the morning and wait at the gate near the place of judgment, and if anybody came with a case to lay before the king, Absalom would call unto him and ask where he came from. If the man said that he was an Israelite, Absalom would say: "You are certainly in the right, but there is nobody here to represent you. If I were judge, any man could come to me with his cause and I would do him justice."

If any man came to bow down to Absalom he would have none of it, but took him by the hand and kissed him. And so Absalom stole the hearts of the men of Israel.

One day he said to the king: "Let me go to Hebron to fulfil a vow which I made to the Lord while I was in Syria."

King David said: "Go in peace."

So Absalom went to Hebron, and he sent spies throughout all the tribes of Israel, saying: "As soon as you hear the sound of a trumpet, then you must proclaim that Absalom rules in Hebron."

Absalom had with him two hundred men from Jerusalem who knew nothing of the conspiracy, and more and more people turned to Absalom.

Then a messenger came to David and warned him and he said to all his servants: "We must flee, or otherwise we shall not be able to escape from Absalom." So he fled from Jerusalem with all his household, but the ark of the Lord and Zadok the priest remained in the city.

So there was war between David and his son Absalom. David divided his army into three parts and he was prepared to go forth with it, but his people said: "You must not go forth, for nobody cares about us except you. You are worth ten thousand of us, so it is better that you should lead us from inside the city."

David said: "I will do whatever you think best."

He stood by the gate and the people came out by the hundreds and thousands. He spoke to his commanders, Joab and Abishai and Ittai, and said: "Deal gently, for my sake, with the young man, Absalom." And all the people heard what he said about Absalom.

A great battle was fought in the wood of Ephraim, and the people of Israel were defeated by the armies of David, and twenty thousand men were killed.

ABSALOM IS KILLED

Absalom met the servants of David. He was riding a horse, and the horse went under a great oak, and Absalom's head was caught up in the thick boughs of the oak, so that he dangled between heaven and earth, and his horse galloped away from beneath him. A man saw him there and told Joab, saying: "I have seen Absalom, hanging in an oak."

Joab said: "Since you saw him why did you not strike him to the ground? I would have given you ten shekels of silver."

The man said: "Not for a thousand shekels of silver would I raise my hand against the king's son, for I heard the king telling you and Abishai and Ittai not to touch the young man Absalom. It would have been as much as my life was worth, for nothing can be hidden from the king, and you yourself would have blamed me."

"I cannot tarry thus with you," said Joab. He took three darts in his hand and thrust them into the heart of Absalom, who was still alive and hanging from the oak. And ten of Joab's young men surrounded Absalom and stabbed him to death.

DAVID RECEIVES THE NEWS

David sat between the two gates and the watchman went up to the roof over the gate by the wall, and saw a man running toward the city. The watchman told the king, and the king said: "If he is alone, he must be coming with news."

Then the watchman saw another man and he said to the king: "The first man runs very much like Ahimaaz the son of Zadok."

The king said: "He is a good man; he will be coming with good news."

Ahimaaz called up to the king and said: "All is well."

Then he fell on his face before the king and said: "Blessed be the Lord God which has delivered up the men who lifted their hand against my lord the king."

The king said: "Is the young man Absalom safe?"

Ahimaaz said: "When Joab sent me

and the other messenger, everything was in great confusion, and I do not know what was happening."

The king said: "Go, and stand aside."

Then the other messenger, Cushi, arrived, and he said: "News, my lord king. The Lord has avenged you on those who rebelled against you."

And the king said to Cushi: "Is the young man Absalom safe?"

Cushi said: "May the enemies of my lord the king and all that seek to harm you, be as Absalom is now!"

The king was greatly distressed, and he went up to the chamber over the gate, weeping and saying: "O my son Absalom, my son, my son Absalom. Would to God I had died for you, O Absalom, my son, my son!"

THE DEATH OF DAVID

NOW King David was old and stricken in years; they wrapped him in clothes but he lost strength daily. The end of his life drew near and he knew that he must die.

He sent for his son Solomon and charged him, saying: "I go the way of all the earth; therefore you must be strong and show yourself to be a man. Keep the commandments of the Lord your God and walk in his ways. Obey his statutes and abide by his word as it is written in the law of Moses. Then the Lord will fulfil his promises that he made to me, saying: 'If thy children take heed to their way, to walk before me in truth with all their heart and all their soul, there shall always be male children for the throne of Israel.' You know what I have endured. Be wise therefore in all that you do."

And in his last words to the people, David spoke of the qualities of kingship in these words: "The God of Israel spoke to me, saying:

'He that ruleth over men must be just, ruling in the fear of God. And he shall be as the light of the morning when the sun rises, as a morning without clouds; as tender grass, springing out of the earth, in clear sunshine after rain.'"

So David slept with his fathers and was buried in the city of David, after reigning over Israel for forty years: seven years in Hebron and thirty-three years in Jerusalem.

And Solomon sat on the throne of David his father, and ruled over his kingdom.

THE TIME OF THE PROPHETS

THE WISDOM OF SOLOMON

AFTER Solomon succeeded his father David on the throne of Israel, he went one day to the holy place Gibeon to offer sacrifice to the Lord, for the temple of the Lord was not yet built. And while Solomon was in Gibeon God appeared to him in a dream, saying: "Ask of me whatever I am to give you."

Solomon answered: "O Lord God, I am your servant. You have made me king instead of David my father, and I am like a little child. I do not know how to go out or come in. I am in the midst of your great people whom you have chosen, so great a people that they cannot be numbered or counted.

"Give, therefore, to your servant an understanding heart to judge your people, that I may judge between good and bad. For who is able to judge so great a people as yours?"

God was much pleased that Solomon asked this thing. And God said to him: "Because you have asked for this thing, and have not asked for long life for yourself, nor for riches for yourself, nor for the life of your enemies, but have asked for understanding to make wise judgments, you will see that I have done just as you asked. Lo, I have given you a wise and understanding heart, so that there has never been anyone like you before, nor shall anyone like you arise after you.

"And I have also given you that which you have not asked, both riches and honour, so that there will not be anyone who is your equal among the kings all your days.

"And if you will walk in my ways, and obey my laws and my commandments, as your father David did, then I will lengthen your days."

Then Solomon awoke and knew that it was a dream. He went to Jerusalem and stood before the ark of the covenant of the Lord, and offered up burnt offerings and peace offerings, and made a feast for all his servants.

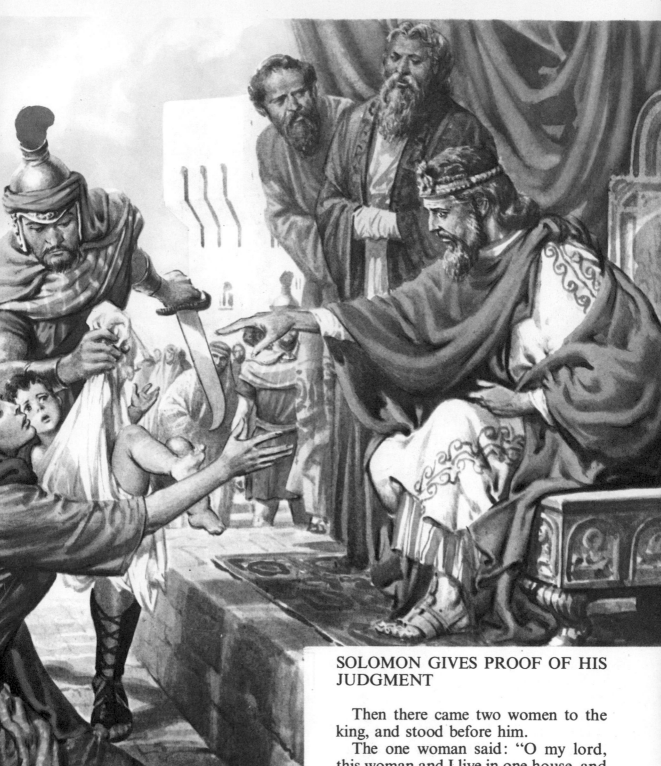

SOLOMON GIVES PROOF OF HIS JUDGMENT

Then there came two women to the king, and stood before him.

The one woman said: "O my lord, this woman and I live in one house, and I bore a child in the house with her. And it happened that three days afterward, this woman bore a child too. We were together, and there was no one else in the house with the two of us.

"This woman's child died in the night and she arose at midnight and took my son from beside me, while your hand-maid slept, and she took him in her arms and laid her dead child in my arms.

"And when I rose in the morning to nurse my child, I saw that it was dead. But when I had looked at it in the daylight, I found that it was not my own son."

The other woman said: "No. the living is my son, and the dead is your son."

And the first woman said: "No, the dead is your son and the living is my son."

Thus they argued before the king.

Then the king said:

"The one says, 'This is my son that is alive, and your son is the dead child,' the other says, 'No, your son is the dead one, and my son is the living'." So the king said: "Bring me a sword." And they brought him a sword. "Divide the living child in two," he said, "and give half to the one and half to the other."

Then the mother to whom the living child belonged spoke to the king, for her heart ached for her son, and she said: "O Lord, give her the living child, but by no means kill it."

But the other said: "Let it be neither mine nor yours, but divide it."

Then the king answered and said: "Give the first woman the living child, and by no means kill it. She is the mother of it."

All Israel heard of the judgment which the king had handed down, and they respected the king. For they saw that the wisdom of God was in him, to give judgments.

And God gave Solomon great wisdom and understanding, and largeness of heart as the sand that is on the seashore. And Solomon's wisdom excelled the wisdom of all the children of the east country and all the wisdom of Egypt. For he was wiser than all men, and his fame spread through all nations round about.

THE BUILDING OF THE TEMPLE

OW in the four hundred and eightieth year after the children of Israel had come out of the land of Egypt, Solomon, in the fourth year of his reign, began to build a temple to the Lord.

The house of the Lord which king Solomon built was ninety feet long and thirty feet broad, and the height of it was forty-five feet. There was a broad porch before the temple, and it had windows of narrow lights, and many chambers.

The house was built of stone made ready before it was brought there, so that there was no sound of a hammer or axe or any tool in the house while it was being built.

The walls and floors and ceilings of the house were of boards of cedar, and Solomon covered the floors with planks of fir.

And he covered the whole house with pure gold, and the whole altar in the holy of holies was covered with pure gold. Within the holy of holies he had two cherubim of olive wood, each fifteen feet high, and their wings touched in the middle of the room. They too were overlaid with gold.

All the walls and the doors were carved with cherubim and with palm trees and flowers, all covered with gold, and in the inner court were three rows of hewed stone columns, and a row of cedar beams.

Solomon caused all the vessels that belonged to the house of the Lord to be made of gold likewise. The altar was of gold, and the candlesticks of pure gold, before the holy of holies, with flowers and lamps and tongs of gold; and bowls and snuffers and basins and spoons and censers of pure gold, and hinges of gold on the doors of the temple.

The house was seven years in the building. Then the work was finished which king Solomon had done for the house of the Lord. And Solomon brought in the things which David his father had dedicated. The silver and the gold and the vessels he put among the treasures of the house of the Lord.

Then Solomon assembled the elders of Israel and all the heads of the tribes, that they might bring the ark of the Lord's covenant into the temple at Jerusalem.

The priests brought the ark of the

covenant into the holy of holies, under the spread wings of the cherubim. There was nothing in the ark except the two tablets of stone which Moses had put there at Horeb when the Lord made a covenant with the children of Israel when they came out of the land of Egypt.

And it came to pass, when the priests had come out of the holy place, that a cloud filled the house of the Lord, so that the priests could not stand to minister, because of the glory of the Lord which filled the house of the Lord.

And Solomon blessed all the congregation of Israel and said:

"Blessed be the Lord God of Israel. I have built a house for the Lord and have set there a place for the ark wherein is the covenant of the Lord, which he made with our fathers, in the days when he brought them out of the land of Egypt."

SOLOMON AND THE QUEEN OF SHEBA

WHEN the queen of Sheba heard of the fame of Solomon, she came to see him and to test him with hard questions. She arrived in Jerusalem with a very great train of attendants, with camels carrying spices, and much gold and precious stones. And when she had come to Solomon, she told him all the things that were on her mind. And Solomon answered all her questions, for there was nothing that he did not know.

And when the queen of Sheba had heard Solomon's wisdom, and seen the house that he had built, the food at his table, his servants, the magnificence of his ministers and his cupbearers and the entrance to the temple which he had built, there was no more spirit in her.

She said to the king: "What I heard in my own country about your wisdom and your deeds was all true. But I could not believe it until I had seen for myself. So I came, and behold, the half was not told me. Happy the men and happy the servants who stand continually before you and listen to your words of wisdom. Blessed be the Lord your God who favours you and has made you ruler over Israel. The Lord loved Israel for ever, therefore he made you king to do judgment and justice."

She gave the king a hundred and twenty talents of gold, and great stores of spices and precious stones. Never before had there been so many spices as those which the queen of Sheba gave to king Solomon.

In exchange king Solomon gave the queen of Sheba everything that she desired and whatever she asked for. And so she went back to her own country, she and her servants.

Solomon grew very rich; he made a great throne of ivory and overlaid it with the best gold. All his drinking vessels were of gold and he had at sea a great navy which brought to his kingdom not only gold but silver and ivory and apes and peacocks. On land Solomon had an army of twelve thousand horsemen and one thousand four hundred chariots.

SOLOMON DIES AND THE KINGDOM IS DIVIDED

King Solomon exceeded all the kings of the earth for riches and wisdom and all the earth sought to hear the wisdom which God had put in his head. But in his riches and his splendour Solomon turned to evil ways. The Lord became angry with him for he burned incense and sacrificed unto other gods. The Lord made adversaries to rise up against him and among those who opposed him was Jeroboam, the son of one of his servants and a mighty man of valour.

And through a prophet, Ahijah the Shihonite, God spoke to Jeroboam saying:

"Because Solomon has not kept my ways and done what is right in my eyes, as did David his father, I will rend the kingdom out of his hands, and will give ten tribes to you. You shall be king over Israel but his son Rehoboam shall reign over one tribe in Jerusalem, the city where I have chosen to put my name."

And God did as he had promised. Solomon had reigned in Jerusalem over all Israel for forty years. He died and was buried in the city of David, his father. And Rehoboam reigned in Solomon's stead, but Israel under Jeroboam rose up against him. Jeroboam was made king over all Israel and reigned for twenty-two years. Rehoboam reigned seventeen years over Jerusalem and there was war between Rehoboam and Jeroboam all their days. And when each king died, he was succeeded by his son.

ELIJAH
A PROPHET
OF ISRAEL

The division in 922 B.C. of the united kingdom of Israel into two parts, the northern kingdom of Israel and the southern kingdom of Judah, was a momentous event in the history of the Hebrews. After about fifty years, a king named Ahab succeeded to the throne of Israel. He married Jezebel, daughter of the king of the Zidonians, and built an altar and a temple to the heathen god, Baal, in his capital city of Samaria. He was sternly rebuked for his evil ways and worship of Baal by the prophet, Elijah.

LIJAH the Tishbite, an inhabitant of Gilead, said to Ahab: "As the Lord God of Israel lives, before whom I stand, there will not be dew nor rain for years, unless I say the word."

Then the word of the Lord came to Elijah, saying: "Get away from here and turn eastward and hide yourself by the brook Cherith, which is this side of Jordan. There you shall drink of the brook, and I have commanded ravens to feed you there."

So he went and did as the Lord had commanded, and lived by the brook Cherith. And the ravens brought him bread and meat in the morning and again bread and meat in the evening, and he drank of the brook.

It came to pass, after a while, that the brook dried up, because there had been no rain in the land.

Then the word of the Lord came to him, saying: "Get up and go to Zarephath, which belongs to Zidon, and live there. You will find I have commanded a widow there to feed you."

ELIJAH HEALS
THE WIDOW'S SON

And when Elijah arrived at the gate of Zarephath he saw that the widow was there gathering sticks.

He called to her and said: "Fetch me, I beg of you, a little water in a vessel, so that I may have a drink." And as she was going to fetch it, he called to her and said: "Please bring me a morsel of bread."

She said: "As the Lord your God lives, I have not a loaf, but only a handful of meal in a barrel, and a little oil in a jar. As you see, I am gathering two sticks, that I may go in and prepare it for myself and my son, so that we may eat it and die."

Elijah said to her: "Do not fear. Go and do as you have said; but make me a little cake of it first, and bring it to me, and afterwards make some for yourself and for your son. For the Lord God of Israel has said: 'The barrel of meal shall not be empty, nor the jar of oil fail, until the day when the Lord sends rain upon the earth.' "

She went and did as Elijah told her, and she and Elijah and her household ate for many days.

But it happened, after these things, that the son of the woman fell sick, and his sickness was so severe that there was no breath left in him.

The woman said to Elijah: "What have I done to you, O man of God? Have you come to me to remind me of my sins, and to kill my son?"

"Give me your son," he said to her, and he took him from her arms and carried him up to a loft where he stayed, and laid him upon his own bed.

Then he cried to the Lord and said: "O Lord my God, have you brought evil upon the widow with whom I am staying, by killing her son?"

Then he stretched himself out upon the child three times and cried to the Lord, and said: "O Lord my God, I beg you, let this child's soul come back to him."

The Lord heard the voice of Elijah, and the soul of the child came to him again, and he breathed. Then Elijah took the child and brought him down from the loft into the house, and gave him to his mother. And Elijah said: "See, your child lives!"

And the woman said to Elijah: "Now by this I know that you are a man of God, and that the word of the Lord which you preach is the truth."

ELIJAH AND THE PRIESTS OF BAAL

AND it came to pass after many days, that the word of the Lord came to Elijah in the third year of the famine, saying: "Go and show yourself to Ahab, and I will send rain upon the earth." And Elijah went to show himself to king Ahab.

When king Ahab saw Elijah, he said to him: "Are you the man who troubles Israel?"

Elijah answered: "It is not I who have troubled Israel, but you and your father's house, by forsaking the commandments of the Lord and following Baalim.

"Now send out and gather together all Israel at Mount Carmel, and the four hundred and fifty prophets of Baal, and the four hundred prophets of the groves who eat at queen Jezebel's table."

So Ahab sent word to all the children of Israel and gathered the prophets together at Mount Carmel.

Then Elijah came before all the people and said: "How long will you waver between two beliefs? If the Lord is God, follow him; if Baal, follow him."

The people answered not a word.

Then Elijah said to the people: "I, and I alone, remain a prophet of the Lord, but the prophets of Baal are four hundred and fifty men. Let them, then, get us two young bulls and let them choose one bull for themselves, and cut it in pieces and lay it on the wood, but put no fire under it. And I will dress the other bull and lay it on the wood and put no fire under it.

"Then you call on the name of your gods, and I will call on the name of the Lord, and the God that answers with fire, let him be God."

And all the people answered and said: "It is well spoken."

Elijah said to the prophets of Baal: "Choose one bull for yourselves and dress it first, for there are many of you. Call on the name of your gods, but do not put any fire under it."

They took the bull which was given them, and they dressed it and called on the name of Baal from morning until noon, saying: "O Baal, hear us." But there was no voice nor any answer, though they leaped upon the altar they had made.

At noon Elijah mocked them and said: "Cry aloud, for he is a god. Either he is talking, or he is busy, or he is on a journey, or perhaps he is asleep and must be awakened."

They cried aloud, and cut themselves, as was their custom, with knives and lances, until the blood gushed out upon their robes.

When midday was past, they worshipped before the altar until time for the evening sacrifice, and still there was neither a voice nor any answer nor any sign that their gods had heard them.

Then Elijah said to all the people: "Come near to me."

All the people gathered around him

Then he walked up to the altar of the Lord which had been broken down. Elijah took twelve stones, according to the number of the tribes of the sons of Jacob which made up Israel. With the stones he built an altar in the name of the Lord, and he made a trench round the altar, large enough to hold two measures of seed. He put the wood in order, and cut the young bull in pieces and laid it on the wood.

Then he said: "Fill four barrels with water and pour it on the burnt sacrifice and on the wood."

When they had done this, he said: "Do it a second time," and they did it a second time. And he said: "Do it a third time," and they did it a third time.

The water ran around the altar, and he filled the trench with water, too.

Then when it was time for the offering of the evening sacrifice, Elijah the prophet came near and said: "Lord God of Abraham, Isaac, and of Israel, let it be known today that you are the God in Israel, and that I am your servant and have done all these things at your command.

"Hear me, O Lord, hear me, that this people may know that you are the Lord God, and that you may have their hearts again."

Then the fire of the Lord came down and consumed the burnt sacrifice and the wood and the stones and the dust, and licked up the water that was in the trench.

When all the people saw it, they fell on their faces and said: "The Lord he is the God; the Lord he is the God."

And Elijah said to them: "Take the prophets of Baal; let not one of them escape."

And they took them; and Elijah brought them down to the brook Kishon and slew them there. And by evening the rains came and thus the famine was ended.

THE STILL SMALL VOICE

A HAB recounted to Jezebel the story of all that Elijah had done, and how he had slain all the prophets of Baal.

So Jezebel sent a messenger to Elijah, saying: "Let the gods do to me and more still, if by this time tomorrow I do not take your life as you have taken theirs."

When Elijah heard this he arose and fled for his life, and went to Beersheba, where he left his servant. And he himself went a further day's journey into the wilderness and sat down under a juniper tree.

He prayed that he might die, and said: "It is enough, Lord. Take away my life, for I am no better than my fathers."

Then he lay down and slept under the tree and an angel awoke him, saying: "Arise and eat."

Elijah saw a cake and jar of water at his head, so he ate and drank, and slept again; and again the angel awakened him to eat. And fortified by the food, he travelled forty days and nights until he arrived at Mount Horeb.

He lived there in a cave and the word of the Lord came to him, asking: "What are you doing here, Elijah?"

Elijah said: "I have cared greatly for the Lord God of hosts, but the children of Israel have forsaken your covenants, thrown down your altars and slain your prophets with the sword. Only I remain, and they are seeking to kill me."

God said: "Go forth, and stand upon the mountain."

He did so, and a great wind blew upon the mountain and smashed the rocks, but the Lord was not in the wind. After the wind came an earth-

quake, but the Lord was not in the earthquake; and after the earthquake a fire, but the Lord was not in the fire; and after the fire, a still small voice.

When Elijah heard the voice, he wrapped his face in his mantle and stood in the opening of the cave.

And the voice said: "What are you doing here, Elijah?"

And Elijah said: "I have cared greatly for the Lord God of hosts, but the children of Israel have forsaken your covenant, and thrown down your altars and slain your prophets with the sword. Only I remain, and they are seeking to kill me."

The Lord said to him: "Go to Damascus and anoint Hazael to be king over Syria; and anoint Jehu, son of Nimshi, to be king over Israel; and Elisha, the son of Shaphat, shall you anoint to be prophet after you."

So Elijah departed and found Elisha whom the Lord had named working at the plough. And Elisha arose and went after Elijah and became his servant.

NABOTH'S VINEYARD

NABOTH the Jezreelite had a vineyard which was situated close to the palace of Ahab, the king of Samaria.

Ahab said to Naboth: "Give me your vineyard, that I may turn it into a herb garden, for it is so near my house. In exchange I will give you a better vineyard, or if you prefer, I will give you its value in money."

Naboth answered: "The Lord forbid that I should give you the land which I have inherited from my forefathers."

Ahab went back to his house, depressed and vexed because of what Naboth had said. He lay down on his bed and turned his face to the wall and refused to eat.

Jezebel, his wife, came in and said: "Why are you so sad that you refuse to eat?"

Ahab said: "Because I asked Naboth to let me have his vineyard, and I offered to pay for it or give him another vineyard in exchange, but he would have none of it."

Jezebel said: "Are you not king of Israel? Get up, eat and be merry, and I shall see to it that you get Naboth's vineyard."

She wrote letters in Ahab's name and sealed them with his seal, and sent them to the elders and the nobles who lived in the same city as Naboth. In the letters she wrote: "Proclaim a fast and set Naboth on high among the people, and set two men, sons of Belial, before him, to testify against him and say that he has blasphemed against God and the king. Then take him out of the city and stone him until he dies."

The elders and nobles of the city did as Jezebel had instructed them. They proclaimed a fast, accused Naboth of blasphemy, and stoned him to death. Then they sent a message to Jezebel, saying: "Naboth is stoned and dead."

When Jezebel heard this, she said to Ahab: "Go and take possession of Naboth's vineyard which he refused to sell to you, for he is no longer alive."

So Ahab went down and took possession of the vineyard of Naboth the Jezreelite.

But the word of the Lord came to Elijah the Tishbite, and he went down to see Ahab, who was in the vineyard which he had taken from Naboth.

And as Elijah came, Ahab said: "Have you found me, O my enemy?"

Elijah said: "I have found you,

because you have sold yourself to work evil in the eyes of the Lord. The Lord will bring evil upon you and destroy your posterity, and the dogs shall eat Jezebel by the wall of Jezreel."

When Ahab heard these words he rent his clothes and fasted and went humbly in sackcloth and ashes. Because of his humility God told Elijah: "I will not bring the evil in his days; but in his son's days I will bring the evil upon his house."

THE PARTING OF ELIJAH AND ELISHA

 ND it came to pass that when the Lord decided to take Elijah up into heaven in a whirlwind, Elijah was with Elisha, his faithful follower, in Gilgal. Setting out from Gilgal together, Elijah and Elisha went to Bethel and Jericho.

And the followers of the prophets who were at Jericho came to Elisha and said to him: "Do you know that the Lord is going to take away your master from you today?"

He said: "Yes, I know it. Hold your peace."

And Elijah said to him: "Wait here, I beg you, for the Lord has told me to go to Jordan."

But Elisha said to him: "As the Lord lives, and as your soul lives, I will not leave you."

So the two went on. And fifty of the followers of the prophets went and stood at a distance to watch. Elijah and Elisha stood beside the Jordan.

Elijah took his mantle and folded it over, and struck the waters so that they were divided on either side, and the two men went across on dry ground.

It happened, when they had crossed over, that Elijah said to Elisha: "Ask what you will of me, before I am taken away from you."

Elisha said: "Let a double portion of your spirit be upon me, I beg of you."

"You have asked a hard thing," Elijah said. "Nevertheless, if you see me when I am taken from you, you shall have your wish; but if not, you shall not have it."

It happened, as they went on and talked together, that a chariot of fire and horses of fire appeared, and swept them apart; and Elijah went up by a whirlwind into heaven.

Elisha saw it, and he cried: "My father, my father! The chariot of Israel and its horsemen!" Then he could not see Elijah any more, and he took hold of his own robe and ripped it in two.

He picked up Elijah's mantle, which had fallen from him, and went back and stood by the bank of the Jordan. He took Elijah's mantle and struck the waters and said: "Where is the Lord God of Elijah?" And when he had struck the waters, they parted on either side of him and Elisha crossed over.

When the followers of the prophets who had come to watch saw him, they said: "The spirit of Elijah rests on Elisha."

And they came to meet him, and bowed themselves to the ground before him.

And the men of Jericho said to him: "You can see that the situation of the city is pleasant, but the water is bad and the ground barren."

Elisha said: "Bring me a new jar and put salt in it."

They did so and he went to the source of the water and threw in the salt and said: "The Lord says that these waters are healed and they will cause no more death or barren lands." So the waters were healed for ever according to the word of Elisha.

ELISHA HEALS A LEPER

Naaman, captain of the army of the king of Syria, was a great man among his master's followers, and honourable. Through him, the Lord had granted freedom to Syria. He was a man of great courage; but he was a leper.

The Syrians had gone out by companies and had brought back as a captive out of the land of Israel a little girl. She was a maidservant to Naaman's wife.

She said to her mistress: "I would to God my lord were with the prophet who is in Samaria, for he would cure him of his leprosy."

When the king of Syria heard what the girl had spoken, he said: "Go now, go, and I will send a letter to the king of Israel."

Naaman departed with the letter, and took with him ten talents of silver, and six thousand pieces of gold, and ten complete changes of clothing.

He delivered to the king of Israel the letter, which said: "When you receive this letter, you will see that I have sent to you with it Naaman, my servant, that you may cure him of his leprosy."

When the king of Israel had read the letter, he tore his clothes and said: "Am I God, to kill and to make alive, that this man sends a man to me to be cured of his leprosy? Take heed, for he seeks to pick a quarrel with me."

Now when Elisha, the man of God, heard that the king of Israel was troubled, he sent word to the king, saying: "Why did you tear your clothes? Let the man come to me, and he shall know that there is a prophet in Israel."

So Naaman came with his horses and his chariot, and stood at the door of the house of Elisha.

Elisha sent a messenger to him, saying: "Go and wash in the Jordan seven times, and your flesh will be healed again, and you will be well."

But Naaman was angry and turned away, saying: "I had thought, 'He will surely come out to me and stand there and call on the name of the Lord his God and strike his hand on the place and cure the leprosy.' Are not Abana and Pharpar, the rivers of Damascus, better than all the waters of Israel? May I not wash in them and be cured?"

His servants spoke to him, and said: "My father, if the prophet Elisha had ordered you to do some difficult thing, would you not have done it? How much better to obey when he says to you, 'Wash and be made well.'"

Then Naaman went and dipped himself seven times in the Jordan, just as the man of God had said, and his flesh was once again like the flesh of a little child, and he was well.

He went back to the man of God, he and all his company, and came and stood before him, and he said: "Now

I know that there is no God in all the earth but in Israel. And so I beg of you to accept a token of your servant's gratitude."

But Elisha said: "As the Lord lives, I will accept nothing. Go in peace."

And Naaman went on his way.

ELISHA'S SERVANT FOLLOWS NAAMAN

But Gehazi, the servant of Elisha, said to himself: "See, my master has refused to accept the gift offered by this Naaman the Syrian. As the Lord lives, I will run after him and obtain something for myself."

So Gehazi followed Naaman, and when Naaman saw him running after him, he came down from his chariot and went to meet him, and said: "Is all well?"

Gehazi said: "All is well. My master has sent me to tell you that two young men of the sons of the prophets have just now arrived from Mount Ephraim, and will you give them a talent of silver and two changes of garments?"

Naaman said: "Be content, take two talents." And he packed two talents of silver and the changes of clothing in two bags and gave them to two of his servants, and they carried them for Gehazi.

When he came to the tower, Gehazi took the bags from them and put them in the house, and told the men to go. Then he went and stood before his master.

And Elisha said to him: "Where have you been, Gehazi?"

He said: "Your servant has not been anywhere."

Elisha said: "Did I not go in spirit with you when the man left his chariot to meet you? Is this the moment to receive money, and to receive garments and olive groves, and vineyards and sheep and oxen and menservants and maidservants? The leprosy of which Naaman was cured has passed over to you and to your descendants for ever more."

And Gehazi went from his presence a leper as white as snow.

THE ANOINTING OF JEHU

The curing of Naaman took place during one of the brief truces between Israel and Syria, which more often than not were fighting against each other. In one battle, Ahab, king of Israel, was killed. He was soon followed to the throne of Israel by Joram, a son. Meanwhile, in the south, Ahaziah, a grandson of Ahab, became king of Judah upon the death of his father, who had married a daughter of Ahab. Jezebel, Ahab's wife, remained in Israel. Such was the situation when Elisha set about helping to fulfil the prophecy of Elijah concerning destruction of the "posterity of Ahab."

 LISHA the prophet called one of his followers and said to him: "Go to Ramoth-Gilead and look for Jehu, the son of Jehoshaphat, the son of Nimshi, and cause him to leave his friends and take him into an inner room. Then take this vial of oil and pour it on his head and say: 'Thus says the Lord, I have anointed you king over Israel.' Then open the door and flee."

So the young man, who was himself a prophet, went to Ramoth-Gilead and told Jehu that he had a message for him. Jehu arose and went into his house, and the prophet poured oil on to his head and said: "Thus says the Lord God of Israel, I have anointed you king over the people of the Lord, even over Israel. And you shall smite the house of Ahab your master, that I may avenge the blood of my servants the prophets, and the blood of all the servants of the Lord, at the hand of Jezebel."

Then the young man opened the door and fled. Jehu went back to his people and one of them said to him:

"Is all well? What did this madman want with you?"

Jehu told them what the young man had said and they blew on trumpets and said: "Jehu is king." So Jehu rode in a chariot towards Jezreel, where king Joram of Israel, son of Ahab, was lying

wounded after a battle with king Hazael of Syria.

A watchman stood on the tower in Jezreel and he saw the company of Jehu approaching and told the king of it. Joram said: "Send a horseman to meet them and ask: 'Do you come in peace?'"

So the horseman went to meet Jehu and said: "The king asks if you come in peace?" Jehu said: "What have you to do with peace? Get behind me."

As he did not return, the watchman sent out another messenger who asked Jehu the same question, and again Jehu answered: "What have you to do with peace? Get behind me."

Then the watchman said: "The messenger reached them, but he has not returned; and the driving is like the driving of Jehu, for he drives furiously."

JEHU SLAYS JORAM

Joram said: "Make ready." His chariot was prepared, and together with Ahaziah, king of Judah, king Joram of Israel went forth to battle, and met Jehu in the land that had belonged to Naboth the Jezreelite. And Jehu drew a bow with all his might and smote Joram between his arms and the arrow went out at his heart, and he sank down in his chariot.

Then Jehu said to Bidkar, his captain: "Take him up and throw him into the field of Naboth the Jezreelite, for today the blood of Naboth and his sons has been avenged on his own ground."

When Ahaziah saw what had happened, he fled by way of a garden house, but Jehu followed and smote him; and he fled to Megiddo and died there. Thus Jehu overcame both Joram of Israel and Ahaziah of Judah.

JEZEBEL IS KILLED

When Jehu came to Jezreel, Jezebel heard about it. She painted her face and dressed her hair and looked down from a window. As Jehu entered through the city gate, she said: "Was there any peace for Zimri who killed his master?"

He looked up to the window and said: "Who is on my side?"

Two or three servants looked down at him, and he said: "Throw her down." So they threw her down, and he trod her underfoot.

When Jehu had come in, he ate and drank, and said: "Go, see now this accursed woman and bury her; for she is a king's daughter."

And thus was fulfilled the prophecy of Elijah the Tishbite concerning queen Jezebel.

THE CROWNING OF JOASH

Jehu completed his destruction of the family of Ahab by slaying seventy of his sons. After this he had all Israel's Baal worshippers put to death. Jehu's slaying of a grandson of Ahab, king Ahaziah of Judah, was to set in motion further killings by Ahaziah's widowed mother, Athaliah, who was eager to be queen of Judah.

 HEN Athaliah of Judah saw that her son Ahaziah was dead, she caused all the royal children to be put to death.

But Jehosheba, the wife of Jehoiada, the high priest, rescued Joash, the son of Ahaziah, by hiding him and his nurse in the sleeping apartment, so that he was not slain. The boy was concealed for six years in the house of the Lord with Jehosheba and Jehoiada, while queen Athaliah reigned in Judah.

In the seventh year Jehoiada fetched all the rulers and the chief captains, and brought them to the house of the Lord, and made a covenant with them.

They swore a solemn oath to him, and he brought them the king's son saying: "This is the thing you shall do. A third of your number shall come into the house of the Lord on the sabbath and keep watch over the king's house. A third shall be at the gate of Sur; and a third at the gate behind the guard, so that the house of the Lord will be safely guarded. The two companies who go off duty on the sabbath will also join in keeping the watch of the house of the Lord. You shall guard the king by surrounding him each man with his sword in hand. If anyone comes within the precincts, he shall be killed. You shall remain with the king both when he goes out and when he comes in."

The captains did as they were commanded, and Jehoiada gave them king David's spears and shields, which were in the temple. The guards stood fully armed throughout the temple, surrounding the king, and Jehoiada presented the young Joash to them and crowned him. They gave him the royal insignia and anointed him, and all the people clapped their hands and said: "God save the king."

When Athaliah heard the noise of the guard and the people, she came to the temple of the Lord. She looked in and saw the king standing by a pillar, as was the custom at a coronation, and the princes and the trumpeters beside him, and all the people rejoicing to the sound of trumpets.

Athaliah rent her clothes and cried: "Treason! Treason!"

Jehoiada said to the captains of the host: "Take her out of the temple and if anybody follows her, put him to death with the sword. She must not die within the precincts of the house of the Lord."

So they seized her and took her on to the road by which horses approached the palace. There she was slain.

Jehoiada made a covenant between the Lord and the king and the people, that they should all be the Lord's people. And the people of the land went into the house of Baal and broke it down. They smashed its altars and its images and they slew Mattan, the priest of Baal, before the altar.

Joash came by way of the guards' gate from the house of the Lord to the king's house, and there he reigned under the name Jehoash.

THE DEATH OF ELISHA

OW Elisha had fallen ill and was on his deathbed. And king Jehoash of Israel, a grandson of Jehu, came to Elisha and wept over him and said: "O my father, my father, the chariot of Israel and the horsemen thereof."

Elisha said to him: "Take a bow and arrows." And he took a bow and arrows.

Elisha said to the King of Israel: "Put your hand on the bow." He did so, and Elisha put his hands upon the king's hands. He said: "Open the window to the east." The king opened it.

Then Elisha said: "Shoot," and the king shot.

"The arrow of the Lord's deliverance," said Elisha, "and the arrow of deliverance from Syria. You shall smite the Syrians in Aphek till you have consumed them. Now, take the arrows." The king took them.

Elisha said: "Strike the ground."

He struck it three times and then did so no more.

The man of God was angry with him and said: "You should have struck five or six times, for then you would have struck Syria until you had destroyed it, whereas now you will strike Syria three times only."

And Elisha died and was buried.

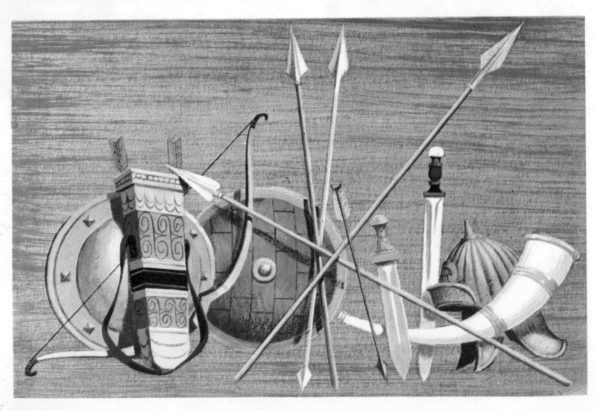

WARNINGS FROM THE PROPHETS

Woe to them that are at ease in Zion,
   and cause the violence to come near;
That lie upon beds of ivory,
   and stretch themselves upon their couches,
And eat the lambs out of the flock,
   and the calves from the midst of the stall,
That chant to the sound of the viol,
   and invent for themselves
   instruments of music, like David;
That drink wine in bowls,
   and anoint themselves with ointments!
Shall not the land tremble for this,
   and everyone mourn that dwells therein?
And it shall come to pass in that day,
   says the Lord God, that I will cause
   the sun to go down at noon,
And I will turn your feast into mourning,
   and all your songs into lamentation.
Behold the days come, says the Lord,
   that I will send a famine in the land;
Not a famine of bread,
   nor a thirst for water,
   but of hearing the words of the Lord.
And they shall wander from sea to sea,
   and from the north even to the east,
They shall run to and fro
   to seek the word of the Lord,
   and shall not find it.

In accordance with Elisha's dying words, Israel won three battles against Syrian forces. But after the prosperous reign of Jeroboam II, son of Jehoash, Israel became weaker and weaker, caught up in a series of internal political intrigues and assassinations.

This beginning of Israel's end was predicted with scorn and vehemence by a visionary shepherd from Judah. This was Amos, the first of many prophets to forecast the downfall of the Hebrew nations. He preached in Israel during the end of Jeroboam's rule around the middle of the eighth century B.C. In particular he attacked the life of luxury and spiritual indifference that he saw as the source of Israel's weakness.

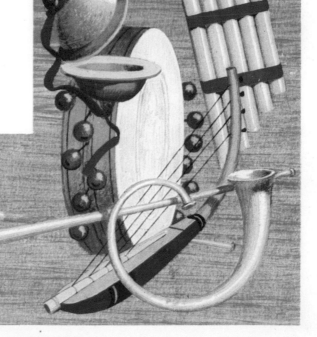

HOSEA'S MESSAGE OF HOPE

Amos was followed closely, in time and in theme, by the prophet Hosea. He preached also in the northern kingdom of Israel, as the dark shadow of a power far more dangerous than Syria stretched closer and closer to Israel's borders. While predicting the approaching disaster, Hosea also held out hope, calling for repentance and promising redemption through God's mercy and love.

O Israel, return unto the Lord your God,
　for you have fallen by your iniquity.
Take with you words,
　and turn to the Lord.
Say unto him, Take away all iniquity,
　and receive us graciously.
His branches shall spread,
　and his beauty shall be as the olive tree.
They that dwell in his shadow shall return;
　they shall revive as the corn
　and grow as the vine.
Who is wise, and he shall understand
　these things;
　prudent, and shall know them?
For the ways of the Lord are right,
　and the just shall walk in them;
But the transgressors shall fall therein.

ISAIAH'S VISION

Both during and after the time of Hosea in Israel, one of the greatest of all Hebrew prophets, Isaiah, was active in Judah, the southern kingdom. Like Israel, Judah had enjoyed a long period of peace and prosperity—during much of the reigns of Jehoash's son, Amaziah, and grandson, Uzziah.

Isaiah was not only a visionary preacher but also a wise statesman and adviser of Judah's kings through years of constant crises. These arose from military threats from without, from traditional opponents such as Syria and Israel, and from a new and dangerous friend, Assyria.

In the year that king Uzziah died, I saw the Lord sitting on a throne lifted up on high, and his train filled the temple. Above it stood the seraphim. Each had six wings: with two he covered his face, with two he covered his feet, and with two he did fly.

One cried to another and said: "Holy, holy, holy is the Lord of hosts. The whole earth is full of his glory."

The posts of the door moved at the voice of him who cried, and the house was filled with smoke. Then I said:

"Woe is me! For I am ruined, because I am a man of unclean lips and I dwell in the midst of people of unclean lips, and now my eyes have seen the king, the Lord of hosts."

Then one of the seraphim flew at me, bearing in his hand a live coal which he had taken from the altar with tongs. He laid it upon my mouth and said:

"Behold, this has touched your lips; your wickedness is taken away, and your sin is removed."

And I heard the voice of the Lord saying: "Whom shall I send? Who will go for us?"

"Here I am," I said. "Send me."

And the Lord said:

"Go and tell this people: 'You hear, but you do not understand. You see, but you do not know what you see.'

"Weigh down the heart of this people and make their ears heavy, and shut their eyes, lest they see with their eyes, and hear with their ears and understand with their hearts, and change their ways and become healed."

Then I said, "How long, O Lord?" And God answered:

"Until the cities are wasted and without inhabitants, and the houses are vacant, and the land is utterly desolate. Then the Lord will have removed the men far away, and the whole land will be forsaken."

RESPITE FOR JERUSALEM

"Behold, a maiden shall conceive,
    and bear a son,
And shall call his name Immanuel,
Butter and honey shall he eat,
That he may know to refuse the evil,
    and choose the good.
For before the child shall know to refuse
    the evil, and choose the good,
The land that you despise shall be
    forsaken of both her kings.
The people that walked in darkness
Have seen a great light;

ZZIAH ruled fifty-two years in Jerusalem and when he died Jotham, his son, ruled in his place. When Jotham died, they buried him in the city of David, and Ahaz, his son, ruled in his place.

Now it came to pass in the days of Ahaz that the king of Syria and the king of Israel attacked Jerusalem, but could not conquer it. And God said to Isaiah, "Go forth and meet Ahaz and say to him:

" 'Take heed and be quiet. Fear not these two smoking firebrands, Syria and Israel. For, although they have made an evil plan against you, it shall not come to pass.' "

Moreover, God spoke to Ahaz, saying:

"Ask for a sign of the Lord your God."

"I will not ask," Ahaz said. "I will not test the Lord."

Then Isaiah said:

"Hear now, O House of David. It is a small thing for you to weary men, but will you weary my God also? The Lord himself shall give you a sign:

Upon those that dwell in the land
  of shadow of death
The light has shined.
For unto us a child is born,
  unto us a son is given:
And the government shall be upon his
  shoulder:
And his name shall be called Wonderful,
  Counsellor, the Mighty God,
The Everlasting Father,
  the Prince of Peace.
Of the spread of his kingdom and his peace
  there shall be no end,
  from now on, even for ever.
The zeal of the Lord of hosts will perform
  this."

Ahaz sent messengers to the king of Assyria, saying:

"Come and save me from the king of Syria and the king of Israel, which rise up against me."

And Ahaz took the silver and the gold that was found in the house of the Lord and in the king's treasury, and sent it as a present to the king of Assyria. Then the king of Assyria answered Ahaz's plea and went out against Damascus and killed the king of Syria.

The Assyrians not only overthrew Damascus and the king of Syria; they also a few years later besieged and captured Samaria, capital of the northern kingdom. The downfall of Samaria in 722 B.C. meant the end of Israel as a nation. The Israelites were marched off and scattered through other parts of the Assyrian Empire.

Meanwhile Judah the southern kingdom managed miraculously to survive. The Assyrians attacked Jerusalem in 701 B.C. but their troops were struck by plague and forced to withdraw. The aged Isaiah saw in these events the deliverance of his people through the working of the hand of God. This was an important function of the prophets: to interpret and demonstrate the actions of God in history.

JOSIAH
A RIGHTEOUS
KING

After king Ahaz's death, his son Heze-kiah reigned, followed by Manasseh, Amon and then Josiah. It was during Josiah's rule, in the last quarter of the seventh century B.C. that one of the major events in Hebrew history occurred, the finding of the Book of the Law, Deuteronomy. This document, which contains many of the rules for behaviour and worship followed by Hebrews and Christians to this day, deeply impressed king Josiah. He tried to put its com-mands into effect by abolishing many of the pagan elements that had crept into the worship of his people.

OSIAH was eight years old when he began to rule, and he ruled thirty-one years in Jerusalem. He did that which was right in the sight of the Lord and followed in the steps of David his fore-father, and turned not aside to the right nor to the left.

And it came to pass in the eighteenth year of king Josiah's reign that the king sent Shaphan the son of Azaliah, the scribe, to the house of the Lord.

And when Shaphan the scribe went to the temple of the Lord, Hilkiah the high priest said to him:

"I have found the Book of the Law in the house of the Lord." And Hilkiah gave the book to Shaphan, and he read it.

Then Shaphan the scribe showed the king the book, saying:

"Hilkiah the priest has delivered this book to me."

And Shaphan read it before the king.

And when the king had heard the words of the Book of the Law he

read into their ears all the words of the book of the covenant which was found in the house of the Lord.

The king stood by a pillar and made a covenant before the Lord, to walk in his ways and to keep his commandments and follow his words and his laws, with all his heart and with all his soul, and to live up to the words of this covenant that were written in the book; and all the people agreed to the covenant.

JOSIAH BANISHES IDOL WORSHIP

Then the king commanded Hilkiah the high priest, and the priests of the second order, and the keepers of the door, to bring forth out of the temple of the Lord all the vessels that were made for Baal and his sacred wood, and for all the other gods; and he burned them outside of Jerusalem in the fields of Kidron, and carried the ashes of them to Bethel.

He put down the idolatrous priests, whom the kings of Judah had ordained to burn incense in the high places in the cities of Judah and in the places round about Jerusalem, and also those who burned incense to Baal, to the sun, and to the moon, and to the planets, and to all the various gods. Josiah destroyed also the workers with ghosts and magic, and the wizards, and the images, and the idols and all the evil things that were to be found in the land of Judah and in Jerusalem, so that he might live up to the words of the law which were written in the book that Hilkiah the priest found in the house of the Lord.

There had been no king like Josiah. For he turned to the Lord with all his heart, and with all his soul, and with all his might, according to all the law of Moses; neither did any come after him who was his equal.

tore his clothes, for he knew his fathers had not listened to the words of this book, to obey all the laws that were written down for them.

The king sent for all the elders of Judah and of Jerusalem. Then he went up to the house of the Lord, taking all the men of Judah and all the inhabitants of Jerusalem with him, both the priests and the prophets and all the people, both small and great, and he

THE FALL OF JERUSALEM

your herds. They shall eat up your vines and your fig trees. And it shall come to pass when you shall say, 'Why does the Lord our God do these things to us?' that I shall answer, 'You have forsaken me and served strange gods in your land. Therefore shall you serve strangers in a land that is not yours.'

"Hear now this, O foolish people, which have eyes and see not, which have ears and hear not."

During king Josiah's reign, another great Hebrew figure appeared as a prophet in Judah. This was Jeremiah, who like Isaiah was both an inspired spokesman for his God and a shrewd analyst of current affairs. Active under five kings of Judah during a time when his country was always at the mercy of stronger powers, Jeremiah often advised compliance. This frequently put him at odds with Judah's leaders.

In the last years of Josiah's rule, Nineveh, the Assyrian capital, fell to the forces of Babylon. Jeremiah saw the rise of this power in the east as an evil omen for Jerusalem and the kingdom of Judah.

 HE words of the Lord came to the prophet Jeremiah, saying:

"I will bring a nation upon you from far away, O house of Israel. It is a mighty nation. It is an ancient nation, a nation whose language you do not know, nor understand. And they shall eat up your harvest and your bread, which your sons and daughters should eat. They shall eat up your flocks and

JUDAH IS CONTROLLED BY FOREIGN POWERS

King Josiah was slain in battle at Megiddo, and his son Jehohoaz reigned in his place. But after three months he was deposed by Pharaoh, king of Egypt, who then made his brother, Jehoiakim, king.

Now Pharaoh demanded tribute of

one thousand talents of silver and one talent of gold from the land of Judah, so Jehoiakim taxed the people to find the silver and gold to give to Pharaoh. He was twenty-five years old when he began to rule, and he did that which was evil in the sight of the Lord.

During his reign, Nebuchadnezzar, king of Babylon, came to Jerusalem, and Jehoiakim became his vassal. After three years he rebelled against him.

But the Lord sent bands of Chaldees

his territory between the Nile and the Euphrates.

Jehoiachin ruled for only three months. Then Nebuchadnezzar, king of Babylon, came up to besiege Jerusalem, and Jehoiachin surrendered himself to Nebuchadnezzar with his mother and his servants, his princes and his officers. The king of Babylon took him prisoner and he also took away all the treasures of the house of the Lord and the treasures of the king's

and Syrians and Moabites and bands of the children of Ammon against Judah, as a punishment for former sins. Jehoiakim fought in vain against them until his death, when Jehoiachin, his son, ruled in his place.

By now the king of Egypt had lost his power and remained behind his own frontiers, for the king of Babylon had taken possession of all

house. And he cut in pieces all the vessels of gold which Solomon had made for the temple of the Lord.

He carried away all the princes, seven thousand mighty men of valour, a thousand craftsmen and blacksmiths —in all ten thousand captives. Only the poorest people were left in the country.

Nebuchadnezzar took Jehoiachin

away to Babylon, and Jehoiachin's mother and his wives and his officers, and all that were strong and likely warriors. All were taken to Babylon.

And the king of Babylon made Mattaniah, uncle of Jehoiachin, king of Judah in his place. And he changed Mattaniah's name to Zedekiah.

Zedekiah was twenty-one years old when he began to rule and he ruled eleven years in Jerusalem. And he did that which was evil in the sight of the Lord, according to all that done by Jehoiakim.

And it came to pass that Zedekiah rebelled against the king of Babylon. So in the ninth year of his reign in the tenth month, in the tenth day of the month, Nebuchadnezzar, king of Babylon, came with all his army and laid siege against Jerusalem.

JEREMIAH FORETELLS THE FATE OF ZEDEKIAH

Then Zedekiah the king sent two priests to Jeremiah the prophet, saying:

"Pray to the Lord our God for us."

At that time, Jeremiah was not in prison, as he often was, but was going about freely among the people. Pharaoh's army had set out from Egypt, and when the Chaldeans heard of this, they departed from their siege of Jerusalem.

The word of the Lord came to Jeremiah, saying:

"This you shall say to the king of Judah: 'Behold, Pharaoh's army which has set out to help you, shall go back to Egypt, and the Chaldeans shall come again and attack this city and burn it down. Do not deceive yourselves, says the Lord, or tell yourselves that the Chaldeans shall go away again, for they shall not depart.

" 'Even if you were to defeat the whole Chaldean army, and there were none left but wounded men, still would

each one of them rise in his tent, and burn this city with fire.' "

But some of the nobles, hearing what Jeremiah had told the king, that the city was going to fall into the hands of Babylon, went to the king and said:

"We entreat you to allow us to put this man to death, for by his words he is sapping the fighting spirit of the people."

"He is in your power," Zedekiah said. "The king can do nothing against your will."

So they took Jeremiah and threw him into the dungeon of Machiah the son of Hammelech, which was a cistern in the court of the prison. They let Jeremiah down with cords into the underground dungeon. There was no water in it, only mud. And Jeremiah sank in the mud.

Now Ebed-melech the Ethiopian, who was one of the king's slaves, heard what had happened to Jeremiah, and he spoke to the king who was sitting in judgment at the gate of Benjamin. He said:

"My Lord King, these men have done wrong in casting Jeremiah the prophet into the dungeon. He will die from hunger there, for there is no more bread in the city."

So the king told Ebed-melech the Ethiopian to take thirty men and rescue Jeremiah from the dungeon before he starved to death.

Ebed-melech took the men and collected some old rags and scraps of material and let them down by ropes into the dungeon. Then he called Jeremiah, saying:

"Put these rags under your armpits to protect you from the rope."

Jeremiah did so, and they pulled him up out of the muddy cistern, and he was sent back into a better prison. King Zedekiah sent for him again, and bade him come to the entrance of the temple.

"One thing I will ask you," said the king. "Hide nothing from me."

"But if I tell you the truth," said Jeremiah, "will you not have me put to death? And if I give you advice, will you not disregard it?"

Then king Zedekiah swore a secret oath to Jeremiah, and said:

"As the Lord our Creator lives, I will not have you put to death, nor will I hand you over to the men who want to kill you."

ZEDEKIAH IGNORES JEREMIAH'S ADVICE

Jeremiah the prophet answered king Zedekiah and said:

"Thus says the Lord, the God of hosts, the God of Israel: If you will go forth to the officers of the king of Babylon, your life will be spared. This city will not be destroyed by fire, and you and your family will survive. But if you will not go forth to the king of Babylon's officers, then this city will be given into the power of the Chaldeans, and they will burn it to the ground, and you will not escape out of their hand."

"I am afraid of the Jews who have gone over to Babylon," said king Zedekiah. "If I surrender, the Chaldeans may hand me over to them, and they will ill-treat me."

"They will not hand you over to the Jews," Jeremiah said. "I beg of you to obey the voice of the Lord, for then all will go well with you, and your life will be spared. If you do not, all your wives and children will be taken by the Babylonians, and because of you the city will be burned with fire."

And king Zedekiah said to Jeremiah:

"Tell no man about this talk of ours and you shall not die. If the nobles hear that I have been talking with you and question you with threats, tell them that you came to plead with me not to be sent back in the dungeon.

The nobles did come and did ask Jeremiah what he and the king had said, and Jeremiah answered as the king had told him. So nobody knew what had been said between them, and nothing more was done about it.

Jeremiah remained in the prison until the day that Jerusalem fell. He was there when Jerusalem was taken.

JERUSALEM IS DESTROYED

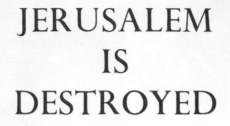

THE Chaldeans laid siege to Jerusalem during eleven years of Zedekiah's reign. And on the ninth day of the fourth month of the siege, the famine spread over the city, and there was no bread for the people in the land.

The city was overcome, and the men of the army fled by night, by way of a gate between two walls, which was near the king's garden, for the Chaldeans were all around the city. And the king went off towards the plain. The army of the Chaldeans pursued the king and overtook him on the plains of Jericho, and all his army was scattered.

So they took the king and brought him up to the king of Babylon at Riblah, and they passed judgment upon him.

They slew the sons of Zedekiah before his eyes, and put out the eyes of Zedekiah, and bound him with fetters of brass, and carried him to Babylon.

A LAMENT FOR JERUSALEM

How lonely sits the city
    that once was full of people!
How like a widow she has become
    that was great among the nations,
    and a princess among the provinces.
Now she is a vassal.
She weeps sadly at night, and her tears
    are on her cheeks.
Among all her lovers she has none to
    comfort her.
All her friends have dealt treacherously
    with her.
They have become her enemies.
In the days of her affliction
    and her miseries
Jerusalem remembered all the pleasant
    things which she had in the days of old.
When her people fell into the hands
    of the enemy, nobody helped her.
Jerusalem has grievously sinned, therefore
    she is removed.
All that honoured her despise her.
Is it nothing to you, all ye that pass by?
Behold and see if there be any sorrow
    like the sorrow which has been done to me,
With which the Lord has afflicted me
    in the day of his fierce anger.

309

SONGS OF THE CAPTIVES

This is the psalm of the exiles in Babylon. A hymn to the Lord and a song of sadness and deep longing for home, it is also a prayer for vengeance upon the Babylonian captors.

By the rivers of Babylon,
There we sat down, yea we wept,
When we remembered Zion.
We hanged our harps
Upon the willows in the midst thereof.
For there they that carried us away
    captive required of us a song;
And they that wasted us required of
    us mirth, saying,
"Sing us one of the songs of Zion."

How shall we sing the Lord's song
In a strange land?
If I forget thee, O Jerusalem,
Let my right hand forget her cunning.

If I do not remember thee,
Let my tongue cleave to the roof of my
    mouth;
If I prefer not Jerusalem
Above my chief joy.

Remember, O Lord, the children of Edom
In the day of Jerusalem,
Who said, "Raze it, raze it,
Even to the foundation thereof."

O daughter of Babylon,
Who art to be destroyed,
Happy shall he be that rewardeth thee
As thou hast served us.
Happy shall he be that taketh and dasheth
Thy little ones against the stones.

Remember, O Lord what has happened to
    us;
Consider and behold our reproach.
Our inheritance is turned over to strangers,
Our houses to aliens.
We are orphans and fatherless,
Our mothers are widows.

The joy of our heart has ceased:
Our dance is turned into mourning.
The crown is fallen from our head:
Woe unto us, that we have sinned.

You, O Lord, remain for ever;
Your throne from generation to generation.
Why do you forget us for ever,
And forsake us for such a long time?
Turn us towards you, O Lord, and we shall
    be turned;
Renew our days as of old.
But you have utterly rejected us;
You are very angry with us.

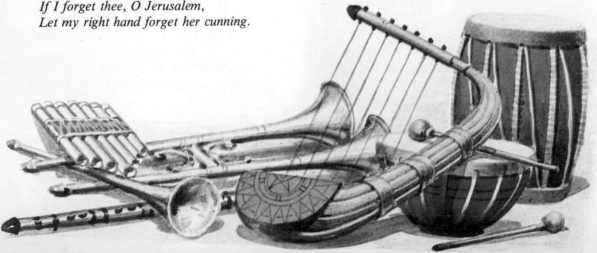

DANIEL IN CAPTIVITY

Some of the trials of the Jews in exile come out in the tales of Daniel who was taken from Jerusalem as a child after the city first became subjected to Babylon. Daniel's role as an often influential foreigner spanned more than half a century from Nebuchadnezzar to the Persian king Cyrus.

WHEN Nebuchadnezzar, the king of Babylon, besieged Jerusalem in the third year of the reign of Jehoiakim, king of Judah, he carried away some of the vessels of the house of God. He carried them to the land of Shinar, to the house of his gods.

Then the king of Babylon told Ashpenaz, the master of his household to choose certain of the children of Israel, of the king's family, and of the princes, children who had no fault and were handsome and bright and quick to learn, who had ability to understand science and were worthy to stand in the king's palace. To these they would teach the wisdom and the language of the Chaldeans.

The king allowed them a daily provision of the king's own food, and of the wine which he drank, to nourish them so that at the end of three years they might stand before him as members of his household.

Now among these were some of the children of Judah: Daniel, Hananiah, Mishael and Azariah. To all these the master of the household gave new names. He gave Daniel the name of Belteshazzar, to Hananiah the name of Shadrach, to Mishael, Meshach, and to Azariah, Abednego.

DANIEL REFUSES
THE KING'S FOOD

But Daniel decided in his heart that he would not pollute himself with the king's meat, which was not the food of the children of Israel, nor with the wine which he drank. Therefore he requested that he might not have to eat it.

Now God had filled the master of the household with love for Daniel. And the master of the household said to him:

"I fear my lord the king, who has given orders for your food and drink. For why should he see your face looking paler and more wan than the children who are in your group? If this happens, you will make me endanger my head with the king."

Then Daniel said to Melzar, whom the master of the household had put over Daniel, Hananiah, Mishael and Azariah:

"Test your servants, please, for ten days. Let them give us peas and beans to eat, and water to drink. Then look at our faces and at the faces of the children who eat of the king's food,

and then deal with your servants according to what you find."

He agreed to test them in this manner, and tried them for ten days. After the ten days, their faces appeared fairer and plumper than those of the children who had eaten of the king's food.

So Melzar took away their helpings of the meat, and the wine that they were supposed to drink, and gave them peas and beans.

As for the four children, God gave them knowledge and skill in all kinds of learning and wisdom: and Daniel had understanding of all visions and dreams.

Now at the end of the time when the king had said they should be brought in, the master of the household took them before Nebuchadnezzar.

The king talked with them, and among them all, none was found like Daniel, Hananiah, Mishael and Azariah: therefore they stayed before the king.

And in all matters of wisdom and understanding in which the king tested them, he found them ten times better than all the magicians and astrologers that were in his realm.

And Daniel stayed on, even until the first year of the reign of king Cyrus.

THE STATUE OF GOLD

EBUCHADNEZZAR the king made a statue of gold ninety feet high and nine feet wide. He set it up on the plain of Dura in the province of Babylon. Then Nebuchadnezzar the king sent out word to gather together the princes, the governors, and the captains, the judges, the treasurers, the counsellors and the sheriffs, and all the rulers of the provinces, to come to see the statue.

And so it happened that the princes, the governors and captains, the judges, the treasurers, counsellors and sheriffs, and all the rulers of the provinces gathered together to see the statue that Nebuchadnezzar the king had set up; and they stood before the statue.

Then a herald cried aloud: "To you it is commanded, O people, that when you hear the sound of the cornet, flute, harp, sackbut, psaltery, dulcimer, and all kinds of music, you shall fall down and worship the golden image that Nebuchadnezzar the king has set

314

up. And anyone who does not fall down and worship shall in that same hour be cast into the middle of a burning fiery furnace."

Therefore when the moment came, when all the people heard the sound of the cornet, flute, harp, sackbut, psaltery, and all kinds of music, they fell down with one accord and worshipped the golden image that had been set up by Nebuchadnezzar.

CHALDEANS ACCUSE THE JEWS

Then certain Chaldeans came up and accused the Jews. They spoke to king Nebuchadnezzar and said:

"O king, live for ever! You, O king, have sent out an order that every man who hears the sound of the cornet, flute, harp, sackbut, psaltery, and dulcimer, and all kinds of music, shall fall down and worship the golden

image, and that whoever does not fall down and worship shall be cast into the middle of a burning fiery furnace.

"There are certain Jews, whom you have put in charge of the affairs of the province of Babylon. They are Shadrach, Meshach and Abednego: these men, O king, have not regarded your wishes. They do not serve your gods, nor worship the golden image which you have set up."

Then Nebuchadnezzar, in his rage and fury, commanded that Shadrach, Meshach and Abednego should be brought before him. Nebuchadnezzar said to them:

"Is it true, O Shadrach, Meshach and Abednego, that you do not serve my gods nor worship the golden image which I have set up? If you are ready when you hear the sound of the cornet, flute, harp, sackbut, psaltery and dulcimer, and all kinds of music, to fall down and worship the image that I have made, all is well; but if you will not worship, you will be cast, the same hour, into the middle of a burning fiery furnace. And who is the God who will deliver you out of my hands?"

THE FIRE LEAVES
THE THREE MEN UNHARMED

And Nebuchadnezzar was full of fury, and his face hardened against Shadrach, Meshach and Abednego.

Therefore he spoke and commanded that the furnace should be heated seven times more than usual. And he commanded the most mighty men in his army to bind Shadrach, Meshach and Abednego, and to cast them into the burning fiery furnace.

Because the king had instructed that the furnace be made exceedingly hot, the flame of the fire killed the men who led Shadrach, Meshach and Abednego to it. But Shadrach, Meshach and Abednego, in the midst of the burning, fiery furnace, were unharmed.

Then Nebuchadnezzar the king was stricken with amazement, and he rose up in haste and summoned his counsellors and said: "Did we not cast three men bound into the midst of the fire?"

"True, O king," they answered.

Then the king said:

"I see four men loose, walking in the midst of the fire, and they are unhurt. And the fourth looks like the Son of God."

And Nebuchadnezzar walked up to the mouth of the burning fiery furnace and said:

"Shadrach, Meshach and Abednego, you servants of the most high God, come out and come here."

Shadrach, Meshach and Abednego walked out of the fire. And all the princes and the captains and governors and the king's counsellors gathered together there and saw these men against whose bodies the fire had no power. Not a hair of their heads was singed, nor were their clothes burned and there was no smell of fire upon them.

Then Nebuchadnezzar spoke and said:

"Blessed be the God of Shadrach, Meshach and Abednego, who has sent his angel and saved his servants who trusted in him, and who defied the king's word and risked their lives that they might not serve or worship any god except their own God.

"Therefore I make a decree: Any people, nation or group which says anything against the God of Shadrach, Meshach and Abednego, shall be cut in pieces and its houses shall be made a rubbish heap; for there is no other god who can save in this way."

Then the king promoted Shadrach, Meshach and Abednego to high offices in the province of Babylon.

THE WRITING ON THE WALL

PON the death of Nebuchadnezzar, his son Belshazzar became king. Belshazzar gave a great feast for a thousand of his lords and drank wine before the thousand.

They brought the golden vessels that had been taken out of the temple of the house of God, and his princes, his wives, and the other women drank from them. They drank wine and they praised the gods of gold, of silver, of brass, of iron, of wood and of stone.

Within the same hour there appeared the fingers of a man's hand, writing upon the wall of the king's palace; and the king saw part of the hand that wrote.

Then the king's face changed, and his thoughts troubled him so that the joints of his legs were loose and his knees knocked together.

The king cried aloud to bring in the astrologers, the Chaldeans, and the soothsayers, and the king said to these wise men of Babylon:

"Whoever reads this writing and tells me the meaning of it shall be clothed in scarlet, and have a chain of gold about his neck, and shall be the third ruler in the country."

All the king's wise men came in, but they could not read the writing nor make known to the king the meaning of it.

Now the queen, called by the king and his lords, came into the banqueting room, and the queen spoke and said:

"O king, live for ever! Do not let your thoughts trouble you, nor let your face change. There is a man in your kingdom who has in him the spirit of the holy gods. In the days of your father, light and understanding and wisdom like the wisdom of the gods was found in him. The king Nebuchadnezzar your father made him master of the magicians, astrologers, Chaldeans and soothsayers, because of his excellent spirit and knowledge and understanding, interpreting of dreams, explaining of hard sentences, and clearing up of doubts, and all this Daniel, whom the king named Belteshazzar, accomplished. Now let Daniel be called, and he will tell you the meaning of this."

Then Daniel was brought in before the king, and the king said to Daniel:

"Are you that Daniel who is one of the children of the captivity of Judah, whom the king my father brought out of the land of the Jews? I have heard of you, that the spirit of the gods is in you, and that light and understanding and excellent wisdom are found in you.

"Now the wise men and astrologers have been brought in before me to read this writing and tell me the meaning of it, but they could not interpret it for me. I have heard of you, and that you can give interpretations and clear meanings.

DANIEL INTERPRETS THE WRITING

Then Daniel answered and said to the king:

"O king, the most high God gave

MENE, MEN
UPHA

TEKEL

RSIN

Nebuchadnezzar, your father, a kingdom and majesty and glory and honour. And because of the majesty that he gave him, all people, nations and languages trembled and feared him. But when his heart was lifted up and his mind hardened in pride, his kingly throne was taken from him; and his glory was taken from him, until he knew that the most high God ruled in the kingdom of men, and that he chooses whomever he wishes to rule over it.

"And you his son, O Belshazzar, have not kept your heart simple, though you knew all this, but you have lifted yourself up against the Lord of Heaven. They have brought you the vessels of his house, and you and your lords, your wives, and other women have drunk wine in them, and you have praised the gods of silver and gold, of brass, iron, wood and stone, which do not see, nor hear, nor know. And the God in whose hands your breath of life is, and whose ways should be yours, him you have not praised.

"This hand then was sent from him and the writing was written by his hand. And this is the writing that was written:

"MENE, MENE, TEKEL, UPHARSIN.

"And this is the meaning of the thing. MENE: God has judged your kingdom and finished it. TEKEL: you have been weighed in the scales and found lacking. UPHARSIN: your kingdom will be divided and given to the Medes and the Persians."

Then Belshazzar commanded that they clothe Daniel in scarlet and put a chain of gold about his neck. And he made a proclamation saying that he was to be the third ruler in the kingdom.

That night Belshazzar, the king of the Chaldeans, was killed. And Darius the Median took his kingdom, being about sixty-two years old.

DANIEL IN THE LIONS' DEN

IT pleased Darius to set over the kingdom a hundred and twenty princes who were to rule the whole kingdom. And over these were three presidents, and of them Daniel was the first. The princes were to give account to them, so that the king would have no troubles.

Daniel was put over the presidents and princes because of his excellent mind. And the king planned to put him over the whole kingdom. Then the presidents and princes tried to find some fault with Daniel concerning the kingdom, but they could find no fault, because he was faithful and loyal, and there was no error or fault to be found in him. And these men said:

"We shall not find any grounds for complaint against Daniel unless it concerns his worship of his God."

So those presidents and princes assembled together before the king and said to him:

"King Darius, live for ever! All the presidents of the kingdom and the governors and the princes, the counsellors and the captains, have consulted together about establishing a royal law, by a firm order, that whoever asks anything of any god or man for thirty days, except of you, O king, shall be cast into a den of lions.

"Now, O king, establish this order, and sign the writing, that it may not be changed, according to the law of the Medes and the Persians, which does not change."

Then king Darius signed his name to the writing.

When Daniel knew that the law was signed and ratified, he went into his house, and his windows being open in his chamber facing Jerusalem, he kneeled down three times a day and prayed and gave thanks to his God just as he had done before.

Then the men came together and found Daniel praying and entreating God. They hurried to the king and reminded him of his order.

"Did you not sign an order that any man asking a favour of any god or man within thirty days, except yourself, O king, shall be thrown into the den of lions?

The king answered and said:

"That is true, according to the law of the Medes and the Persians, which does not change."

Then they answered and said to the king: "That Daniel who is one of the children of the captivity of Judah, does not respect you, O king, nor the decree which you have signed, but makes his request three times a day."

When he heard these words, the king was very much displeased with himself, and he set his heart on saving Daniel. He thought until the setting of the sun about how to save Daniel.

Then the men came before the king and said to him: "Remember, O king, that it is the law of the Medes and the Persians that no order or law which the king lays down can be changed."

Then the king commanded them to

take Daniel and throw him into the den of lions. And the king said to Daniel: "Your God whom you serve so faithfully, surely he will save you."

Then the king went to his palace and passed the night in fasting. No musical instruments were brought in to him, and he did not sleep at all.

Very early in the morning the king arose and hurried to the den of lions. When he came to the den, he cried out in a sorrowing voice to Daniel and said to him: "O Daniel, servant of the living God, has your God, whom you serve so faithfully, been able to save you from the lions?"

Then Daniel said to the king: "O king, live for ever. My God has sent his angel and has shut the lions' mouths, so that they have not hurt me, because I was innocent in his sight; and I have done no harm to you either, O king."

Then the king was exceedingly glad for him, and commanded that Daniel should be brought up out of the den. So Daniel was brought up out of the den, and no wound of any kind was

found on him, because he believed in his God.

Then the king gave commands, and they brought the men who had accused Daniel, and they cast them into the den of lions, and their children and their wives as well. And the lions broke all their bones into pieces.

Then king Darius wrote to all people and nations, and in all the languages of the earth:

"Peace be multiplied to you! I now command that in every part of my kingdom men tremble and fear before the God of Daniel, for he is the living God, unchanging for ever, and his kingdom shall never be destroyed, and his power shall continue to the end. He rescues and saves, and he works signs and wonders in heaven and on earth, he who has saved Daniel from the power of the lions."

So Daniel prospered in the reign of Darius, and in the reign of Cyrus the Persian.

PROPHETS OF THE EXILE

The Bible has little additional information on the seventy years between the destruction of Jerusalem by the Babylonian armies and the rebuilding of the temple there under the Persians. However a general picture emerges of the Jews continuing to practise their religion in distant regions, spurred on by prophets preaching the eventual return to the holy city. One such prophet was the priest Ezekiel who lived and wrote in Babylon.

IT came to pass in the twelfth year of our captivity, in the tenth month, in the fifth day of the month, that one who had escaped from Jerusalem, came to Ezekiel and said:

"The city has fallen."

Then the word of the Lord came to Ezekiel, saying:

"As a shepherd seeks out his flock in the days, so will I seek out my people, and will bring them from all the places where they have been scattered in the cloudy and dark day.

"And I will gather them from the countries, and will bring them to their own land, and feed them upon the mountains of Israel by the rivers, and in all the inhabited places of the country.

"I do this not for your sakes, O house of Israel, but for the holy name's sake, which you have profaned among the heathen. I will sprinkle clean water upon you, and you shall be clean. I will put my spirit within you and cause you to follow my statutes, and you shall keep my laws."

In the twenty-fifth year of captivity, in the fourteenth year after the city had fallen, the hand of the Lord was upon Ezekiel. In the visions of God, he brought him into the land of Israel, and set him upon a very high mountain. And behold there was a man whose appearance was the appearance of brass.

And the man said to him:

"Behold with your eyes all that I show you. Tell all that you see to the house of Israel."

So the spirit took Ezekiel up and brought him into the inner court of the temple, and the glory of the Lord filled the house. Then Ezekiel heard the man speaking to him from the house, while the man stood by him. He said:

"Here is the place of my throne and the place of the soles of my feet, where I will dwell in the midst of the children of Israel for ever. And they shall no longer defile my holy name, neither they, nor their kings."

Ezekiel was deeply aware at all times of the justice and mercy of God.

"If the evil man will turn from the wrongdoing he has committed and keep the statutes of the Lord and do that which is lawful and right, he shall surely live and shall not die. His evil deeds shall not be remembered against him and on account of his righteous acts he shall have life. 'Have I any pleasure that he shall die?' says the Lord. 'Do I not rather rejoice that he shall turn from his wickedness and live?'"

THE RETURN TO JERUSALEM IS FORETOLD

At the end of the period of exile in Babylon a prophet, whose identity is unknown but who is sometimes called Second Isaiah, since his writings form part of the book of that name, wrote telling the Jews that their banishment was over. Babylon was falling and they would soon be allowed to return to Jerusalem.

O, my people, take comfort, take comfort, says your God. Speak tenderly to Jerusalem and cry unto her, that her warfare is ended, for she has received of the Lord's hand double for all her sins. The voice of one that cries in the wilderness:

"*Prepare the way of the Lord.
Make straight in the desert a
    highway for our God.
Every valley shall be exalted,
And every mountain and hill shall be
    made low;
And the crooked shall be made
    straight,
And the rough places plain;
And the glory of the Lord shall be
    revealed,
And all flesh shall see it together,
For the mouth of the Lord has spoken
    it."
The voice said, "Cry."
And he said, "What shall I cry?
All flesh is grass,
And all the goodliness thereof is
    flower of the field.
The grass withers, the flower fades;
But the word of our God shall stand
    for ever."
O Jerusalem, that brings good
    tidings,
Lift up your voice with strength;
Lift it up, be not afraid.
Say unto the cities of Judah,
"Behold your God!"
Behold, the Lord God will come
    with a strong hand,
And his arm shall rule for him;
Behold, his reward is with him,
And his work before him.
He shall feed his flock like
    a shepherd:
He shall gather the lambs with his
    arm.*

THE RETURN TO JERUSALEM

OW in the first year of Cyrus king of Persia, so that the word of the Lord by the mouth of Jeremiah might be fulfilled, the Lord stirred up the spirit of Cyrus. And he made a proclamation throughout all his kingdom, and put it also in writing, saying:

"Thus says the king of Persia: The Lord God of heaven has charged me to build him a house at Jerusalem, which is in Judah.

"Who is there among you who are of his people? May his God be with him, and let him go up to Jerusalem, and build the house of the Lord God of Israel in Jerusalem.

"And let each survivor wherever he is living be assisted by the men of that place with silver and gold, with goods and beasts, besides freewill offerings for the house of God in Jerusalem."

Then rose up the chief of the leaders of Judah and Benjamin, and the priests and the Levites, with all those whose spirits God had raised, to go to Jerusalem to build there the house of the Lord.

And all who were around them filled their hands with vessels of silver, with gold, with goods of all sorts, with beasts and with precious things, and with everything that was willingly offered.

And Cyrus the king brought forth the vessels of the house of the Lord which Nebuchadnezzar had brought out of Jerusalem, and they were brought up from Babylon to Jerusalem.

329

THE TEMPLE IS REBUILT

And now two years after their arrival, all they that were come out of captivity unto Jerusalem set forward the work on the house of the Lord.

But the adversaries of Judah troubled the people in building, and hired counsellors against them, to stop their progress, all the days of Cyrus king of

Persia, even until the reign of Darius king of Persia.

But Darius the king made a decree forbidding any hindrance in the building. And the elders of the Jews built, and finished the temple according to the commandment of Cyrus and Darius, kings of Persia. And the house was finished in the sixth year of the reign of Darius the king.

NEHEMIAH ASKS
THE KING'S PERMISSION

After these things, in the reign of Artaxerxes king of Persia, there was a royal cupbearer named Nehemiah. One day Nehemiah was in the palace at Shushan when some men of Judah arrived, headed by his kinsman Hanani. And Nehemiah asked them for news of those Jews who had not been taken into captivity, and what had happened to the city of Jerusalem. And they said to him:

"Those who remain in the province are in pitiful condition. Although the temple is rebuilt, the wall of Jerusalem is broken down and the gates are burned with fire."

When Nehemiah heard this, he wept and mourned for several days, and fasted, praying to God that the sins of his people might be forgiven and that he might be able to help them.

And it came to pass in the twentieth year of Artaxerxes the king, that Nehemiah took up some wine to give to the king. When he did, he could not conceal his sorrow. But he had never before been sorrowful in the

have found favour in your sight, I would pray you to send me to Judah, to the city of my forefathers' tombs, that I may rebuild it."

Then the king, sitting with the queen by his side, asked:

"How long will your journey be? And when will you return?"

Seeing that the king was willing to let him go, Nehemiah set a date for his return and asked for letters of safe conduct to the governors on the other side of the river, so that they would let him travel through to Judah. He asked also for a letter to Asaph the keeper of the king's forest, allowing him to demand timber to make the beams of the gates and the walls.

All of this was granted to him by the king, together with a military escort for the journey.

Nehemiah came to the governors on the other side of the river and gave them the king's letters. When Sanballat the Horonite and Tobiah the Ammonite, who was his servant, heard that he had come to improve the lot of the children of Israel, they were very angry. But Nehemiah went on to Jerusalem and rested there for three days and nights.

One night he arose with a few of his men and without telling anybody of his intentions—for as yet nobody knew what God meant him to do in Jerusalem—he rode out on a donkey and inspected the city.

He went out by the Valley Gate to the Dragon Well and the Dung Gate, and examined the broken walls and burned-out gates of the city. He passed on to the Gate of the Fountain and the King's Pool, but there was no room for the beast that was under him to pass. So he went on in the darkness beside the brook and looked at that part of the wall, and then turned back and went back into the city through the Valley Gate.

king's presence, so the king said:

"Why do you look so sad? You are not sick, so you must have some secret sorrow."

Nehemiah was frightened and said:

"May the king live for ever! Why should I not grieve since my home city, the grave of my ancestors, is laid waste and its gates consumed with fire?"

"What are you asking for?" said the king.

Nehemiah prayed to God and said to the king:

"If it pleases the king, and if I

THE WALL IS REBUILT

The next day, Nehemiah went to the priests and rulers who still did not know why he had come, and he said to them:

"You see what a sad state Jerusalem is in, and how the gates of the city have been burned by fire. Come, let us build up the wall, so that we can hold up our heads again."

He told them of how God had spoken to him, and also of the king's words, and they said:

"Let us rise up and build."

And they began immediately to make their preparations.

When Sanballat the Horonite and Tobiah the Ammonite and Geshem the Arabian heard what was going to be done, they jeered at Nehemiah and said:

"What are you going to do? Do you propose to rebel against the king?"

Nehemiah answered them, saying:

"The God of heaven will prosper us, and therefore we his servants are going to build. But you have no share and no rights in Jerusalem."

The work was shared out and given to the different families and clans. The high priest and his fellow priests rebuilt and sanctified the Sheep Gate. The Gate of the Fountain was repaired by Shallun the ruler of part of Mizpah. Even women helped in the work of rebuilding.

But when Sanballat and Tobiah and the Arabians and the people of Ammon and Ashod heard that the walls of Jerusalem were being rebuilt and the breaches stopped up, they were very angry. So they plotted to come out and fight against Jerusalem in order to stop the work.

Nehemiah heard of this and he set out a watch for them by night and day. Half of his men laboured at the wall, and the other half stood on the alert, armed with spears and shields and bows, and even the builders worked with their swords at their sides. A trumpeter stood by Nehemiah and he gave his orders to the nobles and the rulers and the rest of the people.

"The work is very widespread, and we are separated from each other on the wall, therefore listen for the trumpet, and if it sounds, wherever you may be, run to it. Our God will fight for us."

Thus they went on with the work, and Nehemiah told the people: "Every man with his servant is to lodge inside Jerusalem, to guard us by night as well as working during the day."

Neither he nor his kinsmen nor his servants nor the guards which followed him took off their clothes, except to wash, during the rebuilding of the wall.

And after fifty-two days the wall was finished.

PSALMS OF JOY

The Psalms formed the hymn book or service book of the Temple, particularly after the return to Jerusalem. They remain to this day the service book both of Judaism and Christianity. Psalm 126, the last given here, was written as a song of homecoming to celebrate the return of the Jews to Jerusalem.

PSALM 23

The Lord is my Shepherd; I shall not want.
He maketh me to lie down in green
     pastures;
He leadeth me beside the still waters.
He restoreth my soul.
He leadeth me in the paths of righteousness
For his name's sake.
Yea, though I walk through the valley
     of the shadow of death,

I will fear no evil, for thou art with me.
Thy rod and thy staff, they comfort me.
Thou preparest a table before me
     in the presence of mine enemies;
Thou anointest my head with oil;
My cup runneth over.
Surely goodness and mercy shall follow me
All the days of my life,
And I will dwell in the house of the Lord
     for ever.

PSALM 24

The earth is the Lord's and the fullness
     thereof,
The world, and they that dwell therein;
For he hath founded it upon the seas,
And established it upon the floods.
Who shall ascend into the hill of the Lord?
Or who shall stand in the holy place?
He that hath clean hands and a pure heart,
Who hath not lifted up his soul
     unto vanity, nor sworn deceitfully.
He shall receive the blessing of the Lord,
And righteousness from the God
     of his salvation.
This is the generation of them that seek him,
That seek thy face, O Jacob.
Lift up your heads, O ye gates,
And be ye lifted up, ye everlasting doors.
And the king of glory shall come in.
Who is this king of glory?
The Lord, strong and mighty,
The Lord, mighty in battle.
Lift up your heads, O ye gates,
Even lift them up, ye everlasting doors;
And the king of glory shall come in.
Who is this king of glory?
The Lord of hosts, he is the king of glory.

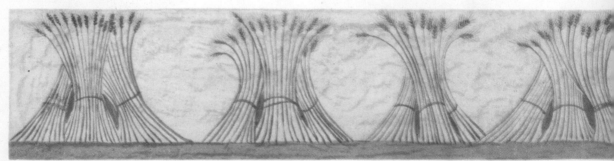

PSALM 100

*Make a joyful noise unto the Lord, all ye
    lands.
Serve the Lord with gladness;
Come before his presence with singing.
Know ye that the Lord, he is God;
It is he that hath made us,
    and not we ourselves;
We are his people,
    and the sheep of his pasture.
Enter into his gates with thanksgiving,
And into his courts with praise;
Be thankful unto him,
    and bless his name.
For the Lord is good, his mercy is
    everlasting,
And his truth endureth to all generations.*

PSALM 126

*When the Lord turned again the captivity
    of Zion,
We were like them that dream.
Then was our mouth filled with laughter,
And our tongue with singing:
Then said they among the heathen,
The Lord hath done great things for them.
The Lord hath done great things for us;
Whereof we are glad.
Turn again our captivity, O Lord,
As the streams in the south.
They that sow in tears shall reap in joy.
He that goeth forth and weepeth,
    bearing precious seed,
Shall doubtless come again with rejoicing,
    bringing his sheaves with him.*

THE TALE OF JONAH

History in the Old Testament ends with the partial restoration of Jerusalem under the leadership of Ezra and Nehemiah. The Old Testament has practically nothing to say about the period after this, the successive eras of Greek and Roman domination when the Old Testament itself was being assembled in its present form.

Though its date of composition is unknown, one of the final books to be accepted as Holy Scripture in the Hebrew Bible was undoubtedly the story of Jonah, which follows. It is one of the shortest books of the Bible, but it is considered by some to be one of the most profound. Beneath its surface, it tells of God's concern for all people, even the Ninevites, long hated by the Hebrews.

HE word of the Lord came to Jonah, son of Amittai, saying: "Arise and go to the city of Nineveh, and preach in it, for its wickedness has offended me."

But Jonah fled before the face of the Lord, and he went down to Joppa, where he found a ship which was bound for Tarshish, in the opposite direction from Nineveh. So he paid his passage and went down into the ship to go to Tarshish, in order to escape the presence of the Lord.

But the Lord sent a great wind out on the sea, and a mighty tempest arose and the ship was in danger of being wrecked. The sailors were afraid and

each one prayed to his god. And they took the cargo and threw it into the sea to lighten the ship.

Jonah was deep inside the ship where he lay fast asleep. So the shipmaster came to him and said: "What do you mean, O sleeper? Arise, call on your God, and if he wills, it may be that we will not perish."

Then the sailors said to each other: "Come let us cast lots, that we may know who is the cause of this evil which has come upon us."

So they cast lots, and the lot fell upon Jonah. And they said to him: "Tell us, we pray you, why this evil has befallen us? What is your occupation? Where do you come from? What is your country and your people?"

"I am a Hebrew," Jonah said to them. "I worship the Lord, the God of heaven, who has made the sea and the dry land."

But Jonah also admitted that he had fled from his God, and then the sailors were exceedingly afraid and they said to him: "Why have you done this? What shall we do to you, in order to calm the sea?"

"Take me up," said Jonah, "and cast me forth into the sea, and it will be calm for you. I know that it is for my sake that this great tempest is upon you."

Nevertheless the men rowed hard to bring the ship to land. But they could not, for the waves were great and the wind was strong against them. Therefore they cried to the Lord: "We beseech you, O Lord, we beseech you not to let us perish for the sake of this man, and do not hold us responsible for an innocent death, since you, O Lord, have done everything according to your will."

Then they took Jonah and threw him into the sea. And the sea stopped its raging. And the men were struck with fear of the Lord, so they offered a sacrifice and made vows to the Lord.

Now the Lord had made ready a great fish to swallow Jonah, and Jonah was in the belly of the fish for three days and three nights. During this time he prayed to the Lord, and at last the Lord spoke to the fish, and it vomited Jonah out on the dry land.

Then the word of the Lord came to Jonah for the second time, saying: "Arise, go to Nineveh, that great city, and preach there the preaching that I tell you."

So Jonah arose and went to Nineveh, according to the word of the Lord. When he reached the city, he walked about in it for a day, and cried: "In forty days Nineveh will be overthrown."

So the people of Nineveh believed in God, and proclaimed a fast and dressed themselves in sackcloth, from the greatest to the very least of them.

Word came to the king of Nineveh, and he rose from his throne and took off his robe, and clothed himself in sackcloth and sat among ashes. And he caused a decree of the king and his nobles to be proclaimed and published throughout Nineveh, saying: "Let neither man nor beast, oxen nor sheep, taste anything. Let them neither eat

nor drink water, but let them all be covered with sackcloth and let them cry to the Lord with all their might. Let each one turn from his evil way, and from all violence. Who can tell if God may not turn and repent, and turn his fierce anger from us, so that we shall not perish?"

God saw their deeds and how they had abandoned their evil ways, and he repented of the evil that he had said he would do to them. He did it not.

GOD ANSWERS JONAH'S ANGER

But Jonah was very displeased and exceedingly angry. He prayed to the Lord, saying: "I pray you, O Lord, did I not say as much when I was still in my own country? That was why I fled from you to Tarshish. For I knew that you are a gracious God and merciful, slow to anger and of great kindness, and repenting of evil. Therefore, now, O Lord, I beg you to take away my life from me: for it is better for me to die than to live."

The Lord answered him: "Is it right of you to be angry?"

So Jonah went out of the city and sat on the east side of it. He made a shelter for himself and sat under it, and there he waited to see what would become of the city.

The Lord God prepared a gourd and made it grow up over Jonah's head to shade him from the noonday sun and ease his grief. So Jonah was very thankful for the gourd.

But early the next morning, God sent a worm which attacked the gourd, so that it withered; and when the sun came up, God sent a violent east wind, and the sun beat down on Jonah's head, and he fainted and longed to die, saying: "It is better for me to die than to live."

Then God said to Jonah: "Is it right for you to be so angry about the gourd?"

Jonah said: "I am quite right to be angry, even unto death."

Then the Lord said to him: "You have had pity on the gourd, though you neither planted it nor tended it; it came up in a night, and it perished in a night.

"Should I not spare Nineveh, that great city, with all its cattle and all its hundred and twenty thousand inhabitants?"

A VISION OF DAYS TO COME

The idea that the tale of Jonah expresses in story form is stated repeatedly by many of the prophets throughout the Old Testament. This is that God's love is both special and far-reaching. It is special in that it is directed towards 'the people of Israel and Judah' with whom God made a covenant at the time of Moses, and far-reaching in that it is not thereby limited to any particular people, time or place.

Its far-reaching qualities are evident in the first of these passages from Micah in which the prophet looks forward to the day of freedom when all nations shall worship God in peace.

But in the last days, it shall come to pass,
  that the mountain of the house
  of the Lord shall be established
  in the top of the mountains,
And it shall be exalted among the hills
  and people shall flock into it
  and many nations shall come, and say,
"Come, and let us go up
  to the mountains of the Lord
  and to the house of the God of Jacob.

And he will teach us of his ways,
  and we will walk in his paths."
For the law shall go forth from Zion
  and the word of the Lord from Jerusalem.
And he shall judge among many people,
  and rebuke strong nations afar off;
And they shall beat their swords
  into ploughshares
  and their spears into pruning hooks.
Nation shall not lift up
  a sword against nation
And they shall not learn war any more.

The special qualities of God's love are clear from the second passage in which first God speaks, then the people of Israel, and finally, in the last verse, Micah himself. Micah's words represent the essence of the prophets' teaching: God requires of his people not sacrifices but lives of justice, kindness and peace.

"O my people, what have I done to you?
  And how have I worried you?
  Give evidence against me.
  I brought you out of the land of Egypt,
  and redeemed you from slavery
  and set before you Moses
  and Aaron and Miriam."

"With what shall we come before the Lord?
  and bow ourselves before the high God?
Shall we come before him
  with burnt offerings,
  with calves of a year old?"

"He has shown you, O man, what is good;
  and what does the Lord require of you,
  but to do justly,
  and to love mercy
  and to walk humbly with your God?"

the
NEW
TESTAMENT

CONTENTS

THE
EARLY
YEARS OF
JESUS

ZACHARIAS AND ELISABETH

THERE was in the days of Herod, the king of Judea, a priest named Zacharias, and his wife Elisabeth. They were both righteous before God, keeping the commandments of the Lord. But they had no children, and they were both well advanced in years.

Now when it was Zacharias' turn to serve in the temple, he went into the temple to burn incense while the whole multitude of the people prayed outside. And an angel of the Lord appeared to him at the right side of the altar, and when Zacharias saw him, he was troubled and fear fell upon him. But the angel said to him:

"Fear not, Zacharias, for your prayer is heard. Your wife shall bear you a son, and you shall call his name John. You shall have joy and gladness and many shall rejoice at his birth. For he shall be great in the sight of the Lord, and shall drink neither wine nor strong drink. He shall be filled with the Holy Spirit. And he shall turn many of the children of Israel to the Lord their God.

"He shall go before him in the spirit and power of Elijah, to turn the hearts of the fathers to the children, and the disobedient to the wisdom of the just, to make ready a people prepared for the Lord."

"How am I to know this is to be?" said Zacharias to the angel. "For I am an old man and my wife too is advanced in years."

The angel answered him, saying:

"I am Gabriel, and I stand in the presence of God. I have been sent to speak to you and to tell you these glad tidings. And, behold, you shall be dumb and unable to speak until these things come about, because you did not believe my words."

The people waiting outside wondered why Zacharias was so long in

the temple. When he came out he could not speak to them, and they sensed that he had seen a vision in the temple, for he made signs to them and remained speechless.

And when his time of service was completed he returned home, and before long his wife Elisabeth knew that she was going to have a child.

AN ANGEL VISITS MARY

HE angel Gabriel was sent by God to a city of Galilee named Nazareth, to a maiden betrothed to a man named Joseph, of the family of David. The name of the maiden was Mary.

The angel appeared to her and said:

"Hail, you who are highly favoured! The Lord is with you; blessed are you among women."

And when she saw him, she was troubled at what he had said and wondered to herself what this greeting could mean. Then the angel continued:

"Fear not, Mary, for you have found favour with God. You shall bring forth a son and shall call his name Jesus. He shall be great, and shall be called the Son of the Highest, and the Lord God shall give him the throne of his forefather David. He shall rule over the house of Jacob for ever, and of his kingdom there shall be no end."

"How shall this be," Mary said to the angel, "seeing that I have no husband?"

The angel answered and said to her:

"The Holy Spirit shall come upon you and the power of the Most High shall overshadow you. The child that is born of you shall be holy and shall be called the Son of God."

"Behold, I am the handmaiden of the Lord," Mary said. "Let it be to me as you have said."

So Mary arose and went into the hill country with haste, to a town of Judah where she went to the house of Zacharias and his wife, her cousin Elisabeth. And when Elisabeth heard her greeting she was filled with the Holy Spirit and she cried out with a loud voice:

"Blessed are you among women, and blessed is the child you shall bear. But why is it that the mother of my Lord should come to me?"

And Mary said:

"*My soul does praise the Lord,*
And my spirit has rejoiced
  in God my Saviour.
For he has regarded the lowliness
  of his handmaiden: for, behold,
  from henceforth all generations
  shall call me blessed:
For he that is mighty has done
  great things for me,
  and holy is his name.
His mercy is on those who fear him
  from generation to generation.
He has showed strength with his arm;
  he has scattered the proud
  in the imagination of their hearts.

He has put down the mighty
  from their thrones and
  has exalted them of low degree.
He has filled the hungry
  with good things,
  and the rich he has sent
  empty away.
He has helped his servant Israel,
  in remembrance of his mercy;
As he spoke to our fathers,
  to Abraham, and to his seed for ever."

Mary remained with Elisabeth for about three months and then returned to her own house.

THE BIRTH OF JOHN THE BAPTIST

Now Elisabeth's time came that she should give birth, and she brought forth a son. Her neighbours and her cousins heard how the Lord had shown great mercy upon her, and they rejoiced with her.

And it came to pass that on the eighth day the child was to be circumcised, and they called him Zacharias, after the name of his father.

But his mother said, "No, he shall be called John." And they said to her, "There is no one of your family that is called by this name." And they made signs to his father, asking how he would have him called.

Zacharias asked for a writing tablet, and wrote: "His name is John." And they all marvelled. Then immediately Zacharias' mouth was opened, and his tongue loosed, and he spoke and praised God. And fear came on all that lived round about them.

Word of all these doings spread throughout all the hill country of Judah, and all that heard of them laid them up in their hearts, saying:

"What kind of child shall this be!"

And his father Zacharias was filled with the Holy Spirit, and prophesied, saying:

"Blessed be the Lord of Israel,
for he has visited and
redeemed his people,
And has raised up a horn
of salvation for us
in the house of his servant David;
As he spoke by the mouth
of his holy prophets,
which have been since
the world began:
That we may be saved from our enemies,
and from the hand of all that hate us,
To perform the mercy promised
to our fathers, and
to remember his holy covenant;
The oath which he swore
to our father Abraham,
That he would grant unto us,
that we being delivered
out of the hand of our enemies,
might serve him without fear,
In holiness and righteousness
before him, all the days of our life:
And you, child, shall be called
the prophet of the Highest,
for you shall go before the face
of the Lord to prepare his ways
To give knowledge of salvation
to his people by remission
of their sins, through the
tender mercy of our God;
whereby the dayspring from
on high has visited us,
To give light to them that sit
in darkness and in the shadow
of death, to guide our feet
into the way of peace."

The child grew and became strong in spirit, and lived in the deserts till the day of his appearance unto Israel.

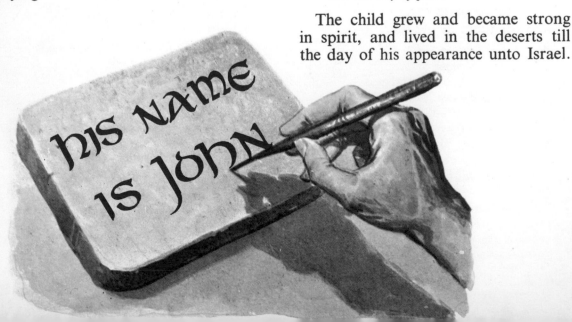

THE BIRTH OF JESUS

IT came to pass in those days that a decree went out from Caesar Augustus, the emperor in Rome, that all the world should be taxed. This taxing was first made when Cyrenius was governor of Syria.

Everyone went to be taxed, each to his own city. And Joseph went up from Galilee, from the city of Nazareth, into Judea, to the city of David which is called Bethlehem, because he was of the house and family of David, to be taxed with Mary his wife who was soon to have a child.

So it came to pass that while they were there the day arrived for her child to be born. She brought forth her firstborn son, and wrapped him in swaddling clothes, and laid him in a manger, because there was no room for them in the inn.

There were in the same country shepherds staying in the field, keeping watch over their flocks by night. And lo, the angel of the Lord came upon them, and the glory of the Lord shone round about them, and they were much afraid.

"Fear not," the angel said to them. "For I bring you good tidings of a great joy that is coming to all people. For to you is born this day in the city of David a Saviour who is Christ the Lord. And this shall be a sign to you: You shall find the babe wrapped in swaddling clothes, lying in a manger."

And suddenly there was with the angel a multitude of the heavenly host praising God and saying:

> *"Glory to God in the highest,*
> *and on earth peace,*
> *good will toward men."*

When the angels had gone away from them into heaven, the shepherds

said to one another, "Let us go into Bethlehem and see this thing which has come to pass, which the Lord has made known to us."

They went with haste and found Mary and Joseph, and the babe lying in a manger. And when they had seen it, they made known throughout the land what they had been told concerning this child. And all who heard it marvelled at the things which were told them by the shepherds. But Mary kept all these things, and pondered them in her heart.

THE PRESENTATION IN THE TEMPLE

Now when the time arrived for the child to be circumcised, he was called Jesus, the name given him by the angel before he was born. And when the days of the purification were over, according to the law of Moses, they brought him to Jerusalem, to present him to the Lord (as it is written in the law of the Lord, "Every firstborn son shall be called holy to the Lord") and to offer a sacrifice according to that which is said in the law of the Lord: "A pair of turtledoves or two young pigeons."

And there was a man in Jerusalem whose name was Simeon, and who was just and devout. The Holy Spirit was in him, and had revealed to him that he should not die before he had seen the Lord's Christ. The Spirit led him that day to the temple, and when the parents brought in the child Jesus, to do for him what the law required, Simeon took him up in his arms, and blessed God and said:

"Lord, now let your servant depart
in peace, according to your word.
For my eyes have seen your salvation,
which you have prepared before
the face of all people;
A light to lighten the Gentiles,
and the glory of your people Israel."

Joseph and the child's mother marvelled at the things which were spoken of him. And Simeon blessed them, and said to Mary: "This child is destined to bring about the fall and rising again of many in Israel. He shall be a sign against which many shall speak (yes, through him a sword shall pierce your own soul also) that the thoughts of many hearts may be revealed."

THE VISIT OF THE WISE MEN

NOW when Jesus was born in Bethlehem of Judea, in the days of Herod the king, there came wise men from the east to Jerusalem, asking: "Where is he that is born King of the Jews? For we have seen his star in the east and are come to worship him."

When Herod the king heard these things, he was troubled, and all Jerusalem with him. And when he had gathered all the chief priests and scribes of the people together, he asked them where Christ should be born. "In Bethlehem of Judea," they said. "For thus it is written by the prophet:

'*And you, Bethlehem, in the land of Judah,*
are not the least among
the princes of Judah.
For out of you shall come a Governor,
that shall rule my people Israel.' "

Then Herod sent secretly for the wise men, and asked them what time the star had appeared. And he sent them to Bethlehem, saying, "Go and search carefully for the young child, and when you have found him, bring me word, that I may come and worship him also."

When they had heard the king, they departed. And, lo, the star which they saw in the east went before them till it came and stood over the place where the young child was. When they saw the star, they rejoiced with

great joy. And when they came into the house, they saw the young child with Mary his mother, and they fell down and worshipped him, and presented to him gifts: gold, frankincense, and myrrh. And being warned by God in a dream that they should not return to Herod, they departed and returned to their own country by another way.

THE FLIGHT INTO EGYPT

HEN the wise men had departed, the angel of the Lord appeared and spoke to Joseph in a dream, saying:

"Arise, and take the young child and his mother, and flee into Egypt, and stay there until I bring you word. For Herod will seek the child to destroy him."

So he arose and took the young child and his mother into Egypt. And there they remained until the death of Herod, that the word of the prophet of the Lord might be fulfilled: "Out of Egypt have I called my son."

When Herod saw that the wise men had deceived him, he was greatly angered. He ordered that all the children under two years old in Bethlehem and the land around should be put to death, in accordance with the time he had learned from the wise men. Then was fulfilled that which was spoken by Jeremiah the prophet:

"In Rama was there a voice heard,
lamenting, and weeping and mourning,
Rachel weeping for her children,
and would not be comforted,
because they were no more."

But when Herod died, an angel of the Lord appeared in a dream to Joseph in Egypt, saying: "Rise up and take the young child and his mother and go into the land of Israel. For those who sought the child's life are dead."

And he arose and took the young child and his mother, and went into the land of Israel. But when he heard that Archelaus reigned in Judea in the place of his father Herod, he was afraid to go there. So, being warned by God in a dream, he turned aside again into the region of Galilee. He went and settled in the city of Nazareth, so that the words which were spoken by the prophets might be fulfilled: "He shall be called a Nazarene."

JESUS AMONG THE TEACHERS

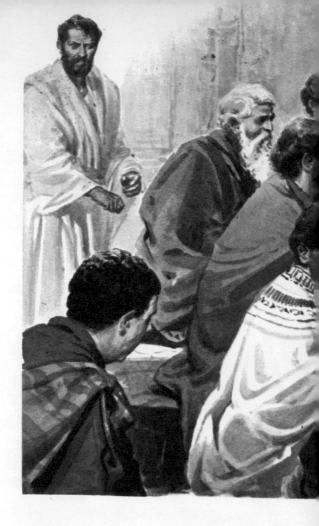

AND the child grew and became strong in spirit and filled with wisdom, and the grace of God was upon him.

Now when he was twelve years old, his parents went up to Jerusalem according to the custom for the feast of the passover. After the passover was ended, and they were returning, the child Jesus stayed behind in Jerusalem.

Joseph and Mary did not know this and, supposing him to have been in their group, went a day's journey before seeking him among their kinsmen and acquaintances. When they did not find him, they turned back again to Jerusalem, seeking him.

After three days, they found him in the temple, sitting among the teachers, both listening to them and asking them questions. And all who heard him were astonished at his understanding and answers.

When his parents saw him, they were amazed. And his mother said to him, "Son, why have you behaved like this to us? Your father and I have been

looking for you and worrying." And he said to them, "Why did you look for me? Did you not know that I must be about my Father's business?" But they did not understand what he was saying to them.

Then he went with them to Nazareth, and was obedient to them, but his mother kept all these things in her heart. Jesus, as he grew up, increased both in wisdom and in favour with God and man.

THE BAPTISM OF JESUS BY JOHN

NOW in the fifteenth year of the reign of Tiberius Caesar, when Pontius Pilate was governor of Judea, and Herod was tetrarch of Galilee, the word of God came unto John the son of Zacharias in the wilderness. And he came into all the country about Jordan, preaching the baptism of repentance for the remission of sins, as it is written in the book of Isaiah the prophet, saying:

"The voice of one crying in the wilderness,
'Prepare ye the way of the Lord,
make his paths straight.
Every valley shall be filled,
and every mountain
and hill shall be made low.
And the crooked shall be made straight,
and the rough shall be made smooth.
And all flesh shall see
the salvation of God.' "

John wore clothing made of camel's hair, and a leather girdle about his waist. And his food was locusts and wild honey.

The people of Jerusalem and all Judea and all the region round about Jordan, went out to him, and were baptized by him, confessing their sins. But when he saw many of the Pharisees and Sadducees come to his baptism, he said to them:

"O generation of vipers, who has warned you to flee from the wrath to come? Do, therefore, deeds that show repentance, and do not just say within yourselves, 'We have Abraham for

forth good fruit is cut down and cast into the fire."

"What shall we do then?" the people asked him. And he answered:

"He who has two coats, let him give to him who has none, and he who has meat, let him give to those that are without."

Then came also tax-collectors to be baptized and said to him, "Master, what shall we do?" And he said to them, "Collect no more than you are instructed to."

Soldiers came to him asking, "And what shall we do?" And he said to them, "Do violence to no man, nor accuse any falsely. And be content with your wages."

People were expectant and wondered in their hearts whether he was the Christ or not. John therefore answered, saying to all of them:

"I indeed baptize you with water, but one mightier than I is coming whose shoes I am not worthy to undo. He shall baptize you with the Holy Spirit and with fire.

"His fork is in his hand, and he will thoroughly clean his floor after the harvest, and will gather his wheat into the granary. But he will burn up the chaff with unquenchable fire."

Then Jesus came from Galilee to Jordan in order to be baptized by John. But John stopped him saying, "I have need to be baptized by you, and do you come to me?"

And Jesus answering said to him, "Let it be so now, for by us must all righteousness be fulfilled."

So John consented. And Jesus, when he was baptized, arose directly from the water. And, lo, the heavens were opened and he saw the Spirit of God coming down like a dove, and alighting upon him. And behold a voice from heaven said:

"This is my beloved Son, in whom I am well pleased."

our forefather.' For I say to you that God is able to raise up children for Abraham from these stones. And now the axe is laid to the root of the trees. Therefore, every tree which brings not

THE TEMPTATION IN THE WILDERNESS

JESUS, full of the Holy Spirit, returned from the Jordan and was led by the Spirit into the wilderness to be tempted by the devil. Jesus fasted forty days and forty nights, and afterwards he was hungry. Then the devil came to him and said, "If you are the Son of God, command that these stones be made bread."

But Jesus answered saying:

"It is written: Man shall not live by bread alone, but by every word that comes out of the mouth of God."

Then the devil took him up into the holy city, and set him on a pinnacle of the temple, and said to him, "If you are the Son of God, throw yourself down. For it is written that he shall put his angels in charge of you to keep you safe, and they shall catch you in their hands, lest you strike your foot against a stone." Jesus said to him:

"It is written also: You shall not tempt the Lord your God."

Again, the devil took him up into a very big mountain, and showed him all the kingdoms of the world, and the glory of them. And he said:

"All these things I will give you, if you will fall down and worship me."

Then Jesus said:

"Away, Satan. For it is written:

You shall worship the Lord your God, and him only shall you serve."

Then the devil left him and, behold, angels came and ministered unto him.

JESUS IN GALILEE

OW Herod, being reproved by John for all the evils which he had done, had John cast into prison, and when Jesus heard this, he departed into Galilee. And leaving Nazareth, he came and dwelt in Capernaum which is on the sea coast.

At this time Jesus began to preach, and to say, "Repent, for the kingdom of heaven is at hand." He was about thirty years of age when he began his ministry.

And as he was walking by the sea of Galilee, he saw Simon and Andrew his brother casting a net into the sea, for they were fishermen. And he went on to one of the boats, which was Simon's, and asked him to push out a little from the shore. Then he sat down and taught the people from the boat.

When he had finished speaking, he said to Simon, "Launch out into the deep water and let down your nets for a catch." And Simon answering said to him, "Master, we have laboured all night and have taken nothing. Nevertheless, at your word I will let down the nets."

When they had done this, they enclosed a great multitude of fish, and their nets broke. Then they called their partners, who were in another boat, that they should come and help them. And they came, and filled both the boats so full that they began to sink.

When Simon saw this, he fell down at Jesus' knees, saying, "Depart from me, for I am a sinful man, O Lord." For he was astonished, and so were all that were with him, at the catch of fish which they had taken.

Then Jesus said to them, "Follow me, and I will make you fishers of men." And immediately they forsook their nets, and followed him.

When he had gone a little further, he saw James the son of Zebedee, and John his brother, who were in their boat mending their nets. He called them, and they left their father Zebedee in the boat with the hired servants, and followed him.

THE MARRIAGE IN CANA

THE third day there was a marriage in Cana of Galilee, and the mother of Jesus was there. Jesus and his disciples were also invited to the wedding. And when they wanted wine, the mother of Jesus said to him, "They have no more wine." Jesus said to her, "Woman, what would you have me do? It is not yet time for me to act." His mother said to the servants, "Whatever he says to you, do it."

Now there were six stone waterpots standing there for the purification rites of the Jews, holding twenty to thirty gallons apiece. Jesus said to the servants, "Fill the waterpots with water." And they filled them to the brim. Then he said to them, "Draw some out now, and take it to the master of the feast." And they took it.

When the master of the feast tasted the water that was made wine, not knowing where it came from (but the servants who had drawn the water knew), the master of the feast called to the bridegroom and said to him, "Every man sets out good wine at the beginning, and when men have drunk well, then that which is worse. But you have kept the good wine until now."

This beginning of miracles Jesus did in Cana of Galilee, and showed his glory, and his disciples believed in him.

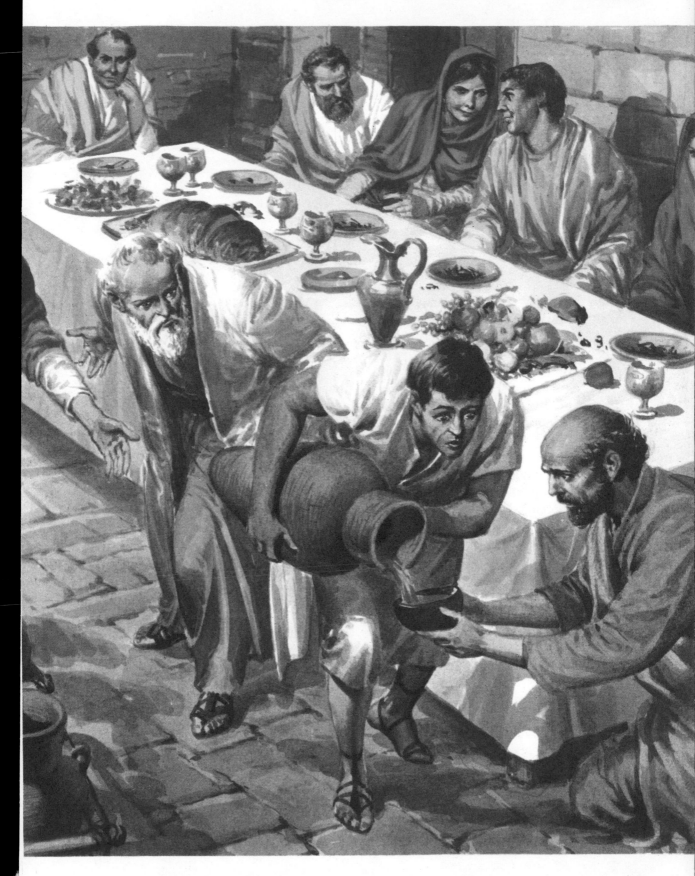

JESUS
PREACHES
IN THE
SYNAGOGUES

AFTER this he went down to Capernaum, with his mother and his brothers and his disciples, and on the sabbath day he entered into the synagogue and taught. And people were astonished at his words, for he taught them as one that had authority, and not as the scribes.

And there was in the synagogue a man with an unclean spirit and he cried out saying:

"Let us alone. What have we to do with you, Jesus of Nazareth? Have you come to destroy us? I know who you are: the Holy One of God."

And Jesus rebuked him saying, "Hold your peace, and come out of him."

The unclean spirit shook him and cried with a loud voice, and then came out of him. And they were all amazed, and they questioned among themselves, saying, "What thing is this? What new doctrine is this? For with authority he commands even the unclean spirits and they do obey him." And immediately his fame spread abroad throughout all the region round about Galilee.

When they left the synagogue, they went into the house of Simon and Andrew, with James and John. Simon's

wife's mother lay sick of a fever, and they told him of her. And he came and took her by the hand, and lifted her up, and immediately the fever left her, and she waited upon them.

That evening, when the sun did set they brought to him all that were diseased and them that were possessed with devils. And all the city was gathered together at the door. He healed many that were sick of various diseases, and cast out many devils.

In the morning, rising up a long while before daylight, he went out and departed into a solitary place, and there prayed. Simon and they that were with him followed after him, and when they found him, they said to him, "All men seek for you." And he said to them, "Let us go into the next towns, that I may preach there also, for that is why I came forth."

And he preached in synagogues throughout all Galilee, and cast out devils.

JESUS HEALS THE LEPER

And there came a leper to him, begging him, and kneeling down and saying to him:

"If you will, you can make me clean."

Jesus, moved with compassion, put forth his hand, and touched him, and said to him, "I will. Be clean." And as soon as he had spoken, immediately the leprosy departed from him, and he was cleansed. Then he sent him away, saying to him, "See that you say nothing to any man, but go your way, show yourself to the priest, and offer for your cleansing those things which Moses commanded."

But he went out and told the news widely, so much that Jesus could no longer openly enter into the city, but stayed outside in desert places. And people came to him from every quarter.

THE PHARISEES QUESTION JESUS

I T came to pass on a certain day, as he was teaching, that there were Pharisees and doctors of the law sitting by, who had come out of every town of Galilee, and Judea, and Jerusalem. And the power of the Lord was present to heal them.

Some men brought in a bed a man who was taken with a paralysis. They sought means to bring him in and lay him before Jesus, but they could not find a way because of the multitude. So they went upon a housetop and let him down through the roof with the bed into the presence of Jesus. And when Jesus saw their faith, he said to him, "Man, your sins are forgiven you."

Then the scribes and the Pharisees began questioning, saying, "Who is this who speaks blasphemies? Who can forgive sins, but God alone?"

But when Jesus sensed what they were thinking, he answered them, and said:

"Why do you question in your hearts, asking whether it is easier to say, 'Your sins are forgiven you,' or 'Rise up and walk'?

"In order that you may know that the Son of man has power on earth to forgive sins," (he said to the paralysed man), "I say to you: Arise, and take up your bed and go into your house."

And immediately he rose up before them, and took up the bed on which he lay, and departed to his own house, glorifying God. And they were all amazed, and they glorified God, and were filled with fear, saying, "We have seen strange things today."

As Jesus went on his way, he saw a man named Matthew sitting at the tax office, and he said to him, "Follow me." And Matthew arose and followed him.

One day, as Jesus sat eating, many tax-collectors and sinners came and sat down with him and his disciples. And when the Pharisees saw it, they said to his disciples, "Why does your master eat with tax-collectors and sinners?"

And Jesus, answering, said to them:

"They that are healthy do not need a physician, but they that are sick. Go and learn what this means: 'I will have mercy, and not sacrifice.' For I have not come to call the righteous, but sinners to repentance."

Then the disciples of John came to him, saying, "Why do we and the Pharisees fast often, while your disciples do not fast?"

And Jesus said to them:

"Do wedding guests mourn, as long as the bridegroom is with them? The days will come when the bridegroom shall be taken from them, and then they shall fast."

THE SABBATH DAY

At that time Jesus went on the sabbath day through the corn. His disciples were hungry and began to pluck ears of corn, and to eat. When the Pharisees saw it, they said to him, "Behold, your disciples are doing what it is not lawful to do upon the sabbath day."

But he said to them:

"Have you not read what David did, and those who were with him, when he was hungry: how he entered into the house of God and ate the showbread, which was not lawful for him to eat, nor for those who were with him, but only for the priests?

"Or have you not read in the law, how on the sabbath days the priests in the temple profane the sabbath and are blameless? But I say to you that in this place is one greater than the temple. For the Son of man is Lord even of the sabbath day."

JESUS HEALS ON THE SABBATH

And he went out from there and went into their synagogue where there was a man who had his hand withered. And they asked him, "Is it lawful to heal on the sabbath day?" so that they might accuse him.

Then Jesus said to them:

"What man is there among you that, if he has a sheep that falls into a pit on the sabbath day, will not take hold of it and lift it out? How much better is a man than a sheep? It is therefore lawful to do good on the sabbath."

Then he said to the man, "Stretch forth your hand." And he stretched it forth and it was restored whole like the other. Then the Pharisees went

out, and held a meeting against him, to plan how they might destroy him.

Now there is at Jerusalem by the sheep market a pool. Around it lay a great multitude of invalid folk, of blind, lame and withered, waiting for the water to move. For an angel of the

Lord went down at certain seasons into the pool and troubled the water. And whoever stepped in first after the troubling of the water was cured of whatever disease he had.

THE INVALID AT THE POOL

A certain man was there who had had a sickness for thirty-eight years. When Jesus saw him and knew that he had been lying there a long time, he said to him, "Do you wish to be made healthy?"

The invalid man answered, "Sir, I have no man to put me in the pool when the water is troubled, and while I am going, another steps down before me."

is not lawful for you to carry your bed." He answered them, "He that made me healthy said to me, 'Take up your bed and walk.'"

Then they asked him, "What man is the one who said to you, 'Take up your bed and walk?'" But he that was healed did not know who it was, for Jesus had gone away, a crowd being in the place.

Afterwards, Jesus found him in the temple, and said to him, "Behold, you are well. Sin no more, lest a worse thing come to you." The man departed, and told the priests that it was Jesus who had healed him. And therefore the authorities persecuted Jesus, and tried to slay him, because he had done these things on the sabbath day.

Jesus said to him, "Rise, take up your bed, and walk." And immediately the man was made healthy, and took up his bed, and walked.

Now that day was the sabbath. Therefore the Jews said to him that was cured, "It is the sabbath day. It

But Jesus answered them, "My Father is for ever at work, and so am I." Therefore his enemies tried even more to kill him, because he not only had broken the sabbath, but said also that God was his Father, making himself equal with God.

THE TWELVE APOSTLES
ARE CHOSEN

And it came to pass in those days that he went out into a mountain to pray, and continued all night in prayer to God. And when it was day, he called to him his disciples, and of them he chose twelve, whom he also named apostles. And he gave to them power to cast out unclean spirits, and to heal all kinds of sickness and all disease.

Now the names of the twelve apostles are these: The first, Simon, who is called Peter, and Andrew his brother; James the son of Zebedee and John his brother; Philip and Bartholomew; Thomas and Matthew the publican; James the son of Alpheus and Lebbeus, whose surname was Thaddeus; Simon the Canaanite; and Judas Iscariot, who betrayed him.

And he came down with them, and stood in the plain, with the company of his disciples and a great multitude of people from all Judea and Jerusalem, and from the sea coast of Tyre and Sidon, which came to hear him and to be healed from their diseases. And they that were troubled with unclean spirits were healed. And the whole multitude tried to touch him, for goodness went forth from him and healed every one of them.

THE SERMON ON THE MOUNT

ND seeing the multitudes, he went up into a mountain. And when he had found a suitable place, his disciples came to him, and he opened his mouth and taught them saying:

"Blessed are the poor in spirit,
for theirs is the kingdom of heaven.
Blessed are they that mourn,
for they shall be comforted.
Blessed are the meek,
for they shall inherit the earth.
Blessed are they which do hunger
and thirst for righteousness,
for they shall be filled.
Blessed are the merciful,
for they shall obtain mercy.
Blessed are the pure in heart,
for they shall see God.
Blessed are the peacemakers,
for they shall be called
the children of God.
Blessed are they which are persecuted
for righteousness' sake,
for theirs is the kingdom of heaven.
Blessed are you, when men
shall revile you, and persecute you,
and shall say all manner of evil
against you falsely, for my sake.
Rejoice, and be exceeding glad,
for great is your reward in heaven,
for so persecuted they the prophets
which were before you.

"You are the salt of the earth. But if the salt has lost its flavour, how shall it be salty again? It is then fit for nothing but to be thrown out and trodden underfoot.

"You are the light of the world. A city that is set on a hill cannot be hidden.

"Men do not light a candle and put it under a bushel, but on a candlestick, where it gives light to all that are in the house.

"Let your light so shine before men that they may see your good works and glorify your Father who is in heaven.

THE LAW AND THE PROPHETS

"Do not think that I have come to destroy the old law or the prophets. I have not come to destroy but to fulfil. For truly I say to you, till heaven and earth pass away, not one dotting of an 'i' nor crossing of a 't' will be removed from the law until all is fulfilled.

"Therefore whoever breaks one of the least of these commandments, and teaches men to do so, shall be called the lowest of all in the kingdom of heaven.

For I say to you that unless your goodness excels that of the scribes and the Pharisees, you shall never enter the kingdom of heaven.

"You have heard it said by men in the days of old, 'You shall not kill, and whoever kills shall be in danger of punishment.' But I say to you that whoever is angry with his brother without cause will be in danger of punishment by God. And whoever curses his brother shall be in danger of hell fire.

"Therefore, if you bring your offering to the altar, and there remember that your brother has any grievance against you, leave your offering there before the altar, and go and be first reconciled to your brother, and then come and make your offering.

"Agree with your adversary quickly while you are on the way to court with him, lest at any time the adversary deliver you to the judge, and the judge deliver you to the officer, and you be cast into prison. Truly I say to you, you shall never come out of there, till you have paid the last penny.

"Again, you have heard that it has been said by men of old, 'You shall

not swear falsely, but shall perform as you swear in your oaths.' But I say to you, swear not at all, neither by heaven, for it is God's throne, nor by earth, for it is his footstool; neither by Jerusalem, for it is the city of the great King. Nor shall you swear by your head, because you cannot make one hair white or black. But let what you have to say be simply 'Yes' or 'No,' for whatever is more than these comes from evil.

"You have heard that it has been said, 'An eye for an eye, a tooth for a tooth.' But I say to you, do not resist an injury. Whoever strikes you on the right cheek, turn to him also the other. If any man wants to sue you for your coat, let him have your cloak as well, and whoever compels you to go one mile, go with him two. Give to him that asks, and if anyone wishes to borrow from you, do not turn away.

THE LOVE OF ENEMIES

"You have heard that it has been said, 'You shall love your neighbour and hate your enemy.' But I say to you, love your enemies, bless those who curse you, do good to those who hate you, and pray for those who persecute you, so that you may be the children of your Father in heaven. For he makes his sun rise on the evil and on the good alike, and sends his rain on the just and on the unjust.

"For if you love those who love you, what reward do you deserve? Do not even tax-collectors do the same? And if you greet your brothers only, what do you do more than others? Do not even tax-collectors do so? Be therefore perfect, even as your Father who is in heaven is perfect.

"Take care that you do not do your good deeds before men, to be seen by them. Otherwise you will have no reward from your Father who is in heaven. When you give charity, do not sound a trumpet before yourself as the hypocrites do in the synagogues and in the streets, to have the praise of men. Truly I say to you, they have their reward in that. But when you give alms, let not your left hand know what your right hand does, so that your charity may be in secret. And your Father who sees what you do in secret shall reward you openly.

THE LORD'S PRAYER

"And when you pray, you shall not be as the hypocrites are, for they love to pray standing in the synagogues and on the corners of the streets, so that they may be seen by men. Truly I say to you: that is their reward. But you, when you pray, go into your room and when you have shut the door, pray to your Father who is unseen. And your Father who sees that which is in secret shall reward you openly.

"And when you pray, do not use idle phrases as the heathen do, for they think they shall be heard for their many words. Therefore do not be like them, for your Father knows everything you need, before you ask him. In this manner therefore pray:

"Our Father who art in heaven,
Hallowed be thy name.
Thy kingdom come.
Thy will be done on earth,
  as it is in heaven.
Give us this day our daily bread.
And forgive us our debts,
  as we forgive our debtors,
And lead us not into temptation,
  but deliver us from evil:
For thine is the kingdom, and the power,
  and the glory, for ever. Amen.

"For if you forgive men their offences, your heavenly Father will also forgive you. But if you do not forgive men their offences, neither will your Father forgive your offences.

"Moreover, when you fast, do not look sad like the hypocrites. For they disfigure their faces so that they may appear to fast. Truly I say to you, they have their reward. But you, when you fast, anoint your head, and wash your face, so that you do not appear to fast to men, but to your Father. And your Father who sees that which is in secret shall reward you openly.

TREASURE IN HEAVEN

"Do not collect for yourselves treasures on earth, where moth and rust do damage, and where thieves break through and steal. But collect for yourselves treasures in heaven, where neither moth nor rust do damage, and where thieves do not break through and steal. For where your treasure is, there will be your heart also.

"The lamp of the body is the eye. If therefore your eye is sound, your whole

body shall be full of light. But if your eye is evil, your whole body shall be full of darkness. If therefore the light that is in you is darkness, how great is that darkness!

"No man can serve two masters, for either he will hate one and love the other, or else he will stand by one and despise the other. You cannot work for both God and worldly wealth. Therefore I say to you, do not worry about your well-being, what you shall eat, or what you shall drink, nor about your body and what you shall put on. Is not life more than food, and the body more than clothing?

"Behold the fowls of the air. They sow not, nor do they reap, nor gather into barns. Yet your heavenly Father feeds them. Are you not much better than they? Which of you by taking thought can add one minute to his life? And why do you worry about clothing? Consider the lilies of the field and how they grow. They do not work, nor do they spin. And yet I say to you that even Solomon in all his glory was not dressed like one of these. Therefore, if God so clothes the grass of

the field, which today grows and to-morrow is cast into the oven, shall he not much more clothe you, O you of little faith?

"Therefore do not worry saying, 'What shall we eat?' or 'What shall we drink?' or 'With what shall we be clothed?', for your heavenly Father knows that you need all these things. But seek first the kingdom of God, and his righteousness, and all these things shall be yours as well. Take therefore no thought for tomorrow, for tomorrow shall take care of itself. The troubles of today are enough for today.

"Judge not, that you be not judged. For by what judgment you make, you shall be judged, and with what measure you give, so shall you be measured. Why do you see the speck that is in your brother's eye, but do not notice the log that is in your own eye? How can you say to your brother, 'Let me pull out the speck from your eye,' when, behold, there is a log in your own eye? You hypocrite, first cast out the log from your own eye, and then you shall see clearly to cast out the speck from your brother's eye.

"Do not give that which is holy to the dogs, nor cast your pearls before swine, lest they trample them under their feet, and turn again and attack you.

"Ask, and it shall be given you. Seek, and you shall find. Knock, and it shall be opened to you. For every one that asks receives, and he that seeks finds, and to him that knocks it shall be opened. What man is there among you who, if his son asks bread, will give him a stone? Or if he ask a fish, will give him a serpent?

THE GOLDEN RULE

"If you then, being evil, know how to give good gifts to your children, how much more shall your Father who is in heaven give good things to them that ask him? Therefore, whatever you want that men should do to you, do so to them. For this is the law and the prophets.

"Enter in at the narrow gate, for wide is the gate and broad is the way that leads to destruction, and there are many who go in that way. Because narrow is the gate, and narrow is the way which leads to life, and there are few that find it.

BY THEIR FRUITS...

"Beware of false prophets which come to you in sheep's clothing, but inwardly are ravenous wolves. You shall know them by their fruits. Do men gather grapes from thorns, or figs from thistles? Every good tree brings forth good fruit, but a bad tree brings forth bad fruit. A good tree cannot bring forth bad fruit, nor can a bad tree bring forth good fruit. Every tree that does not bring forth good fruit is cut down, and cast into the fire. Therefore, by their fruits you shall know them.

"Not everyone that says to me, 'Lord, Lord,' shall enter into the kingdom of heaven, but he shall that does the will of my Father who is in heaven. Many will say to me that day, 'Lord, Lord, have we not prophesied in your name, and in your name cast out devils, and in your name done many wonderful works?' And then I will say to them, 'I never knew you. Depart from me, you that practise evil.'

"Therefore, whoever hears these sayings of mine, and does them, I will liken to a wise man who built his house upon a rock. The rain came down, and the floods came, and the winds blew and beat against that house, but it did not fall, for it was founded upon a rock. And every one that hears these sayings of mine and does them not, shall be like a foolish man who built his house upon the sand. And the rain came down, and the floods came, and the winds blew and beat against that house, and it fell. And great was the fall of it."

And it came to pass, when Jesus had ended these sayings, the people were astonished at his doctrine. For he taught them as one having authority, and not as the scribes.

THE MINISTRY OF JESUS CONTINUES

NOW when he had ended all his sayings in the audience of the people, he entered into Capernaum. There a certain centurion had a servant who was dear to him, who was sick and ready to die. And when he heard of Jesus, he sent to him the elders of the Jews, begging him to come and heal his servant. When the elders came to Jesus they spoke to him saying, "He deserves that you should do this, for he loves our nation and he has built us a synagogue."

Then Jesus went with them, and when he was not far from the house, the centurion sent friends to him, saying, "Lord, do not trouble yourself, for I am not worthy that you should enter my house, nor have I thought myself worthy to come to you. But say the word and my servant shall be healed. For I am a man of authority, having under me soldiers; I say to one, 'Go,' and he goes, and to another, 'Come,' and he comes, and to my servant, 'Do this,' and he does it."

When Jesus heard these things, he marvelled, and, turning around, he said to the people that followed him, "I say to you, I have not found such great faith, no, not in Israel." And when they that were sent returned to the house they found the servant healed that had been sick.

JESUS HEALS THE WIDOW'S SON

The next day, he went into a city called Nain, and many of his disciples went with him and many people. Now when he came to the gate of the city, behold, there was a dead man being

carried out, the only son of his mother who was a widow. And many people of the city were with her.

When the Lord saw her, he had compassion on her, and said to her, "Weep not." Then he went over and touched the coffin, while they that carried it stood still. And he said, "Young man, I say to you, arise." And he that was dead sat up and began to speak. And Jesus delivered him to his mother.

And there came a great fear on all, and they glorified God, saying that a great prophet had risen up among them, and that God had visited his people.

JESUS SENDS WORD TO
JOHN THE BAPTIST

The disciples of John told him of all these things. And John called two of them and sent them to Jesus, saying, "Are you he that is to come, or are we to look for another?"

In the same hour when the men came, he cured many of their sicknesses and plagues, and evil spirits. Then Jesus answered:

"Go your way, and tell John what things you have seen and heard, how the blind see, the lame walk, the lepers are cleansed, the deaf hear, the dead are raised, and to the poor the gospel is preached. And blessed is he who shall not be offended by me."

When the messengers of John had departed, he began to speak to the people concerning John:

"What did you go into the wilderness to see? A reed shaken by the wind? What did you go out to discover? Behold, they who are gorgeously dressed and live delicately are in kings' courts. But what did you go out to see? A prophet? Yes, I say to you, and much more than a prophet. This is he of whom it is written: 'Behold, I send my messenger who shall prepare your way before you.' For I say to you, among those that are born of women there is not a greater prophet than John the Baptist. But he that is least in the kingdom of God is greater than he.

"To what therefore shall I compare the men of this generation? What are they like? They are like children sitting in the market place, and calling to one another and saying, 'We have piped for you, and you have not danced; we cried for you, and you have not wept.' For John the Baptist came neither eating bread nor drinking wine, and you say, 'He has a devil.' The Son of man has come eating and drinking, and you say, 'Behold, a gluttonous man and a drunkard, a friend of publicans and sinners.' "

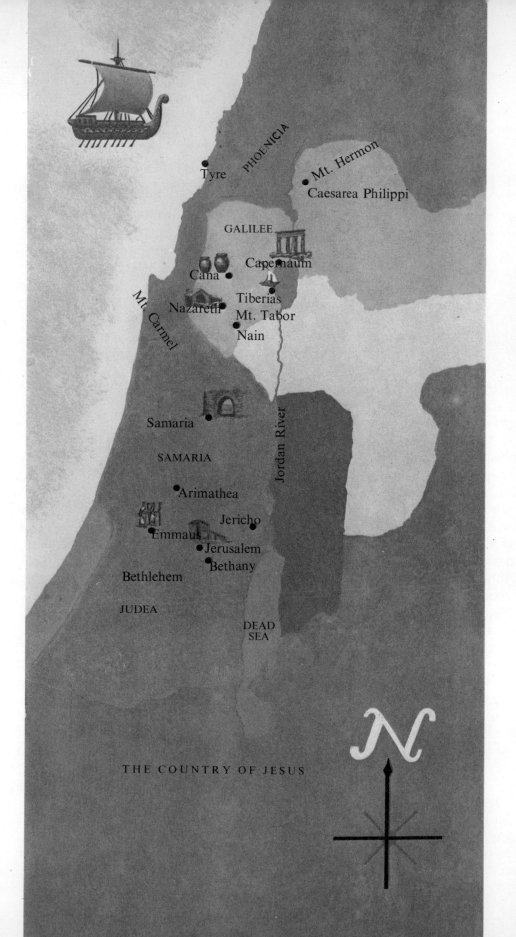

Tyre

PHOENICIA

Mt. Hermon

Caesarea Philippi

GALILEE

Capernaum

Cana

Tiberias

Nazareth

Mt. Tabor

Mt. Carmel

Nain

Jordan River

Samaria

SAMARIA

Arimathea

Jericho

Emmaus

Jerusalem

Bethany

Bethlehem

JUDEA

DEAD
SEA

THE COUNTRY OF JESUS

N

JESUS PREACHES ON FORGIVENESS

THE scribes and the Pharisees brought to him a woman caught doing wrong, and when they had placed her before him, they said, "Master, this woman was caught doing wrong, in the very act. Now Moses in the law commanded that such a person should be stoned. But what do you say?" This they said to test him, that they might be able to accuse him.

Jesus stooped down and with his finger wrote on the ground as though he had not heard them. When they continued asking him, he stood up and said to them, "He that is without sin among you, let him first cast a stone at her." And again he stooped down and wrote on the ground.

When they heard it, they went away one by one, beginning with the eldest, and Jesus was left alone, except for the woman. Then Jesus stood up and seeing no one but the woman said to her, "Woman, where are your accusers? Has no man condemned you?" She said, "No man, Lord." And Jesus said to her, "Neither do I condemn you. Go, and sin no more."

One of the Pharisees asked Jesus to eat with him. And he went into the Pharisee's house and sat down to dinner. Now there was a woman in the city who was a sinner, and when she learned that Jesus was having dinner at the Pharisee's house, she brought an alabaster box of ointment and stayed at his feet, behind him, weeping. She began to wash his feet with tears, and wipe them with the hair of her head, and kissed his feet and anointed them with ointment.

When the Pharisee who had invited him saw this, he said to himself, "This man, if he were a prophet, would have known who and what kind of woman this is who touches him, for she is a sinner." Jesus answering said to him, "Simon, I have something to say to you." And he said, "Master, speak on."

"There was a certain creditor which had two debtors. One owed him much, and the other a little. When they had nothing to pay, he forgave them both freely. Tell me then, which of them will love him most?"

"I suppose the one to whom he forgave the most," Simon said. And Jesus said to him, "You have judged rightly." Then turning to the woman, he said to Simon, "Do you see this woman? I came into your house, and you gave me no water for my feet, but she has washed my feet with tears and wiped them with the hairs of her head. You gave me no kiss, but this woman, since the moment I came in, has not stopped kissing my feet. You did not anoint my head with oil, but this woman has anointed my feet with ointment.

"Therefore, I say to you, her sins, which are many, are forgiven, for she loved much. But he to whom little is forgiven, loves little."

And he said to her, "Your sins are forgiven."

Then they that sat at dinner with him began to say within themselves, "Who is this that forgives sins also?"

And he said to the woman, "Your faith has saved you. Go in peace."

Then a man possessed with a devil, blind and dumb, was brought, and Jesus healed him so that he both spoke and saw. And all the people were amazed and said, "Is this not the Son of David?" But when the Pharisees heard it, they said, "This fellow casts out devils only through Beelzebub the prince of the devils."

Jesus knew their thoughts and said to them: "Every kingdom divided against itself is brought to ruin, and every city or house divided against itself cannot stand. If Satan casts out Satan, he is divided against himself. How then shall his kingdom stand?

"If I cast out devils through Beelzebub, through whom do your children cast them out? Therefore, they shall be your judges. But if I cast out devils through the spirit of God, then the kingdom of God has come to you. Or else, how can one enter a strong man's house and plunder his goods, unless he first tie up the strong man? Then he will plunder his house. He that is not with me is against me, and he that does not gather with me scatters.

"Therefore I say to you, all manner of sin and blasphemy shall be forgiven men, but blasphemy against the Holy Spirit shall not be forgiven men. Whoever speaks a word against the Son of man shall be forgiven, but whoever speaks against the Holy Spirit shall not be forgiven, neither in this world nor in the world to come. Every idle word that men shall speak, they shall give account of in the day of judgment. For by your words you shall be justified, and by your words you shall be condemned."

Then certain of the scribes and Pharisees said, "Master, we wish to see a sign from you." But he answered:

"An evil and indulgent generation seeks a sign, but there shall be no sign given to it except the sign of the prophet Jonah: As Jonah was three days and three nights in the whale's belly, so shall the Son of man be three days and three nights in the heart of the earth."

JESUS PREACHES IN PARABLES

IT came to pass that he went throughout every village and city, preaching and showing the glad tidings of the kingdom of God. The twelve apostles were with him, and certain women which had been healed of evil spirits and sicknesses: Mary called Magdalene, out of whom went seven devils, and Joanna the wife of Chuza, Herod's steward, and Susanna, and many others, who cared for him out of their means.

By the seaside, great multitudes were gathered together about him, so he went into a boat and addressed the multitude who stood on the shore.

THE SOWER

And he spoke many things to them in parables, saying:

"A sower went out to sow his seed. And as he sowed, some fell by the wayside, and the fowls came and ate them up. Some fell on stony places where they had not much earth. And when the sun rose they were scorched, and because they had no root, they withered away. And some fell among thorns, and the thorns sprang up and choked them. But others fell into good ground and brought forth fruit, some a hundredfold, some sixtyfold, some thirtyfold."

And when he had said these things, he cried, "He that has ears to hear, let him hear." Then his disciples asked him, saying, "What does this parable mean?" And he said:

"To you is given to know the mysteries of the kingdom of God, but to the others I speak in parables, that seeing they still may not see, and hearing they still may not understand. Now the meaning of the parable is this:

"The seed is the word of God. Those by the wayside are they who hear. Then the devil comes and takes away the word out of their hearts, lest they should believe and be saved.

"Those on the rock are they who, when they hear, receive the word with joy, and having no roots, they believe for a while, but in time of temptation fall away.

"Those which fell among thorns are they who, when they have heard, go forth and are choked with the cares and riches and pleasures of this life, so that their faith never ripens.

"But the seed on the good ground are they who, with honest and good hearts, having heard the word, keep it and bring forth fruit with patience."

THE GRAIN OF MUSTARD SEED

He put forth another parable to them, saying:

"The kingdom of heaven is like a grain of mustard seed, which a man took and sowed in the field. It is indeed the least of all seeds, but when it is grown it is the greatest among plants, and becomes a tree, so that the birds of the air come and build nests in its branches."

THE TARES

Another parable he gave to them, saying:

"The kingdom of heaven is like a man who sowed good seed in his field, but while he slept, his enemy came and sowed tares among the wheat, and went his way. So when the blades sprang up and brought forth fruit, the tares appeared also.

"So the servants of the man came and said to him, 'Did you not sow good seed in the field? From where then have come the tares?'

" 'An enemy has done this,' he said to them, and the servants asked, 'Do you wish then that we go and gather them up?' But he said, 'No, lest while you gather up the tares, you root up the wheat with them also. Let both grow together until the harvest, and in the time of harvest, I will say to the reapers, "Gather together first the tares and bind them in bundles to burn them. But gather the wheat into my barn." ' "

THE MEANING OF THE TARES

All these things Jesus spoke to the multitude in parables. He did not speak to them without a parable, so that it might be fulfilled which was spoken by the prophet, saying:

"I will open my mouth in parables. I will utter things which have been kept secret since the foundation of the world."

Then Jesus sent the multitude away and went into a house, and his disciples came to him, saying, "Explain to us the parable of the tares of the field."

And when they were alone together, he answered:

"He that sows the good seed is the Son of man. The field is the world; the good seed are the children of the kingdom. But the tares are the children of the wicked one. The enemy that sowed them is the devil. The harvest is the end of the world; the reapers are the angels. Therefore, as the tares are gathered and burned in the fire, so shall it be at the end of the world.

"The Son of man shall send forth his angels, and they shall gather out of his kingdom all things that offend, and those who do evil, and they shall throw them into a furnace of fire. There shall be a wailing and a gnashing of teeth. Then the righteous shall shine forth like the sun in the kingdom of their Father. Who has ears to hear, let him hear."

THE NET OF FISH

"Again, the kingdom of heaven is like a net that was cast into the sea and gathered all kinds of fish. When it was full, they drew it to shore and sat down and put the good into vessels, but cast the bad away.

"So it shall be at the end of the world. The angels shall come forth and separate the wicked from the just and shall cast them into the furnace."

JESUS IN NAZARETH

WHEN Jesus had finished these parables, he departed and went into his own country, to Nazareth where he had been brought up. And as his custom was he went into the synagogue on the sabbath day, and stood up to read. The book of the prophet Isaiah was given to him, and when he opened the book he found the place where it was written:

"The Spirit of the Lord is upon me, because he has anointed me to preach the gospel of the poor.

"He has sent me to heal the broken-hearted, to preach deliverance to the captives, and recovering of sight to the blind, to set at liberty those who are oppressed, and to preach the acceptable year of the Lord."

He closed the book and gave it back to the minister and sat down. And the eyes of all them that were in the synagogue were fastened on him. And he began to say to them, "To-day this Scripture is fulfilled in your ears."

All wondered at the gracious words that came from him, and they said, "Is this not Joseph's son? Is this not the carpenter, the son of Mary, the brother of James and Joseph, and of Jude and Simon? And are not his sisters here with us?" And they took offence at him.

But Jesus said to them, "A prophet is not without honour except in his own country and among his own kin, and in his own house."

And he marvelled because of their unbelief.

And all those in the synagogue, when they heard these things, were filled with wrath, and rose up and thrust him out of the city, and led him up to the edge of the hill on which their city was built, that they might throw him down.

But he, passing through the midst of them, went his way.

JESUS CALMS THE STORM

Now it came to pass on a certain day that he went into a boat with his disciples, and said to them, "Let us go over to the other side of the lake." So they set sail. But as they sailed, he fell asleep, and there came down a storm of wind on the lake, and the boat was filled with water, so that they were in danger. The disciples awoke him saying, "Master, Master, we are sinking."

Then Jesus arose and rebuked the wind and the raging of the water, and they ceased and there was a calm. And he said to the disciples, "Where is your faith?"

They were frightened, and wondered at this, saying to one another, "What manner of man is this? For he commands even the winds and the water and they obey him."

And they came to the other side of the lake, into the country of the Gadarenes. When Jesus stepped forth on the land, he met a certain man who had had devils a long time, and wore no clothes, nor lived in any house, but had his dwelling among the tombs.

When the man saw Jesus, he cried out, and fell down before him, and with a loud voice said, "What have I done to you, Jesus, Son of God most high? I beg you, do not torment me." (For Jesus had commanded the unclean spirit to come out of the man, for often it had seized him, and though he had been kept bound with chains and in fetters, he broke the bonds and was driven by the devil into the wilderness).

"What is your name?" Jesus asked him. And he said, "Legion," because many devils were within him. And he begged Jesus not to command them to go out of the country.

Now there was a herd of many swine feeding on the mountain, and he begged him to let them enter into the swine. He allowed them, and the devils went out of the man and entered into the swine, and the herd ran violently down a steep slope into the lake, and were drowned.

When they that fed the swine saw what was done, they fled, and went and told it in the city and in the country. Then people went out to see what was done. They came to Jesus and found the man, out of whom the devils had departed, sitting at the feet of Jesus, clothed, and in his right mind. And they were afraid.

Those who had seen it told them by what means he that was possessed of the devils was healed. Then the whole multitude of the country of the Gadarenes begged Jesus to depart from them, for they were taken with great fear. So he went back into the boat. Then the man out of whom the devils were departed asked that he might go with him, but Jesus sent him away, saying, "Return to your own house, and show what great things God has done to you." So he went his way and told throughout the whole city what great things Jesus had done to him. And people marvelled greatly.

JESUS RESTORES JAIRUS' DAUGHTER TO LIFE

When Jesus had returned again by boat to the other side of the lake, many people gathered about him while he was by the water. There came to him one of the rulers of the synagogue, Jairus by name. When he saw Jesus, he fell at his feet, and pleaded greatly saying, "My little daughter lies at the point of death. I pray you, come and lay your hands on her, that she

may be healed, and she shall live." Jesus went with him, and many people followed and thronged about him.

On the way, there was a woman who had suffered a flow of blood twelve years, and had been treated many times by physicians. She had spent all that she had, and was no better but had grown worse. She had heard of Jesus and came in the crowd behind him and touched his garment. For she said, "If I may only touch his clothes, I shall be well."

Immediately, the bleeding ceased and she felt in her body that she was healed. Then Jesus, feeling instantly that virtue had gone forth from him, turned around in the crowd, and said, "Who touched my clothes?"

His disciples said to him, "You see the multitude thronging about you, and do you say, 'Who touched me?'"

He looked round about to see her who had done this thing. Then the woman, fearing and trembling, knowing what was done in her, came and

And he allowed no man to follow him, except Peter, and James, and John, the brother of James. And he went to the house of the ruler of the synagogue. He saw there many weeping and wailing greatly, and when he had gone in, he said to them, "Why do you make this noise and weep? The girl is not dead, but sleeps."

They laughed at him. But when he had put them all out, he took the father and the mother of the girl, and those that were with him, and went in where

fell down before him, and told him all the truth. And he said to her, "Daughter, your faith has made you whole. Go in peace, and be healed of your plague."

While he was still speaking, there came from the ruler of the synagogue's house some men who said to Jairus, "Your daughter is dead, why trouble the Master any further?" But as soon as Jesus heard this, he said to the ruler of the synagogue, "Be not afraid. Only believe."

the girl was lying. Then he took the girl by the hand and said to her, "Talitha cumi," which means, being interpreted, "Little girl, I say to you, arise."

Immediately the girl arose, and walked—for she was twelve years old —and they were filled with great astonishment.

But he told them strictly that no man should know of it, and commanded that she should be given something to eat.

THE BEHEADING OF JOHN THE BAPTIST

OW Herod the tetrarch heard of all that was done by Jesus, and he was perplexed, because some said that it was John the Baptist, risen from the dead. Some said that Elijah had appeared, and others that one of the old prophets had risen again. But when Herod heard of these things, he said, "It is John, whom I beheaded. He has risen from the dead."

For Herod himself had had John put in prison, for the sake of Herodias, his brother Philip's wife, whom he had married. John had said to Herod, "It is not lawful for you to have your brother's wife." Therefore Herodias had a quarrel against him. She would have had him killed, but she could not. For Herod feared John, knowing that he was a just and holy man.

But on his birthday, Herod gave a supper for his lords, high captains, and the leading men of Galilee, and the daughter of Herodias came and danced, and pleased Herod and those who sat with him. And the king said to the girl, "Ask of me whatever you will, and I will give it to you." He swore to her, "Whatever you ask of me, I will give it to you, up to half of my kingdom."

The girl went forth and said to her mother, "What shall I ask?" And her mother said, "The head of John the Baptist."

So she went directly to the king and said, "My wish is that you give me in due course, on a platter, the head of John the Baptist."

Then the king was very sorry, but because of his oath and those who sat with him, he could not reject her demand. So immediately the king sent an executioner and commanded that John's head be brought. And the executioner went and beheaded him in the prison, and brought his head on a platter, and gave it to the girl. And the girl gave it to her mother.

When his disciples heard of it, they came and took his body and laid it in a tomb, and went and told Jesus. When Jesus heard of it, he went by boat out into a deserted place, with his apostles.

THE FEEDING OF THE MULTITUDE

THE people saw them departing, and many knew him, and ran on foot from all cities, and were there before them. And Jesus, when he arrived, saw many people and was moved with compassion toward them, because they were like sheep not having a shepherd. And he began to teach them many things.

Now later in the day his disciples came to him and said, "This is a deserted place, and it is late. Send them away, so that they may go into the country round about, and into the villages, and buy themselves bread. For they have nothing to eat."

He answered and said to them, "Give them something to eat." And they said to him, "Shall we go and buy two hundred pennyworth of bread, and give it to them to eat?"

"How many loaves do you have?" he answered, "Go and see."

One of his disciples, Andrew, Simon Peter's brother, said to him, "There is a lad here who has five barley loaves and two small fishes. But what are they among so many?"

Jesus said, "Make the men sit down." Now there was much grass in the place, so the men sat down, in number about five thousand. And Jesus took the loaves, and when he had given thanks, he distributed them to the disciples, and the disciples to

those who were sitting. They did like-wise with the fishes.

When they were filled, he said to his disciples, "Gather up the pieces that remain, so that nothing is lost."

Therefore, they gathered them to-gether, and filled twelve baskets with the leftovers of the five barley loaves, which remained over and above to those who had eaten.

JESUS WALKS ON THE WATER

Jesus sent the multitudes away, and asked his disciples to get into a boat and to go ahead of him to the other side of the lake toward Capernaum. Then he went up into a mountain to pray, and when the evening came, he was there alone.

But the boat was now in the midst of the sea, tossed by the waves, for the wind was against them. And in the fourth watch of the night, Jesus went to them, walking on the sea.

When the disciples saw him walking on the sea, they were troubled and said, "It is a spirit." And they cried out for fear. But Jesus spoke to them, saying, "Be of good cheer. It is I. Be not afraid."

Peter answered him and said, "Lord, if it is you, let me come to you on the water."

"Come," he said. And Peter came down out of the boat, and he walked on the water, to go to Jesus. But when he saw the strong wind, he was afraid and began to sink. "Lord, save me," he cried, and immediately Jesus stretched forth his hand and caught him, and said to him, "O you of little faith, why did you doubt?"

And when they had come into the boat, the wind ceased. Then they that were in the boat worshipped him, saying "Truly you are the Son of God."

JESUS QUOTES ISAIAH

When they had crossed the water, they came into the land of Gennesaret, and when the men of that place learned of him, they brought to him all that were diseased, and asked that they might only touch the hem of his garment. And as many as touched it were made perfectly well.

Then scribes and Pharisees from Jerusalem came to Jesus, saying, "Why

do your disciples revolt against the tradition of the elders? They do not wash their hands when they eat bread."

He answered and said, "You hypocrites! Well did Isaiah prophesy of you, saying:

" 'This people honours me with their lips, but their heart is far from me. And in vain do they worship me, teaching for doctrines the commandments of men.' For, laying aside the commandments of God, you hold to the tradition of men, attending to such little things as the washing of pots and cups."

Then he called the multitude and said to them, "Hear, and understand. Not that which goes into the mouth, but that which comes out of the mouth, does harm to a man."

Then his disciples came and said to him, "Did you know that the Pharisees were offended after they heard this saying?" But he answered and said:

"Every plant which my heavenly Father has not planted shall be rooted up. Let them alone. They are blind leaders of the blind. And if the blind lead the blind, both shall fall into the ditch."

"Explain to us this parable," Peter said to him. And Jesus said:

"Are you also still without understanding? Do you still not understand that whatever goes in at the mouth goes only into the belly. But those things which come out of the mouth come forth from the heart, and they defile a man. For out of the heart come evil thoughts, murders, wrongdoing, thefts, blasphemies, false witness. These are the things which defile a man. But to eat with unwashed hands defiles no one."

From there, Jesus went into Tyre and Sidon. Then he returned to the sea of Galilee, through the region of the Decapolis. Next he came in a ship to

413

Dalmanutha, then to Bethsaida. In all these places he preached and healed.

And when Jesus came into the coasts of Caesarea Philippi, he asked his disciples, "Who do men say that I, the Son of man, am?" And they said, "Some say you are John the Baptist, some, Elijah, and others, Jeremiah or one of the prophets."

"But who do you say that I am?" he asked. And Simon Peter answered and said, "You are the Christ, the Son of the living God."

Jesus said to him, "Blessed are you, Simon, son of Jonah, for flesh and blood have not revealed it to you, but my Father who is in heaven.

"And I say also to you that you are Peter, the rock, and upon this rock I will build my church. And the gates of hell shall not prevail against it. I will give to you the keys of the kingdom of heaven, and whatever you bind on earth shall be bound in heaven, and whatever you loose on earth shall be loosed in heaven." Then he told his disciples that they should tell no man that he was Jesus the Christ.

JESUS FORETELLS THE CRUCIFIXION

From that time forth, Jesus began to tell his disciples how he must go to Jerusalem, and suffer many things from the elders and chief priests and scribes, and be killed, and be raised again the third day. Then Peter began to rebuke him, saying, "Be it far from true, Lord. This shall not happen to you."

But he turned and said to Peter: "Get thee behind me, Satan. You are an offence to me, for you are not concerned with the things of God, but those of men."

Then Jesus said to his disciples:

"If any man wishes to come after me, let him deny himself and take up his cross and follow me. For whoever wishes to save his life, shall lose it, and whoever will lose his life for my sake shall find it. For what shall it profit a man if he shall gain the whole world and lose his own soul? Or what shall a man give in exchange for his soul? Whoever therefore shall be ashamed of me and of my words in this indulgent and sinful generation, of him also shall the Son of man be ashamed, when he comes in the glory of his Father with the holy angels, to reward every man according to his works."

And he said to them, "Truly I say to you that there are some of them that stand here who shall not taste of death till they have seen the kingdom of God come with power."

THE TRANSFIGURATION

After six days, Jesus took Peter, James, and John his brother, and brought them up into a high mountain, and was transfigured before them: his face shone like the sun and his clothing was as white as light. And, behold, there appeared to them Moses and Elijah talking with him.

Then Peter said, "Lord, it is good for us to be here. If you will, let us make three tabernacles here, one for you, one for Moses, and one for Elijah."

While he still spoke, behold, a bright cloud overshadowed them, and a voice came out of the cloud, saying: "This is my beloved Son, in whom I am well pleased. Listen to him." And when the disciples heard it, they fell on their faces and were much afraid.

But Jesus came and touched them, and said: "Arise and do not be afraid." And when they had lifted up their eyes, they saw no man, except Jesus alone.

As they came down the mountain, Jesus commanded them, saying, "Tell

the vision to no man, until the Son of man has risen again from the dead." And his disciples asked him, saying, "Why then do the scribes say that Elijah must come first?"

Jesus answered, "Elijah truly must come first and restore all things. But I say to you, that Elijah has come already, and they did not know him, but have done to him whatever they pleased. Likewise shall the Son of man also suffer from them."

Then the disciples understood that he spoke to them of John the Baptist.

JESUS INSTRUCTS THE DISCIPLES

 N the next day, when they had come down from the mountain, many people met them. And a man in the crowd cried out, "Master, I beg you, look at my son, for he is my only child. A spirit has taken him and at times he cries out suddenly and often he falls into the fire, and often into the water. I brought him to your disciples, but they could not cure him."

Then Jesus answered and said, "O faithless and perverse generation, how long shall I be with you? How long shall I bear you? Bring him here to me." And Jesus rebuked the devil, and he departed out of him, and the child was cured from that very hour.

Then the disciples came to Jesus privately and said, "Why could we not cast it out?" And Jesus said to them, "Because of your unbelief. For truly I say to you, if you have faith as small as a grain of mustard seed, you shall say to this mountain, 'Move hence to yonder place,' and it shall move, and nothing shall be impossible to you. However, this happens only by prayer and fasting."

They departed and passed through Galilee, and Jesus taught his disciples, saying, "The Son of man shall be delivered into the hands of men, and they shall kill him, and after he is killed, he shall rise the third day." But they did not understand his words, and were afraid to ask him.

And he came to Capernaum, and in a house he asked them, "What was it you disputed among yourselves on the way?" But they held their silence, since on the way they had disputed among themselves about who should be the greatest.

Then Jesus sat down and called the twelve, and said to them, "If any man desires to be first, he must be last of all, and servant of all." And he took a child and placed him in the midst of them and, taking him in his arms, he said, "Whoever shall receive

one such child in my name, receives me. And whoever receives me, receives not me, but him that sent me."

Then John said, "Master, we saw someone casting out devils in your name, and we forbade him, because he does not follow us." But Jesus said, "Do not forbid him, for there is no man that does a miracle in my name that can easily speak evil of me. For he that is not against us is for us. Whoever shall give you a cup of water to drink in my name, because you belong to Christ, truly I say to you, he shall not lose his reward.

"And whoever shall offend one of these little ones that believe in me, it is better for him that a millstone were hanged around his neck, and he were cast into the sea.

"And if your hand offends you, cut it off. It is better for you to enter into life maimed than to have two hands to go into hell, into the fire that shall never be put out. And if your foot causes you to sin, cut it off. It is better for you to enter lame into life than having two feet to be cast into hell. And if your eye offends you, pluck it out. It is better for you to enter into the kingdom of God with one eye, than having two eyes to be cast into hell.

"Moreover, if your brother trespasses against you, go and tell him his fault between you and him alone. If he shall hear you, you have gained your brother. But if he will not hear you, then take with you one or two witnesses, so that every word may be established. And if he will not hear them, tell it to the church. But if he refuses to hear the church, let him be like a heathen and a publican to you.

"I say to you that if two of you agree on earth concerning anything that they shall ask, it shall be done for them by my Father who is in heaven. For where two or three are gathered together in my name, there am I in the midst of them."

THE PARABLE OF THE UNMERCIFUL SERVANT

Then Peter came to him and said, "Lord, how often shall my brother sin against me, and I forgive him? Up to seven times?"

Jesus said to him, "I say to you, not seven times, but seventy times seven.

"Thus the kingdom of heaven is like a certain king who had a servant that owed him ten thousand talents. Because he could not pay, his lord ordered him to be sold, and his wife and children and all that he had, and payment be made. The servant there-fore fell down and worshipped him, saying, 'Lord, have patience with me, and I will pay you all.' Then the lord of that servant was moved with compassion and freed him and forgave him the debt.

"But the same servant went out and found one of his fellow servants who owed him a hundred pence, and he laid hands on him, and took him by the throat, saying, 'Pay me what you owe.' And his fellow servant fell down at his feet and begged him, saying, 'Have patience with me, and I will pay you all.' And he would not, but went and cast him into prison, till he should pay the debt.

"So when his fellow servants saw what was done, they were very sorry, and came and told to their lord all that was done.

"Then his lord, after calling him forth, said to him, 'O wicked servant, I forgave you all that debt, because you begged me. Should you not also have had compassion on your fellow servant, even as I had pity on you?' And his lord was angered and delivered him to the torturers, till he should pay all that was due to him. So likewise shall my heavenly Father do also to you, if you do not forgive from your hearts your brothers' trespasses."

It came to pass that when Jesus had finished these sayings, he departed from Galilee and came into the coasts of Judea beyond the Jordan. And great multitudes followed him, and he healed them there.

As he went along the road, a certain man said to him, "Lord I will follow you wherever you go." Jesus said to him, "Foxes have holes and birds of the air have nests, but the Son of man has nowhere to lay his head."

He said to another, "Follow me." But the man said, "Lord, allow me first to go and bury my father." Jesus said to him, "Let the dead bury their dead, but you go and preach the kingdom of God."

And another said, "Lord, I will follow you, but let me first go bid them farewell who are at my home." And Jesus said to him, "No man, having put his hand to the plough, who looks back, is fit for the kingdom of God."

SEVENTY MORE DISCIPLES ARE APPOINTED

After these things, Jesus appointed seventy more disciples and sent them two by two ahead of him into every city and place where he himself would come. And he said to them:

"The harvest truly is great, but the labourers are few. Pray, therefore, to the Lord of the harvest, to send forth labourers into his harvest.

"Go your ways. Behold, I send you forth as lambs among wolves. Carry neither purse, nor money, nor shoes, and salute no man along the way. And into whatever house you enter, first say, 'Peace be to this house.'

"And remain in the same house, eating and drinking such things as they give, for the labourer is worthy of his hire. Do not go from house to house.

"Into whatever city you enter, and they receive you, eat such things as are set before you, and heal the sick that are therein, and say to them, 'The kingdom of God is near.' But whatever city you enter that receives you not, go your ways out into the streets of the same, and say, 'Even the very dust of your city, which clings to us, we wipe off against you. Nevertheless, be sure of this, that the kingdom of God is near.' But I say to you that it shall be more tolerable in that day for Sodom than for that city.

"He that hears you, hears me, and he that despises you, despises me, and he that despises me, despises him that sent me."

THE GOOD SAMARITAN

A certain lawyer stood up and tested him, saying, "Master, what shall I do to inherit eternal life?" Jesus answered, "What is written in the law? How do you read it?"

The lawyer said, "You shall love the Lord your God with all your heart, and with all your soul, and with all your strength, and with all your mind, and your neighbour as yourself."

And Jesus said to him, "You have answered right. Do this, and you shall live." But the lawyer, wishing to justify himself, said to Jesus, "And who is my neighbour?" And Jesus answering said:

"A certain man went down from Jerusalem to Jericho and fell among thieves who stripped him of his clothing, and wounded him, and departed, leaving him for dead. And by chance there came a certain priest that way, and when he saw him, he passed by on the other side. And likewise a Levite, when he was at the place, came and looked at him, and passed by on the other side.

"But a certain Samaritan, as he journeyed, came where he was, and when he saw him, he had compassion on him. He went to him and bound up his wounds, pouring on oil and wine, and put him on his own beast, and brought him to an inn and took care of him.

"And the next day, when he departed, he gave some money to the innkeeper and said to him, 'Take care of him, and whatever more you spend, when I come again, I will repay you.'

"Now which of these three, do you think, was a neighbour to him that fell among the thieves?"

And the lawyer said, "He that showed mercy on him." Then Jesus said to him, "Go, and do likewise."

THE RICH YOUNG RULER

A certain ruler asked him, saying also, "Good Master, what shall I do to inherit eternal life?" And Jesus said to him, "Why do you call me good? There is none good but one, that is, God. You know the commandments: Do not commit adultery. Do not kill. Do not steal. Do not bear false witness. Honour they father and mother."

And he answered and said to Jesus, "Master, all these things I have observed from my youth." Then Jesus looking at him, loved him, and said to him, "One thing you lack: Go your way, sell whatever you have, and give to the poor, and you shall have treasure in heaven. Then come, take up the cross, and follow me."

The young man was sad at these words, and went away grieved. For he had great possessions.

And Jesus looked round about, and said to his disciples, "How hard it shall be for them that have riches to enter into the kingdom of God!" The disciples were astonished at his words, but Jesus answered again and said to them, "Children, how hard it is for them that trust in riches to enter into the kingdom of God! It is easier for a camel to go through the eye of a needle than for a rich man to enter into the kingdom of God."

They were astonished beyond measure, and said among themselves, "Who then can be saved?" And Jesus looking upon them said, "With men it is impossible, but not with God. For with God all things are possible."

Then Peter said, "Behold, we have forsaken all and followed you. What shall we have therefore?" And Jesus said to them:

"Truly I say to you which have followed me that, in the day when the Son of man shall sit in the throne of his glory, you also shall sit upon twelve thrones, judging the twelve tribes of Israel. And everyone that has forsaken houses, or brothers, or sisters, or father, or mother, or wife, or children, or lands, for my name's sake, shall receive a hundredfold, and shall inherit everlasting life.

"But many that are first shall be last, and the last shall be first.

THE LABOURERS
IN THE VINEYARD

"For the kingdom of heaven is like an householder who went out early in the morning to hire labourers for his vineyard. When he had agreed with his labourers on a silver piece a day, he sent them into his vineyard.

"He went out about nine o'clock and saw others standing idle in the market place; and said to them, 'Go to my vineyard too, and whatever is right I will give you.' And they went their way. He went out about noon and again at mid-afternoon, and did likewise. And near the end of the day he went out, and found others standing idle, and said to them, 'Why do you stand here idle?' They said to him, 'Because no one has hired us.' He said to them, 'Go to my vineyard, too, and whatever is right, you will receive.'

"So when evening came, the lord of the vineyards said to his steward, 'Call the labourers and give them their wages, beginning from the last to the first.'

"And when those came who were hired near the end of the day, each one received a silver piece. So when the first came, they supposed that they would receive more; but they likewise each received a silver piece.

"When they had received it, they murmured against the man of the house, saying, 'These last have worked only one hour, and you have made them equal to us who have borne the burden and heat of the day.' But he answered one of them, and said, 'Friend, I do you no wrong. Did you not agree with me on a silver piece? Take what is yours and go your way. I will give to the last the same as to you. Is it not lawful for me to do what I will with what is mine? Is your eye greedy, because I am generous?'

"So the last shall be first, and the first last."

JOY IN HEAVEN

All the publicans and sinners drew near to Jesus to hear him. And the Pharisees and scribes murmured, saying, "This man receives sinners and eats with them." Then Jesus spoke this parable to them, saying:

"What man of you, having a hundred sheep, if he loses one of them, does not leave the ninety and nine in the wilderness, and go after that which is lost, until he finds it? And when he has found it, he lays it on his shoulders, rejoicing. And when he comes home, he calls together his friends and neighbours, saying to them, 'Rejoice with me, for I have found my sheep which was lost.' I say to you that likewise there shall be more joy in heaven over one sinner that repents than over ninety and nine just persons who need no repentance.

"Or what woman, if she has ten pieces of silver and loses one, does not light a candle and sweep the house and seek diligently till she finds it?

And when she has found it, she calls her friends and her neighbours together, saying, 'Rejoice with me, for I have found the piece which I had lost.' Likewise, I say to you, there is joy in the presence of the angels of God over one sinner who repents.'"

THE PRODIGAL SON

And Jesus said:

"A certain man had two sons. The younger of them said to his father, 'Father, give me the portion of goods that I will inherit.' So he divided his property between them. And not many days after, the younger son gathered all together and took a journey into a far country, and there wasted his wealth in riotous living. And when he had spent all, there arose a mighty famine in that land, and he began to be in want. So he went and hired himself out to a citizen of that country, who sent him into his fields to feed pigs. He was ready to fill himself with the husks the pigs ate, for no man gave

him anything. When he came to himself, he said, 'How many hired servants of my father's have bread enough and to spare, while I am perishing with hunger. I will arise and go to my father, and will say to him, 'Father, I have sinned against heaven and before you. I am not worthy any more to be called your son. Make me one of your hired servants.'

"He rose up and went to his father. But when he was still a long way off, his father saw him, and had pity; and ran and fell on his neck and kissed him. The son said to him: 'Father, I have sinned against heaven, and in your eyes, and am no longer worthy to be called your son.'

"But the father said to his servants, 'Bring out the best robe, and put it on him. And put a ring on his hand, and shoes on his feet. And bring out the fatted calf and kill it, and let us eat and be merry. For this son of mine was dead, and is alive again. He was lost and is found.'

"And they began to be merry.

"Now his elder son was in the field. And as he came and drew near the house, he heard music and dancing. He called one of the servants and asked what these things meant. He said to him, 'Your brother has come home. And your father has killed the fatted calf because he has him back, safe and sound.'

"He was angry, and would not go in. So his father came out and pleaded with him. He answered his father, saying, 'Lo, these many years I have served you, never at any time disobeying any of your commandments. And yet you never gave me a kid, so that I might make merry with my friends. But as soon as this other son of yours came, who has eaten up your wealth in riotous living, you killed the fatted calf for him.'

"And the father said to him, 'Son, you are always with me, and all that I have is yours. It is fitting that we should make merry, and be glad; for this your brother was dead, and is alive again; was lost, and is found.'

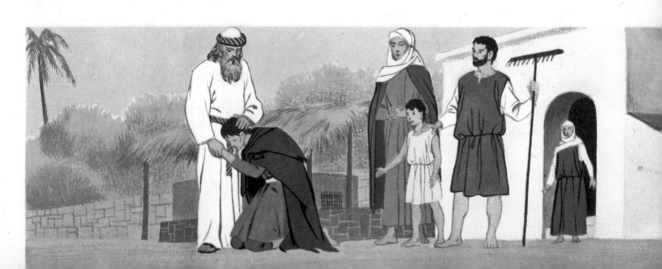

THE RICH MAN AND
THE BEGGAR

"There was a certain rich man, who was clothed in purple and fine linen, and dined sumptuously every day. And there was a certain beggar named Lazarus who lay at his gate, covered with sores, and desiring from the rich man's table. The dogs even came and licked his sores.

"It came to pass that the beggar died, and was carried by the angels to Abraham's side. The rich man also died, and was buried. And in hell he lifted up his eyes, being in torment; and saw Abraham afar off, and Lazarus with him.

"He cried out and said, 'Father Abraham, have mercy on me, and send Lazarus, that he may dip the tip of his finger in water, and cool my tongue. For I am tormented in this flame.'

"But Abraham said, 'Son, remember

that you in your lifetime received your good things, and Lazarus bad things; but now he is comforted and you are tormented. And besides all this, there is a great gulf set between you and us; so that those who would pass from here to you cannot; neither can they who would pass from your side come to us.'

"Then the rich man said, 'I beg you then, father, to send him to my father's house; where I have five brothers, so that he may warn them, lest they also come into this place of torment.'

"Abraham said to him, 'They have Moses and the prophets, let them listen to them.' And he said, 'No, father Abraham, but if one went to them from the dead, they would repent.'

"And Abraham said to him, 'If they do not listen to Moses and the prophets, they will not be persuaded; even though one rises from the dead.'"

THE JOURNEY TO JERUSALEM

AS Jesus was on his way to Jerusalem, he passed through the midst of Samaria and Galilee. And as he entered a certain village, there met him ten men that were lepers, who stood afar off. And they lifted up their voices and cried, "Jesus, Master, have mercy on us." And when he saw them, he said to them, "Go and show yourselves to the priests." And it came to pass that as they went they were healed. And one of them, when he saw that he was healed, turned back, and with a loud voice glorified God, and fell down on his face at his feet, giving him thanks. And he was a Samaritan.

And Jesus said, "Were there not ten healed? But where are the nine? Only this stranger has returned to give glory to God." And he said to him, "Arise, go your way; your faith has made you whole."

A PARABLE OF PRAYER

Jesus spoke this parable to certain men who were proud of their own righteousness and looked down upon others: "Two men went up into the temple to pray, the one a Pharisee, the other a tax gatherer.

"The Pharisee stood and prayed by himself in these words: 'God, I thank you that I am not like other men, greedy, unjust, indulgent, or like this tax gatherer! I fast twice in the week, and I give a tenth of all I own to charity.'

"But the publican, standing far off, would not lift up so much as his eyes to heaven, but beat upon his breast, saying, 'God be merciful to me, a sinner.'

"I tell you, this man went down to his house justified rather than the other. For everyone that exalts himself shall be humbled, and he that humbles himself shall be exalted."

JESUS PREPARES THE DISCIPLES

They were on the road going up to Jerusalem, and Jesus went before them. And as the disciples followed, they were amazed and afraid. Then he called again the twelve and began to tell them what things should happen to him, saying:

"Behold, we go up to Jerusalem. The Son of man shall be delivered to the chief priests and to the scribes, and they shall condemn him to death and shall deliver him to the Gentiles. And they shall mock him, and shall beat him, and shall spit upon him, and shall kill him. And the third day he shall rise again."

James and John, the sons of Zebedee, came to him saying, "Master, will you do for us whatever we shall desire?" He said to them, "What do you want that I should do for you?"

baptized with the baptism that I am baptized with?"

They said to him, "We can." And Jesus said to them, "You shall indeed drink of the cup that I drink of, and with the baptism that I am baptized you shall be baptized. But to sit on my right hand and on my left hand is not mine to give, but it shall be given to them for whom it has been prepared."

When the other ten heard it, they began to be much displeased with James and John. But Jesus called them to him and said to them, "You know that they which rule over the Gentiles exercise strong authority over them. But it shall not be so among

"Grant us," they said, "that we may sit, one on your right hand and the other on your left hand, in your glory."

But Jesus said to them, "You know not what you ask. Can you drink of the same cup that I drink of, and be

you: Whoever will be great among you, shall be your servant, and whoever of you will be the greatest, shall be a servant to all. For even the Son of man came not to be ministered to, but to minister, and to give his life as a ransom for many."

Jesus entered and passed through Jericho. And there was a man named Zaccheus, the chief among the tax collectors, who was rich and who tried to see Jesus, to learn who he was. But he could not because of the crowd, for he was small in size. So he ran ahead and climbed up into a sycamore tree to see him, for he was to pass that way.

When Jesus came to the place, he looked up and saw him and said to him, "Zaccheus, make haste and come down, for today I must stay at your house." And he made haste and came down, and received him joyfully.

When the people saw it, they all murmured, saying, "He has gone to be a guest with a man that is a sinner."

Then Zaccheus stood and said to the Lord, "Behold, Lord, half of my goods I give to the poor. And if I have taken anything from any man by false accusation, I repay him fourfold."

And Jesus said to him, "This day salvation has come to this house, inasmuch as he also is a son of Abraham. For the Son of man has come to seek and to save that which was lost."

JESUS AT THE HOME OF MARY AND MARTHA

Now it came to pass, as they went, that he entered into a certain village called Bethany, and a certain woman named Martha received him into her house. She had a sister called Mary, who sat at Jesus' feet and heard his word. But Martha was busy with much serving and came to him and said, "Lord, do you not care that my sister has left me to serve alone? Tell her therefore that she should help me."

Jesus answered and said to her, "Martha, Martha, you are careful and troubled about many things. But only one thing is needful. Mary has chosen that good part, which shall not be taken away from her."

LAZARUS IS RAISED FROM THE DEAD

On another occasion Lazarus, the brother of Mary, was sick. So his sisters sent word to Jesus, saying, "Lord, he whom you love is sick." For Jesus loved Martha, and her sister, and Lazarus.

When he heard therefore that he was sick, he stayed two days more in the place where he was. After that he said to his disciples, "Our friend Lazarus sleeps, but I go, that I may awake him out of sleep."

Then his disciples said, "Lord, if he sleeps, he shall be well." Then Jesus said to them plainly, "Lazarus is dead. And I am glad for your sakes that I was not there, in order that you may believe. Nevertheless, let us go to him."

Then Thomas, who was called the Twin, said to his fellow disciples, "Let us go also, that we may die with him."

When Jesus came, he found that Lazarus had lain in the grave four days already. And since Bethany was close to Jerusalem, about two miles away, many of the Jews had come to Martha and Mary, to comfort them concerning their brother.

Now Martha, as soon as she heard that Jesus was coming, went and met him, but Mary sat still in the house. Martha said to Jesus, "Lord, if you had been here, my brother would not have died. But I know that even now whatever you will ask of God, God will give it to you."

rection, and the life. He that believes in me, though he is dead, shall live. And whoever lives and believes in me shall never die. Do you believe this?"

She said to him, "Yes, Lord, I believe that you are the Christ, the Son of God, which was to come into the world." And when she had so spoken she went her way, and called Mary her sister secretly, saying, "The Master has come, and calls for you." As soon as Mary heard that, she arose quickly and came to him.

Now Jesus was not yet in the town, but was in that place where Martha met him. The Jews then who had seen her in the house, and had comforted her, when they saw Mary rise up hastily and go out, followed her, saying, "She goes to the grave to weep there."

"Your brother shall rise again," said Jesus. And Martha said, "I know that he shall surely rise again in the resurrection at the last day."

Jesus said to her, "I am the resur-

When Mary had come to where Jesus was and saw him, she fell down at his feet, saying to him, "Lord, if you had been here, my brother would not have died."

When Jesus saw her weeping, and also the Jews weeping that came with her, he groaned in the spirit and was troubled, and said, "Where have you laid him?"

They said to him, "Lord, come and see." Jesus wept, and the Jews said, "Behold how much he loved him!" And some of them said, "Could not this man, who opened the eyes of the blind, have caused that Lazarus should not have died?"

Jesus therefore groaning again within himself came to the grave. It was a cave, and a stone lay upon it. Jesus said, "Take away the stone."

Then Martha said, "Lord, by this time he is decaying, for he has been dead four days." But Jesus said to her, "Did I not say to you that if you

would believe, you would see the glory of God?"

They took away the stone from the grave, and Jesus lifted up his eyes and said, "Father, I thank you for having

heard me. And I know that you hear me always, but because of the people who stand here, I said it, that they might believe that you have sent me."

And when he had thus spoken, he cried in a loud voice, "Lazarus, come forth."

And he that was dead came forth, bound hand and foot with grave clothes, and his face was bound about with a napkin. Jesus said to them, "Unbind him, and let him go."

Then many of the people who had come with Mary and had seen the things which Jesus did, believed in him. But some of them went their ways to the Pharisees, and told them what things Jesus had done.

JESUS' ENEMIES PLOT TO KILL HIM

Then the chief priests and the Pharisees held a council, and said, "What are we to do? This man does many miracles. If we let him alone, all men will believe in him, and the Romans shall come and take away both our holy place and our nation."

One of them, named Caiaphas, being the high priest that year, said to them, "You know nothing and do not realize that it is expedient for us that one man should die for the people, and that the whole nation should not perish."

This was not his own opinion, but being high priest that year, he prophesied that Jesus should die for the nation. And not for the nation only, but also that he should gather together the children of God that were scattered abroad.

From that day forth, they planned together how to put him to death.

Jesus therefore walked no longer openly among the Jews, but went into a country near the wilderness, into a city called Ephraim, and there continued with his disciples.

THE SUPPER AT BETHANY

Now the Jews' passover was near at hand, and many went out of the country up to Jerusalem before the passover, to purify themselves. There they looked for Jesus and spoke among themselves, as they stood in the temple, "What do you think? Do you believe that he will not come to the feast?" For both the chief priests and the Pharisees had given a commandment that, if any man knew where he was, he should announce it, that they might seize him.

Then Jesus six days before the passover came to Bethany, where Lazarus was whom he had raised from the dead. There they made him a supper, and Martha served. But Lazarus was one of them that sat at the table with him.

Mary took a pound of ointment of spikenard, very costly, and anointed the feet of Jesus, and wiped his feet with her hair. And the whole house was filled with the odour of the ointment.

Then said one of his disciples, Judas Iscariot, Simon's son, who was to betray him, "Why was not this ointment sold for three hundred pence, and given to the poor?" This he said, not that he cared for the poor, but because he was a thief, and had the money bag and would take what was put in it.

Then Jesus said, "Let her alone. For the day of my burying has she kept this. The poor you always have with you, but me you do not have always."

Many people knew that he was there, and they came not only for Jesus' sake, but that they might see Lazarus also, whom he had raised from the dead. But the chief priests consulted together in order that they might put Lazarus also to death, because he was the cause of many of the Jews going away from them, and believing in Jesus.

THE CRUCIFIXION AND THE EARLY CHURCH

THE ENTRY INTO JERUSALEM

IT came to pass that when Jesus was near Bethphage and Bethany, at the hill called the Mount of Olives, he sent forth two of his disciples, saying:

"Go into the village near by and upon entering you shall find a colt tied on which no man has ever sat. Loose him and bring him here. And if any man asks you, 'Why do you loose him?' say to him, 'Because the Lord has need of him.' "

The two disciples went their way and found it as he had said to them. As they were loosing the colt, the owners said to them, "Why do you loose the colt?" And they said, "The Lord has need of him."

They brought him to Jesus and they laid their garments upon the colt, and they set Jesus upon it. And as he rode, they spread their clothes on the road.

When he had come near the slope of the Mount of Olives, the whole multitude of his disciples began to rejoice and praise God with a loud voice for all the mighty works that they had seen, saying, "Blessed be the king that comes in the name of the Lord. Peace in heaven, and glory in the highest."

Then some of the Pharisees from among the multitude said to him, "Master, rebuke your disciples."

He answered and said to them, "I tell you that if they should hold their peace, the stones would immediately cry out."

He had come near to the city, and when he saw it he wept over it, saying:

"If only you knew, in this day of yours, the things which concern your peace! But they are hid from your eyes. The days shall come that your enemies shall build a trench around you and keep you in on every side. They shall throw you to the ground and your children within you. They shall

not leave you one stone on another, because you did not acknowledge the time when God visited you."

And when he entered Jerusalem, all the city was moved, saying, "Who is this?" And the multitude said, "This is Jesus the prophet of Nazareth of Galilee."

JESUS DRIVES OUT MONEYCHANGERS

Jesus went into the temple of God, and drove out all them that sold and bought in the temple, and overturned the tables of the moneychangers, and the seats of them that sold doves and said to them, "My house shall be called the house of prayer, but you have made it a den of thieves."

And the blind and the lame came to him in the temple and he healed them.

But when the chief priests and scribes saw the children crying in the temple and saying, "Hosanna to the son of David," they were much displeased.

They said to him, "Do you hear what they say?" Jesus answered saying, "Yes, have you never read, 'Out of the mouth of babes, O God, you have drawn perfect praise'?"

And he left them and went out of the city into Bethany, and he lodged there.

THE FIG TREE WITHERS AWAY

On the next day, when they were coming from Bethany, Jesus was hungry. Seeing a fig tree far away that had leaves, he went to see whether he might find any fig on it. But when he came to it, he found nothing but leaves, for it was not yet the time for figs.

And he said to it, "Let no fruit grow on you from now and for ever." And immediately the fig tree withered away.

When the disciples saw it, they marvelled, saying, "How soon the fig tree has withered away!" Jesus answered and said to them, "Truly I say to you, you if you have faith and doubt not, shall not only do this which was done to the fig tree, but also if you say to this mountain, 'Be removed and be cast into the sea,' it shall be done. All things you ask in prayer, believing, you shall receive."

THE GREEDY WORKMEN

When Jesus came into the temple, the chief priests and the elders of the people came to him as he was teaching, and said, "By what authority do you do these things, and who gave you this authority?"

Jesus would not answer their question, but he began to speak to them in parables, saying:

"A certain man planted a vineyard and hedged it round about and dug a wine press in it, and built a tower, and then let it out to workmen, and went to a distant land.

"When the time of harvest drew near, he sent his servants to the workmen to collect the fruits of the vineyard. But the workmen took his servants, and beat one, and killed another, and stoned another.

"Again he sent other servants, and they did likewise to them. Last of all he sent his son to them, saying, 'They will respect my son.'

"But when the workmen saw the son, they said among themselves, 'This is the heir. Come, let us kill him and let us seize his inheritance.'

"And they caught him, and threw him out of the vineyard, and killed him.

"When the lord of the vineyard comes, what will he do to those workmen?" Jesus asked.

They said to him:

"He will miserably destroy those wicked men, and will rent out his vineyard to other workmen, who will pay him his share of the fruits when they ripen."

When the chief priests and Pharisees had heard his parable, they knew that he spoke of them. But when they tried to lay their hands on him, they were afraid of the multitude because it took him for a prophet.

GOD AND CAESAR

The Pharisees watched Jesus, and they sent forth spies who pretended to be honest men, that they might make use of his words to deliver him into the power and authority of the governor.

The spies questioned him, saying, "Master, we know that you are true and teach the truth, showing no favour, but truly teaching the way of God. Tell us therefore whether you think it is lawful for us to give tribute to Caesar or not?"

But he saw their craftiness and said to them, "Why do you try to trap me? Show me a coin. Whose name and image has it?"

They answered and said, "Caesar's." And he said to them, "Give therefore to Caesar the things which are Caesar's and to God the things which are God's."

And they could not twist his words before the people. They marvelled at his answer, and held their peace.

THE WIDOW'S PENNY

Jesus looked up and saw the rich men casting their gifts into the treasury. He saw also a certain poor widow casting in two pennies. And he said:

"Truly I say to you, that this poor widow has cast in more than all of them. For all these others have given offerings to God out of their abundance. But she in her poverty has given all she had to live upon."

THE UNWORTHY GUEST

Jesus spoke to them again by a parable, saying:

"The kingdom of heaven is like a certain king who prepared a marriage for his son, and sent forth his servants to call them that were invited to the wedding. And they would not come.

"Again, he sent out other servants, saying, 'Tell them that are invited that I have prepared my dinner. My oxen and my fat cattle are killed and all things are ready. Tell them to come to the marriage.'

"But they made light of it, and went their ways, one to his farm, another to his merchandise. And the rest took his servants and treated them spitefully, and slew them.

"When the king heard of this, he was angry. He sent forth his armies and destroyed those murderers, and burnt up their city.

"Then he said to his servants, 'The wedding is ready, but those who were invited were not worthy. Go therefore into the highways, and as many as you shall find, invite them to the marriage.'

"So those servants went out into the highways and gathered together as many as they found, both bad and good, and the wedding was furnished with guests.

"When the king came in to see the guests, he saw a man among them who did not have on a wedding robe. And he said to him, 'Friend, how did you come in here not having a wedding robe?'

"The man answered nothing.

"Then the king said to his servants, 'Bind him hand and foot and take him away, and cast him into outer darkness.'

"There shall be weeping and gnashing of teeth. For many are called, but few are chosen."

JESUS AND THE DISCIPLES

AS Jesus went out of the temple, one of his disciples said to him, "Look, Master, at these stones and these buildings!" He said, "As for these things which you see, the days shall come when there shall not be left one stone upon another that has not been thrown down."

And as he sat upon the Mount of Olives, his disciples came to him privately, saying, "Tell us. When shall these things be? And what shall be the sign of your coming and of the end of the world?"

And Jesus answered and said to them:

"Take care that no man deceives you. For many shall come in my name, saying, 'I am Christ,' and shall deceive many. You shall hear of wars and rumours of wars, but see that you do not become troubled, for all these things must come to pass. This is not the end yet.

"For nation shall rise against nation, and kingdom against kingdom. There shall be famines and pestilences and earthquakes in different places. All this is the beginning of sorrows.

"Then there shall be great troubles such as there have not been since the beginning of the world, troubles that there never have been and there never shall be. And unless those days were to be shortened, no living things could be saved. But for the sake of my chosen ones, those days shall be shortened.

THE END OF TIME

"The sun shall be darkened, and the moon shall not give her light, and the stars shall fall from heaven, and the powers of the heavens shall be shaken.

"Then the sign of the Son of man shall appear in the heavens, and then shall all the tribes of the earth mourn. And they shall see the Son of man coming in the clouds of heaven with power and great glory. And he shall send his angels with a great sound of a trumpet, and they shall gather together his chosen ones from the four winds, from one end of heaven to the other.

"Now learn a lesson from the fig tree: When its branch is still tender and puts forth leaves, you know that summer is near. So likewise you, when you see all these things, know that it is near, even at the doors.

"Truly I say to you, this generation shall not pass until all these things are fulfilled. Heaven and earth shall pass away, but my words shall not pass away.

"No man knows the day and the hour, not even the angels of heaven, but my Father only. Watch therefore, for you do not know what hour your Lord will come. But know this, that if the man of the house had known what

time the thief would come, he would have watched and would not have allowed his house to be broken into.

"Therefore, be ready also. For at the time when you do not think it, the Son of Man is coming. Blessed is the servant whom his lord shall find doing his duty when he comes. Truly I tell you, he shall make him ruler over his goods.

THE WISE AND FOOLISH BRIDESMAIDS

"Thus the kingdom of heaven shall be like ten bridesmaids who took their lamps and went forth to meet the bridegroom. Five of them were wise and five were foolish.

"They that were foolish took their lamps but took no oil with them. The wise ones took oil in vessels with their lamps.

"As the bridegroom was late, they you. Go instead to them that sell, and buy for yourselves.'

"While they went to buy, the bridegroom came and they that were ready went in with him to the marriage, and the door was shut. Afterwards the other bridesmaids came, saying, 'Lord, Lord, open the door to us.' But he answered and said, 'Truly, I do not know you.'

"Watch therefore, for you know neither the day nor the hour in which the Son of man comes.

all slumbered and slept. But at midnight the cry went up, 'Behold, the bridegroom comes. Go out to meet him.' Then all the bridesmaids rose up and trimmed their lamps. And the foolish said to the wise, 'Give us some of your oil, for our lamps have gone out.' But the wise answered, saying, 'We cannot, lest there should not be enough both for us and for

THE UNPROFITABLE SERVANT

"Again the kingdom of heaven is like a man setting off for a distant country who called together his servants and delivered to them his goods. To one he gave five talents, to another two, and to another one—to each according to his special abilities. Then he set off on his journey.

"He who received the five talents went and traded with them and made five more. And likewise he who received two gained two more. But he who received one went and dug in the earth and hid his lord's money.

"After a long time, the lord of those servants came home and reckoned with them. He who had received five talents came and brought five more, saying, 'Lord, you gave me five talents. Behold, I have earned five more beside them.'

"His lord said to him, 'Well done, good and faithful servant. You have been faithful over a few things, I will make you ruler over many things. Come, share with your lord his joy.'

"Then he who had received the one talent came and said, 'Lord, I knew that you are a hard man harvesting where you have not sown, and gathering where you have not threshed. And I was afraid, and went and hid your money in the earth. Lo, here you have what is yours.'

"His lord said to him, 'Well done, good and faithful servant. You have been faithful over a few things, I will make you ruler over many things. Come share with your lord in his good fortune.'

"Then he who had received two talents came and said, 'Lord, you gave me two talents. Behold, I have earned two more beside them.'

"His lord answered and said to him, 'You wicked and lazy servant! You knew that I reap where I have not sown, and gather where I have not threshed. Therefore you should have loaned out my money and then at my returning I should have had my money back with interest.

"Therefore take the talent from him, and give it to him who has ten talents. For to every one who has, more shall be given, and he shall have plenty. But from him who has not, shall be taken away even that which he has. Now cast the unprofitable servant into outer darkness.

"There shall be weeping and gnashing of teeth.

THE DAY OF JUDGMENT

"When the Son of man shall come in his glory, and all the holy angels with him, then shall he sit upon his glorious throne, and before him shall be gathered all nations. And he shall separate them one from another, as a shepherd divides his sheep from the goats. He shall set the sheep on his right hand, but the goats on the left.

"Then the King shall say to those on his right hand, 'Come, you blessed of my Father, inherit the kingdom prepared for you from the beginning of the world. For I was hungry, and you gave me food. I was thirsty and you gave me drink. I was a stranger, and you took me in. I was naked and you clothed me. I was sick and you visited me. I was in prison and you came to me.'

"Then shall the righteous answer him, saying, 'Lord, when did we see you hungry, and feed you? Or thirsty, and give you drink? When did we see you a stranger, and take you in? Or naked, and clothe you? Or when did we see you sick, or in prison, and come to you?'

"And the King shall answer and say to them, 'Truly I tell you, inasmuch as you have done it to one of the least of these my brothers, you have done it to me.'

"Then he shall also say to those on his left hand, 'Be off, you accursed ones, into everlasting fire, prepared for the devil and his angels. For I was hungry and you did not feed me,

thirsty and you gave me nothing to drink. I was a stranger and you did not take me in. I was naked and you did not clothe me. I was sick and in prison and you did not visit me.'

"Then they too will answer him, saying, 'Lord, when did we see you hungry, or thirsty, or a stranger, or naked, or sick, or in prison, and did not help you?'

"Then shall he answer them saying, 'Truly I say to you, inasmuch as you did not do it to one of the least of these my brothers, you did not do it to me.'

"And these shall go away into eternal punishment, but the righteous into eternal life."

JUDAS PLOTS TO BETRAY JESUS

And it came to pass when Jesus had finished all these sayings, that he said to his disciples, "You know that after two days is the feast of the Passover and the Son of man is to be betrayed and crucified."

Then the chief priests and the scribes and the elders of the people assembled together in the palace of the high priest, who was called Caiaphas. And they discussed how they might take Jesus by trickery and kill him.

But they said:

"Not on the feast day, lest there be an uproar among the people."

Then one of the twelve, called Judas Iscariot, went to the chief priests and said to them:

"What will you give me, if I deliver him to you?"

And when the chief priests heard him, they were glad and made an agreement with him for thirty pieces of silver. Judas accepted and from that time on he sought above all an occasion when the crowd would be absent.

447

THE LAST SUPPER

On the day of unleavened bread, when the Passover lamb was to be sacrificed, Jesus sent forth two of his disciples, saying, "Go into the city and prepare the Passover feast, so that we may eat."

And the two disciples asked him:

"Where are we to prepare it?"

He said, "When you have come into the city, you will meet a man carrying a pitcher of water. Follow him into the house he enters. And say to the man of the house, 'The Master says, "Where is the guest chamber where I shall eat the Passover feast with my disciples?"' And he will show

you a large room, furnished. Make ready there.''

They went and found it all as he had told them, and they prepared the Passover feast.

When the evening came, Jesus sat down with the twelve. And he said to them, "How greatly I have desired to eat this Passover with you before I suffer. For I tell you, I will not eat another until it is fulfilled in the kingdom of God.''

And as they were eating, Jesus took bread and blessed it, and breaking it into pieces he gave it to them, saying, "Take, eat; this is my body which is given for you. Do this in remembrance of me.''

After supper he took the cup and when he had given thanks, he gave it to them saying:

"Drink you all of it; for this is the new testament in my blood, which is shed for you and for many, for the forgiveness of sins. Take this, and divide it among you. For I say to you, I will not drink of the fruit of the vine until I drink it anew with you in my Father's kingdom."

When the supper was ended, Jesus rose from the table, laid aside his garments, and took and fastened a towel about him. Pouring water into a basin he began to wash the disciples' feet and to wipe them with the towel he had wrapped around him.

When he came to Simon Peter, Peter said to him, "Lord, do you wash my feet?"

Jesus answered and said to him, "What I am doing you do not understand now, but you will understand after."

Peter said to him, "You shall never wash my feet."

Jesus answered him, saying, "If I do not wash you, you have no part with me."

Then Peter said to him, "Lord, not my feet only, but also my hands and

my head." But Jesus answered and said, "He who is clean needs only to wash his feet to be clean all over. And you are clean—but not all of you." Jesus added the words "not all of you" for he knew who was to betray him.

"DO AS I HAVE DONE TO YOU"

After he had washed their feet and had taken his garments and was seated again, he said to them, "Do you know what I have done to you? You call me Master and Lord, and you speak well, for so I am. If I then, your Lord and Master, have washed your

feet, you also ought to wash one another's feet. For I have given you an example, that you should do as I have done to you.

"Truly, truly I say to you, the servant is not greater than his lord, nor is he that is sent greater than he that sent him. If you know these things, happy are you if you do them.

JESUS REVEALS HIS BETRAYER

"I speak not of you all. I know whom I have chosen, for the scripture must be fulfilled which says,

'*He who eats bread with me*
Has lifted up his heel against me.'"

When Jesus had spoken, he was deeply troubled and said: "Truly, truly I say to you that one of you shall betray me."

Then the disciples looked at one another, not knowing of whom he spoke. Now close beside Jesus at the table was one of the disciples whom he loved. Simon Peter therefore beckoned to this disciple that he should ask who it was of whom Jesus spoke. Then he, leaning towards Jesus, said to him. "Lord, who is it?"

Jesus answered, "It is he to whom I shall give a piece of bread, when I have dipped it in the bowl." And when he had dipped the bread, he gave it to Judas Iscariot, the son of Simon.

And after Judas took the bread, Satan entered into him. Then Jesus said to him, "What you must do, do quickly."

Now no one at the table knew why he said this to him. For some of them thought, since Judas had the purse, that Jesus had told him to buy the things that would be needed for the festival, or that he should give something to the poor.

Then having received the bread, Judas went out immediately. And it was night.

FAREWELL TO THE DISCIPLES

WHEN Judas had departed, Jesus said, "My children, for only a little while longer shall I be with you. You shall seek me, but as I said to the Jews, now I say to you: Where I am going, you cannot come.

"I give you a new commandment, that you love one another. As I have loved you, so also should you love one another. By this all people will know that you are my disciples, if you have love for one another.

"Greater love has no man than this: that a man lay down his life for his friends. You are my friends, if you do whatever I command you. I shall call you no longer servants, for a servant does not know what his lord does; but I have called you friends, for all that I have heard from my Father I have made known to you.

"Do not let your hearts be troubled. You believe in God; believe in me too. In my Father's house are many mansions. If it were not so, I would have told you. I go to prepare a place for you. And if I go and prepare a place for you, I will come again and take you back with me: that where I am, you may be also."

Simon Peter said to him, "Lord, where are you going?"

Jesus answered him, "Where I am going, you cannot follow me now, but you shall follow me later."

Peter said to him, "Lord, why cannot I follow you now? I would lay down my life for your sake."

Jesus answered him, "Will you lay down your life for my sake? Truly I say to you, the cock will not crow before you have denied me three times."

And he said to them, "When I sent you out without purses or shoes, did you lack anything?"

They said, "Nothing."

Then he said to them, "But now, he who has a purse, let him take it, and also his wallet. And he who has no sword, let him sell his robe and buy one. For I tell you, the writing in the scripture must be fulfilled in me: 'And he was counted among the outlaws.' For there is a purpose to things concerning me."

And they said, "Lord, see, here are two swords."

And he said to them, "It is enough."

THE GARDEN OF GETHSEMANE

WHEN they had sung a hymn, they went out of the city to the Mount of Olives. Then Jesus said to them, "You will all desert me this night. For it is written, 'I will smite the shepherd, and the sheep of the flock will be scattered.' But after I have risen again, I will go before you into Galilee."

Peter answered and said to him, "Though everyone else may desert you, I will never desert you." Jesus said to him again, "I tell you truly that tonight before the cock crows, you shall deny me three times."

But Peter said to him, "Even though I should die with you, I would never deny you." And all the disciples said likewise.

Then Jesus went forth with them to a place over the brook Cedron, where there was a garden called Gethsemane. And he said to his disciples, "Sit here while I go over yonder and pray."

He took with him Peter and the two sons of Zebedee, and he began to be sorrowful and heavy of heart. Then he said to them, "My soul is exceeding sorrowful, even unto death. Stay you here and watch with me."

JESUS PRAYS

He went on a little farther and fell to his face and prayed, saying, "O my Father, if it is possible, let this cup pass from me. Nevertheless, let not my will but your will be done."

And there appeared to him an angel from heaven, strengthening him. Then, being in agony, he prayed more earnestly, and his sweat was like great drops of blood falling to the ground.

And he came back to the disciples and found them asleep, and said to Peter, "What, could you not watch with me one hour? Watch now, and pray that you do not fall into temptation. The spirit is indeed willing, but the flesh is weak."

He went away again a second time and prayed, saying, "O Father, if this cup of suffering cannot pass from me unless I drink it, your will shall be done." And he came and found them asleep again, for their eyes were heavy. Then he left them and went away again and prayed a third time, saying the same words.

And when he returned, he found them asleep again, and he said to them, "Sleep on now and take your rest. It is enough. The hour has come when the Son of man shall be betrayed into the hands of sinners."

Then he said, "Rise up. Let us go. Behold he that betrays me is at hand."

THE BETRAYAL

While he was still speaking, Judas, one of the twelve, came, and with him a great multitude with swords and clubs, from the chief priests and the elders of the people.

Now he that betrayed him gave them a signal, saying, "Whomever I shall kiss, he is the one. Hold him fast."

And with that he came to Jesus and said, "Hail, Master," and kissed him.

Jesus said to him, "Friend, why have you come?" Then they came and laid hands on Jesus and took him.

Simon Peter, having a sword, drew it and struck the high priest's servant, and cut off his right ear. But Jesus said to him, "Put up your sword again in its place. For all who draw the sword shall die by the sword. Do you think that I could not now pray to my Father and he would immediately give me more than twelve legions of angels? But how then would the scriptures be fulfilled which say that it must be thus?" And he touched the man's ear and healed him.

At the same time he said to the multitudes, "Have you come out as if against a thief, with swords and clubs, to take me? I sat daily with you, teaching in the temple, and you laid not a hand on me."

But all this was done that the scriptures of the prophets might be fulfilled. Then all the disciples forsook him, and fled.

PETER DENIES JESUS

They who had arrested Jesus led him to Caiaphas, the high priest, where the scribes and elders were assembled. But Peter followed him at a distance to the high priest's palace, and went in and sat with the servants, to see the end.

Now the chief priests and elders and all the council sought false witnesses against Jesus, so that they could put him to death. But they found nothing. Although many people came to testify falsely, still they found nothing.

At last two false witnesses came and said, "This fellow said, 'I am able to destroy the temple of God and to build it again in three days.'"

The high priest arose and said to him, "Do you answer nothing? What is it that these witnesses say against you?"

But Jesus held his peace. Then the high priest said to him, "I ask you by the living God that you tell us whether you are the Christ, the Son of God."

Jesus said to him, "You have said so. But I say to you: In the days to come, you shall see the Son of man sitting on the right hand of Power, and coming on the clouds of heaven."

Then the high priest tore his clothes, saying, "He has spoken blasphemy. What further need have we of witnesses? Behold, now you have heard his blasphemy. What think you?"

They answered and said, "He deserves to die."

Then they did spit in his face, and strike him, while others hit him with the palms of their hands, saying, "Prophesy to us, you Christ! Who is it that struck you?"

Simon Peter meanwhile remained outside with the servants. And the maid at the door said to him, "Are you not one of this man's disciples?"

And he said, "I am not."

The servants and officers had made a fire of coals for it was cold and they were standing by it, warming themselves. Peter stood there also and they said to him, "Are you not, too, one of his disciples?"

He denied it and said, "I am not."

Then one of the high priest's servants and a kinsman to the one whose ear Peter had cut off said, "Did I not see you in the garden with him?"

Peter then denied it again and immediately the cock crew.

Then the Lord turned and looked at Peter and Peter remembered the words of Jesus, "Before the cock crows, you will deny me three times." And Peter went out and wept bitterly.

JUDAS HANGS HIMSELF

Then Judas, who had betrayed him, when he saw that Jesus was condemned, repented and brought the thirty pieces of silver back to the chief priests and elders, saying, "I have sinned in that I have betrayed innocent blood."

They said, "What is that to us? That is your affair."

Then he threw down the pieces of silver in the temple, and went out and hanged himself.

And the chief priests took the silver pieces and said, "It is not lawful for us to put them into the treasury, because it is the price of blood." They discussed it, and bought with the silver the potter's field, to bury strangers in. That is why that field has been called the Field of Blood until this day.

THE TRIAL

When the morning came, all the chief priests and elders of the people planned together against Jesus, to put him to death. And when they had bound him, they led him away to the hall of judgment and delivered him to Pontius Pilate, the Roman governor. They themselves did not go into the judgment hall, lest they should be ceremonially defiled, for they wanted to eat the Passover supper.

So Pilate came out to them and said, "What charge do you bring against this man?"

They answered and said to him, "If he were not a wrongdoer, we would not have delivered him to you."

Then Pilate said to them, "Take him and judge him according to your law."

But the Jews said to him, "It is not lawful for us to put any man to death."

Pilate went back into the judgment hall and called Jesus to him, and said to him, "Are you the King of the Jews?"

Jesus said to him, "Are you asking this of yourself, or did others say this about me?"

Pilate said, "Am I a Jew? Your own nation and the chief priests have delivered you to me. What have you done?"

Jesus answered, "My kingdom is not of this world. If my kingdom were of this world, my servants would have fought against my being delivered to the Jews. No, my kingdom is elsewhere."

Then Pilate said to him, "Are you a king, then?"

Jesus answered, "You say I am a king. To this end was I born, and for this cause I came into the world, that I should testify to the truth. Everyone who is on the side of truth listens to my voice."

PILATE GIVES WAY

And Pilate said to him, "What is truth?" Then Pilate went out again to the people and said to them, "I find in him no fault at all. But you have a custom, that I should release to you one prisoner at the Passover. Do you wish therefore that I release to you the King of the Jews?"

The chief priests and elders persuaded the people that they should ask for a notable prisoner, Barabbas, and put Jesus to death.

So they all cried out saying, "Not this man, but Barabbas." Barabbas was a robber and a murderer.

As Pilate was sitting on the judgment seat, his wife sent a message to him, saying, "Have nothing to do with that just man; for I have suffered many things this day in a dream concerning him."

So Pilate asked them again, "Which of the two shall I release to you? Barabbas, or Jesus which is called Christ?" And they said, "Barabbas." So Pilate

said, "What shall I do then with Jesus that is called Christ?" And they all said, "Let him be crucified."

And the governor said, "Why? What evil has he done?" But they cried out all the more, saying, "Let him be crucified."

So Pilate, seeing that he could not prevail on them and that there was an uproar, took water and washed his hands before the multitude, saying, "I am innocent of the blood of this just person."

stripped him and put on him a scarlet robe. Having braided a crown of thorns, they put it upon his head, and a reed in his right hand. They bowed the knee before him and mocked him saying, "Hail, King of the Jews!" They spat upon him and struck him with their hands. Taking the reed, they struck him upon the head. And after they had mocked him, they took the robe off him and put his own clothes on him. Then they led him away to crucify him.

Then all the people answered and said, "Let his blood be on us, and on our children."

And the voices of them and of the chief priests prevailed. And Pilate gave sentence that it should be as they required. And he released Barabbas to them, and delivered Jesus to be crucified.

Then the soldiers of the governor took Jesus into the common hall and brought to him a band of soldiers. They

JESUS IS CRUCIFIED

They took Jesus and led him away; and he, bearing his cross, went forth to a place called the Place of a Skull, which is called in Hebrew Golgotha.

And as they led him along, they laid hold on one Simon, a Cyrenian, coming from the country, and they laid the cross on him that he might carry it, behind Jesus.

And there followed him

group of people, and of women, bewailing him and lamenting him.

But Jesus turned to them and said, "Daughters of Jerusalem, weep not for me, but weep for yourselves and your children. For the days are coming in which people shall say to the mountains, 'Fall on us!' and to the hills, 'Cover us!' "

There were also two others, criminals, led out with him to be put to death. And when they had come to the place, which is called the Skull or

each soldier. They took his robe too. Now the robe was without seams, woven from the top down. Therefore they said among themselves, "Let us not tear it, but let us draw lots for it, to see whose it shall be." This was in order that the scripture might be fulfilled which says,

"They parted my clothing among them,
and for my robe they did cast lots."

All these things, therefore, the soldiers did.

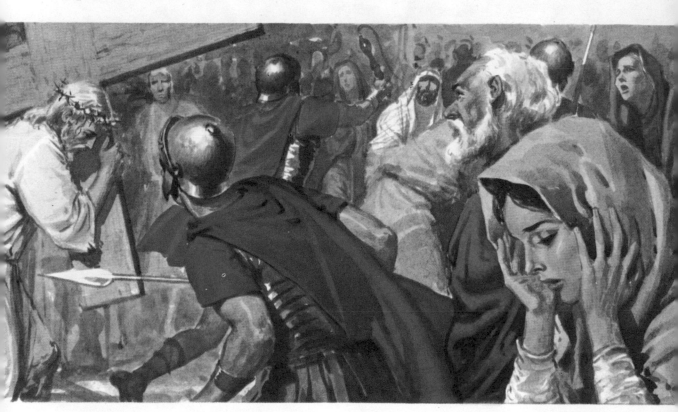

Golgotha, they crucified him there, with the two criminals, one on the right hand, the other on the left.

Then Jesus said:

"Father, forgive them, for they know not what they do."

THE ROBE IS DIVIDED

And the soldiers, when they had crucified Jesus, took his garments, and divided them into four parts, one to

Now close by the cross of Jesus stood his mother, and his mother's sister, Mary the wife of Cleophas, and Mary Magdalene.

When Jesus saw his mother and a disciple whom he loved standing by, he said to his mother, "Woman, behold your son."

Then he said to the disciple, "Behold your mother." And from that hour that disciple took her into his own home.

THE CROWD MOCKS JESUS

People stood by watching him, and others who passed by shouted abuse at him, wagging their heads and saying, "If you are the Son of God, come down from the cross." And the chief priests and rulers did likewise, saying, "He saved others; himself he cannot save. If he be the King of Israel, let him now come down from the cross and we will believe him. He trusted in God; let him deliver him now, if he will have him; for he said 'I am the Son of God.'"

Now from noon until three in the afternoon there was darkness all over the land.

And at three Jesus cried with a loud voice, "My God, my God, why have you forsaken me?" Knowing that all things were now completed that the scriptures might be fulfilled, Jesus said, "I thirst." One who stood by, ran and

filled a sponge with vinegar. Putting it upon a lance he gave it to him to drink sticking it in his mouth and saying: "Let us see whether his God will come to save him."

Over Jesus' head was a sign written in letters of Greek, Latin and Hebrew, reading, "This is the King of the Jews."

And one of the criminals who were crucified with him scoffed at him, saying, "If you are Christ, save your-self and us." But the other rebuked him, saying, "Do you not fear God, seeing that you are also condemned? And we are here justly, for we receive the due return for our deeds, but this man has done nothing wrong."

And he said to Jesus, "Lord, remember me when you come into your kingdom."

And Jesus said to him, "Truly I tell you today you shall be with me in paradise."

461

JESUS GIVES UP THE GHOST

The sun was darkened, and the veil of the temple was torn in two from top to bottom. The earth quaked, rocks split, and graves were opened.

And when Jesus had cried with a loud voice, he said, "Father, into your hands I commend my spirit." And after this, he said, "It is finished," and bowed his head and gave up the ghost.

Now when the captain of the guard saw the earthquake and all those things that were done, he praised God, saying, "Truly this man was the Son of God."

All the people who had come to watch the spectacle, seeing the things which were done, beat their breasts and went away.

And those who knew him, and the women who had followed him from Galilee stood afar off, watching these things.

THE BODY IS BURIED

The people, that the bodies should not remain on the crosses on the sabbath day, asked Pilate that he have them taken away. But when the soldiers came to Jesus, one of them with a spear pierced his side and forthwith there came out blood and water.

When evening was come, behold, a disciple of Jesus, a rich man named Joseph of Arimathea came secretly to

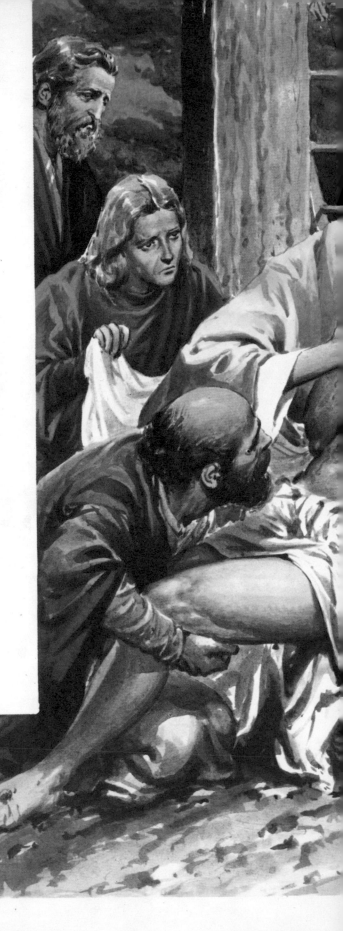

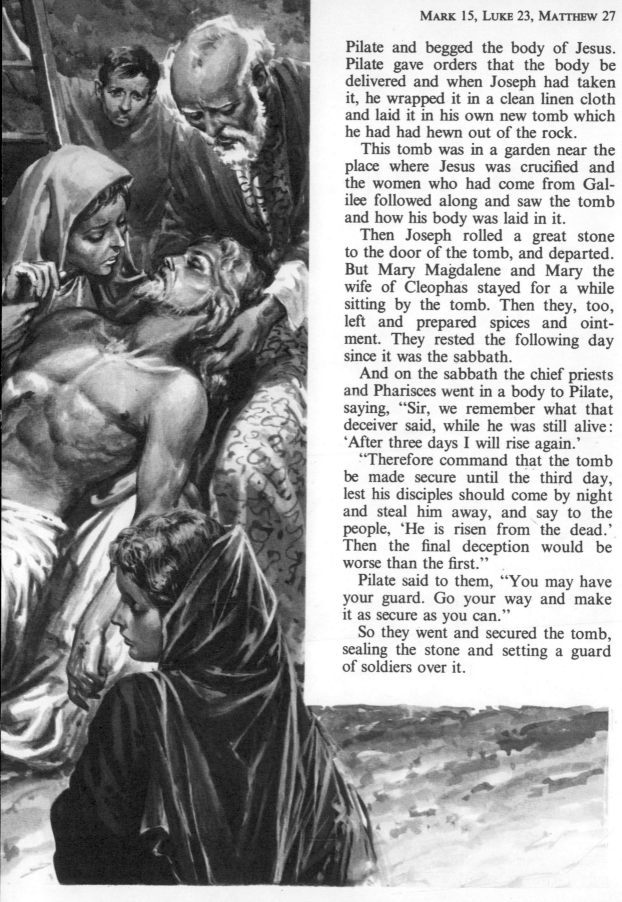

Pilate and begged the body of Jesus. Pilate gave orders that the body be delivered and when Joseph had taken it, he wrapped it in a clean linen cloth and laid it in his own new tomb which he had had hewn out of the rock.

This tomb was in a garden near the place where Jesus was crucified and the women who had come from Galilee followed along and saw the tomb and how his body was laid in it.

Then Joseph rolled a great stone to the door of the tomb, and departed. But Mary Magdalene and Mary the wife of Cleophas stayed for a while sitting by the tomb. Then they, too, left and prepared spices and ointment. They rested the following day since it was the sabbath.

And on the sabbath the chief priests and Pharisces went in a body to Pilate, saying, "Sir, we remember what that deceiver said, while he was still alive: 'After three days I will rise again.'

"Therefore command that the tomb be made secure until the third day, lest his disciples should come by night and steal him away, and say to the people, 'He is risen from the dead.' Then the final deception would be worse than the first."

Pilate said to them, "You may have your guard. Go your way and make it as secure as you can."

So they went and secured the tomb, sealing the stone and setting a guard of soldiers over it.

THE RESURRECTION

 T the end of the sabbath, as it began to dawn on the first day of the week, Mary Magdalene and Mary the wife of Cleophas came to see the tomb. And, behold, there was a great earthquake, for the angel of the Lord descended from heaven and came back and rolled the stone from the entrance, and sat on it. His face was like lightning and his garments were white as snow.

For fear of him, the guards trembled and fainted away as if they were dead men. But the angel spoke to the women and said, "Fear not. For I know that you seek Jesus, who was crucified. He is not here, for he has risen, as he said. Come, see the place where the Lord lay.

"And now go quickly and tell his disciples that he has risen from the dead, for, behold, he goes ahead of you into Galilee, where you shall see him. There, I have told you."

They departed quickly from the tomb with fear and great joy, and ran to bring word to his disciples. And as they went to tell them, Jesus met them, saying, "All hail." And they came and held him by the feet and worshipped him.

Then Jesus said to them, "Be not afraid. Go and tell my brothers to go into Galilee, and there they shall see me."

THE APPEARANCE TO THE DISCIPLES

On that same day, two of his disciples went to a village called Emmaus which was about seven miles from Jerusalem. They talked together about all these things which had happened. And it came to pass that while they discussed and reasoned together, Jesus

himself came near and went with them. But they did not recognize him.

He said to them, "What manner of conversation is this that you make, one to another, as you walk and are so sad?"

One of them, whose name was Cleophas, answered, "Are you a stranger in Jerusalem? Have you not heard of the things that have come to pass there in these days?"

Jesus said to them, "What things?"

They said, "Concerning Jesus of Nazareth, who was a prophet mighty in deed and word before God and all the people, and how the chief priests and our rulers delivered him to be condemned to death and have crucified him. We had hoped that he was the man who would lead Israel.

"Today is the third day since these things were done, and certain women astonished us by telling us about how they went to the tomb where he was buried and had a vision of angels, who said that he was alive.

"Certain of our company went to the tomb, and found it was as the women had said, but they did not see him."

Then Jesus said to them, "O fools, and slow of heart to believe all that the prophets have spoken." And beginning at Moses and all the prophets, he explained to them the things in all the scriptures concerning himself.

And they drew near to the village where they were going and Jesus was going to walk on, but they stopped him, saying, "Stay with us, for it is toward evening and the day is far spent." So he went in and remained with them.

THE BREAKING OF BREAD

As he sat eating with them, he took bread and blessed it and broke it, and gave it to them. Then their eyes were opened, and they knew him. But he had vanished out of their sight. Then they said to one another, "Did not our hearts burn within us while he talked with us on the road, and while he explained to us the scriptures?"

And they returned to Jerusalem in the same hour and found the eleven gathered together and they said, "The Lord is risen indeed, and has appeared to Simon." They told what things were done on the way to Emmaus and how he became known to them in breaking the bread.

THE TAKING OF FOOD

As they thus spoke, Jesus himself stood in the midst of them and said to them, "Peace be unto you."

But they were terrified and much afraid and supposed that they had seen a spirit.

And he said to them, "Why are you troubled? And why do thoughts arise in your hearts? Behold my hands and my feet; that it is I myself. Handle me and see. For a spirit does not have flesh and bones, as you see me have."

And when he had thus spoken, he showed them his hands and his feet.

And while they still did not believe for joy, and wondered, he said to them, "Have you here any food?" And they gave him a piece of a broiled fish and of a honeycomb. And he took it, and did eat before them.

Then he said to them, "These are the words which I spoke to you while I was still with you, that all things must be done that were written in the law of Moses and in the Prophets and in the Psalms concerning me."

He opened their minds so that they might understand the scriptures, and said, "Thus it is written that it was necessary for Christ to suffer and to rise from the dead on the third day, and that repentance and forgiveness of sins should be preached in his name among all nations, beginning at Jerusalem. And you are witnesses of these things."

THOMAS DOUBTS

But Thomas, one of the twelve, called Didymus (the Twin), was not with them when Jesus came. The disciples therefore said to him, "We have seen the Lord." But he said to them, "Unless I see in his hands the print of the nails, and put my finger into the print of the nails, and thrust my hand into his side, I will not believe."

After eight days, when the disciples were again in the room, and Thomas was with them, Jesus came to them, though the doors were shut, and stood among them and said, "Peace be unto you."

Then he said to Thomas, "Reach out your finger and touch my hands, and reach your hand here and thrust it into my side, and do not be faithless, but believe."

Thomas answered and said to him, "My Lord and my God."

Jesus said to him, "Thomas, because you have seen me you have believed. Blessed are they who have not seen, yet have believed."

AT THE SEA OF TIBERIAS

After these things, Jesus showed himself again to his disciples at the sea of Tiberias. There were together Simon Peter and Thomas called Didymus and Nathanael of Cana, and the sons of Zebedee, and two others of his disciples.

Simon Peter said to them, "I go afishing." They said to him, "We also go with you." So they went forth and entered a boat immediately. They fished all night long and still caught nothing.

When the morning came, Jesus stood on the shore, but the disciples did not know that it was Jesus. He said to them, "Children, have you any food?"

"No," they answered him.

Then he said to them, "Cast your net on the right side of the boat and you will find fish." They cast therefore and they were not able to draw the net for the catch of fish. Therefore John, the disciple whom Jesus loved, said to Peter, "It is the Lord." And

of great fishes, one hundred and fifty-three of them. And although there were so many, the net was not broken.

Jesus said to them, "Come and dine." And knowing that it was the Lord, none of them dared to ask him, "Who are you?"

So Jesus took the bread that was lying there and gave it to them and the fish likewise.

This was the third time that Jesus showed himself to his disciples after he had risen from the dead.

JESUS ASCENDS INTO HEAVEN

Jesus appeared to his disciples for forty days, speaking of things concerning the kingdom of God. And while he was with them he commanded them not to leave Jerusalem, but to wait there for a promise from the Father. He said:

"For John truly baptized with water, but you shall be baptized with the Holy Spirit not many days from now. You shall receive power after the Holy Spirit has come upon you. You shall be witnesses for me in Jerusalem, and in all Judea, and in Samaria, and to the outermost parts of the earth."

Then Jesus led his disciples out as far as Bethany, and he lifted up his hands and blessed them. And while they looked on, he was taken up and a cloud received him out of their sight.

While they looked steadily toward heaven as he went up, behold, two men stood beside them in white robes and said to them, "You men of Galilee, why do you stand gazing up into heaven? This same Jesus who was taken up from you into heaven shall come again in the same way as you have seen him go."

And they worshiped him, and returned to Jerusalem with great joy, and were continually in the temple praising and blessing God.

when Simon Peter heard that it was the Lord, he wrapped his fisher's coat round him (for he was naked), and cast himself into the sea.

The other disciples came in a little boat, for they were not far from land, and they dragged the net filled with fish. As soon as they had come to land, they saw a fire of coals there and fish laid on it, and some bread.

Jesus said to them, "Bring the fish that you have caught." Simon Peter went and pulled the net to land, full

THE COMING OF THE HOLY SPIRIT

WHEN the day of Pentecost had come, the disciples were all gathered together in one place. And suddenly there came a sound from heaven like a rushing mighty wind, and it filled all the house where they were sitting.

And there appeared to them tongues of flame which sat upon each of them. And they were all filled with the Holy Spirit, and began to speak in other languages, as the Spirit led them to speak.

Now there were living in Jerusalem Jews, devout men, from every nation under heaven. And when this news spread, the multitude came together and were confounded because every man heard them speak in his own language.

They were all amazed and marvelled, saying to one another, "Behold, are not all these who speak Galileans? How is it that each of us hears his own language from where he was born? Parthians and Medes and Elamites, and the dwellers of Mesopotamia, and of Judea and Cappadocia and Pontus and Asia, of Phrygia and Pamphylia, of Egypt and the parts of Libya around Cyrene, and strangers from Rome, Jews and proselytes, Cretans and Arabs, we hear them speak in our own tongues of the wonderful works of God."

They were all amazed and wondered, saying to one another, "What does this mean?"

Others, mocking, said, "These men are full of new wine."

But Peter, standing up with the eleven (for they had chosen Matthias to take the place of the traitor Judas), lifted up his voice and said to them, "You men of Judea, and all you who live in Jerusalem, listen to my words and know this: These men are not

drunken, as you suppose, for it is only the ninth hour of the day. But this is that which was spoken by God to the prophet Joel: 'And it shall come to pass in the last days, that I will pour out my Spirit upon all men. And your sons and your daughters shall prophesy, and your young men shall see visions and your old men shall dream dreams.' " And he told them of Jesus the Christ, the Son of God.

Then those who gladly received his word were baptized, and that same day were added to them about three thousand souls. They followed faithfully the apostles' teaching and fellowship, breaking bread together and praying.

And fear came upon every soul and many wonders were done by the apostles. All that believed were together and owned all things in common. They sold their possessions and goods and divided the money among all the people, as each had need of it.

Daily they went together to the temple, and from house to house they ate with gladness and singleness of heart, praising God and having favour with all the people. And the Lord added to their number daily those who would be saved.

A LAME BEGGAR HEALED

Now Peter and John went together into the temple at the hour of prayer, being the third hour of the afternoon. And a certain man, lame from birth, was laid daily at the gate of the temple which is called Beautiful, to ask alms of those who enter the temple.

Seeing Peter and John about to go into the temple, he asked alms of them. And Peter, fixing his eyes upon him, said, "Look at us." He looked at them, expecting to receive something from them. Then Peter said to him, "Silver and gold I have none, but what I have I give you. In the name of Jesus Christ of Nazareth, rise up and walk."

And he took him by the right hand and lifted him up. Immediately his feet and ankle bones received strength, and he, leaping up, stood and walked, and entered with them into the temple, walking and leaping and praising God.

The people saw him walking and heard him praising God, and they knew that it was he who had sat begging at the gate Beautiful of the temple; they were filled with amazement and wonder at what had happened to him.

When Peter saw this, he said to the people, "You men of Israel, why do you marvel at this? Why do you stare at us so, as though by our own power or holiness we have made this man walk?

"The God of Abraham and of Isaac, and of Jacob, the God of our fathers, is thus glorifying his Son, Jesus, whom you delivered up and denied in the presence of Pilate, when he was determined to let him go. But you denied the Just and Holy One, and demanded that a murderer be set free for you. You killed the Prince of life, whom God has raised from the dead. Of that we are witnesses. And his name, through faith in his name, has made this man strong whom you well know."

THE APOSTLES ARE ARRESTED

As they spoke to the people, the priests and the captain of the temple and the Sadducees came upon them

However, many of those who heard the word believed, and the number of them grew to about five thousand.

The next day, the rulers and elders and scribes, Annas the high priest, and Caiaphas, and John and Alexander and as many as were of the family of the high priest gathered together at Jerusalem.

They conferred among themselves, saying:

"What shall we do with these men? That a notable miracle was done by them is clear to all the people of Jerusalem, and we cannot deny it. But so that it spreads no further, let us threaten them, that they speak hereafter to no man in this name." And they called them, and commanded them not to speak at all nor teach in the name of Jesus.

But Peter and John answered and said to them:

"Whether it is right in the sight of God to listen more to you than to God, you judge. For we can only speak of the things which we have seen and heard."

And when they had threatened them further, they let them go, finding no way to punish them because of the people.

Then great wonders were worked among the people by the hands of the apostles, so much so that the people brought forth the sick into the streets and laid them on beds and couches so that at least the shadow of Peter passing by might fall upon some of them.

There came a multitude from the cities around Jerusalem, bringing sick folk and those who were troubled with evil spirits. And they were healed, every one.

Then the high priest rose up, and all the Sadducees who were with him, and they were filled with indignation. They laid their hands upon the apostles and put them in the common prison.

and were angered that they taught the people and preached the resurrection from the dead, through Jesus. They arrested them and held them until the next day, for it was evening.

THE APOSTLES ESCAPE

But the angel of the Lord opened the prison doors by night, and brought them out, and said, "Go, stand up in the temple and speak to the people all the words of this life." And when they heard that, they went into the temple early in the morning, and taught.

Now the high priest and they that were with him called together the council and all the senate of the children of Israel, and sent to the prison to have them brought. When the officers went and did not find them in the prison, they returned, saying, "The prison we found shut securely and the keepers standing outside before the doors, but when we opened them, we found no man within."

Then someone came and told them, "Behold, the men whom you put in prison are standing in the temple and teaching the people." And when the high priest and the captain of the temple and the chief priests heard these things, they wondered what would come of them.

STEPHEN, THE FIRST MARTYR

The apostles chose seven men to help them with their daily affairs, and among these was Stephen, a man full of faith and of the Holy Spirit. He did great wonders and miracles among the people. Some members of the synagogue disputed with him, but they were not able to stand up to his wisdom and the spirit with which he spoke.

So they got some men to say, "We have heard him speak blasphemous words against Moses and against God." And they stirred up the people and the elders and the scribes, and they came upon him and seized him and brought him before the council.

They set up false witnesses who said, "This man never ceases speaking blasphemous words against this holy place and the law.

"We have heard him say that this Jesus of Nazareth shall destroy this place and shall change the customs which Moses gave us."

And all those who sat in the council looked at him, and saw that his face was like the face of an angel.

Then the high priest said, "Are these things so?"

STEPHEN MAKES HIS DEFENCE

Stephen said, "Men, brothers and fathers, listen. The Most High does not dwell in temples made with hands, for as the prophet says, 'Heaven is my throne, and the earth is my footstool. What house will you build me?' says the Lord. 'Or what is the place of my rest? Has not my hand made all these things?'

"You stubborn people, heathen in heart and heathen in hearing! You always resist the Holy Spirit. As your fathers did, so do you. Which of the prophets did not your fathers persecute? And they killed those who foretold the coming of the Just One; whom you have just now betrayed and murdered—you who received the law from the angels but have not kept it!"

When they heard these things, they were cut to the heart and ground their teeth at him. But he, being full of the Holy Spirit, looked steadily up into heaven and saw the glory of God, and Jesus standing on the right hand of God.

He said, "Behold, I see the heavens opened and the Son of man standing on the right hand of God."

Then they cried out with a loud voice, and stopped up their ears, and ran upon him all at once. They threw him out of the city and stoned him. And the witnesses laid down their cloaks at the feet of a young man whose name was Saul.

As they stoned Stephen, he called upon God, saying, "Lord Jesus, receive my spirit." He kneeled down and cried out with a loud voice, "Lord, do not count this sin against them." And when he had said this, he fell asleep in death.

SAUL IS CONVERTED

Not only did Saul consent to Stephen's death but he was directing heavy persecution against the church in Jerusalem, entering into every house and dragging out men and women to put them into prison. Breathing out threats of slaughter against the disciples of the Lord, Saul went to the high priest and asked from him letters to the synagogue in Damascus, so that if he found any who followed Christ's way, whether they were men or women, he might bring them bound to Jerusalem.

But as he journeyed, approaching Damascus, suddenly there shone around him a light from heaven, and he fell to the earth and heard a voice saying to him, "Saul, Saul, why do you persecute me?" And he said, "Who are you, Lord?" And the Lord said, "I am Jesus, whom you persecute."

Then he, trembling and astonished, said, "Lord, what do you want me to do?" And the Lord said to him,

"Arise and go into the city, and you shall be told what you must do."

The men who journeyed with him stood speechless, hearing a voice but seeing no man.

Saul arose from the earth, and when he opened his eyes, he could see no man. But they led him by the hand and brought him into Damascus. For three days he was without sight, and neither ate nor drank.

Now there was a certain disciple in Damascus named Ananias. And the Lord said to him in a vision, "Ananias." And he answered, "Yes, I am here, Lord."

The Lord said to him, "Arise and go into the street called Straight, and ask in the house of Judas for a man called Saul of Tarsus. For he is praying and has seen in a vision a man named Ananias coming in and putting his hand upon him that he might receive his sight."

Then Ananias said, "Lord, I have heard from many people about this man and how much evil he has done to your saints at Jerusalem. And here he has authority from the chief priests to arrest all that call upon your name."

But the Lord said to him, "Go your way, for he is chosen by me to carry my name to the Gentiles, and kings, and the children of Israel. For I shall show him how greatly he must suffer for my name's sake."

SAUL BECOMES A CHRISTIAN

Ananias went his way and entered the house, and putting his hands on Saul, said, "Brother Saul, the Lord, even Jesus who appeared to you on the road as you came, has sent me that you might receive your sight and be filled with the Holy Spirit."

Immediately it was as if scales fell from his eyes, and he received his sight at once, and arose and was baptized.

When he had eaten, he was stronger, and he stayed on for some days with the disciples who were in Damascus. He began preaching in the synagogues that Christ is the Son of God. And all who heard him were amazed, and said, "Is this not he who destroyed those who called on Christ's name in Jerusalem, and came here in order to bring them bound to the chief priests?"

But Saul increased all the more in strength, and confounded his foes who lived in Damascus, by proving that Jesus was indeed the Christ.

After many days had passed, they plotted to kill him. But Saul knew that they were lying in wait for him, and that they watched the gates day and night to kill him. So the disciples took him by night and let him down over the wall in a basket. And when Saul came to Jerusalem, he joined the disciples there.

477

THE TEACHING OF PETER

There was a certain man in Caesarea called Cornelius, a centurion of the Roman army. He was a devout man, one who feared God with all his household, who gave much alms to the people and prayed to God constantly.

on him, and when he had told them of all these things, he sent them to Joppa.

On the next day, as they went on their journey and drew near to the city, Peter went up on to the housetop for his noonday prayers. And while he was there, the men whom Corne-

He saw in a vision one afternoon an angel of God come to him and say, "Cornelius." When he looked at him, he was afraid and said, "What is it, Lord?"

And the angel said to him, "Your prayers and your alms have come up before God as a memorial. Now send men to Joppa, and call for one Simon whose other name is Peter. He is staying with one Simon, a tanner, whose house is by the seaside. He shall tell you what you ought to do."

When the angel who spoke to Cornelius had gone away, he called two of his household servants and a devout soldier from among them who waited

lius had sent, having made enquiry for Simon's house, stood before the gate. They called and asked whether Simon called Peter was staying there.

In the midst of Peter's prayers, the Holy Spirit said to him, "Behold, three men seek you. Arise therefore, go down and go with them. Do not worry about anything, for I am the one who has sent them."

Then Peter went down to the men and said, "Behold, I am the one whom you seek. Why have you come?" And they said, "Cornelius the centurion, a just man and one who fears God, a man of good reputation among the whole Jewish nation, was told by a holy angel of God to send for you to come to his house, so that he could hear you speak."

Then he called them in and gave them lodging. And the next day Peter went away with them, and certain of the brothers from Joppa went with him.

any man is unclean. Therefore I came to you without question as soon as I was sent for. I ask now for what purpose you have sent for me?"

Cornelius told him of his vision. Then Peter began to speak and said, "Truly I can see that God favours no person, but among every people he

PETER AND THE CENTURION

The following day, they entered Caesarea and Cornelius was waiting for them, having called together his kinsmen and close friends. As Peter came in, Cornelius met him and fell down at his feet and worshipped him. But Peter lifted him up, saying, "Stand up, I myself also am a man."

As they talked, he went in and found that there were many gathered together. And Peter said to them, "You know that it is an unlawful thing for a man that is a Jew to keep company or visit with anyone of another people. But God has taught me not to feel that

who fears him and does what is right is acceptable to him."

While Peter was speaking to them, the Holy Spirit fell on all those who heard his words. And all those believers among the Jews who had come with Peter were astonished because the gift of the Holy Spirit was poured out even upon the Gentiles. For they heard them speak in strange words and glorify God. Then Peter said, "Can any man deny them water to be baptized, these who have received the Holy Spirit as well as we?" And he commanded them to be baptized in the name of the Lord. They begged him to remain with them for some days.

PETER IS IMPRISONED

Now about that time, Herod the king reached out to strike certain of the followers of Christ. He had James the brother of John killed with the sword. And, because he saw it pleased the people, he proceeded further to seize Peter too.

When he had arrested him, he put him in prison and delivered him to four squads of soldiers to guard him, intending after the Passover to bring him forth to the people. So Peter was kept in prison, but the prayers of the church were made unceasingly to God for him.

When Herod was about to bring him forth, that same night Peter was sleeping between two soldiers, bound with two chains. And the keepers at the doors guarded the prison. And, behold, an angel of the Lord came to him, and a light shone in the prison, and he struck Peter on the side and raised him saying, "Arise quickly." And his chains fell off his hands.

The angel said, "Dress yourself and put on your sandals." He did so. Then the angel said, "Wrap your robe around you and follow me."

PETER ESCAPES

He went out and followed him. But Peter did not believe that it was true which was done by the angel, and thought he was seeing a vision.

When they had passed the first and second guard, they came to the iron gate that led into the city. It opened to them of its own accord, and they went out and passed on through one street, and then the angel departed from him.

When Peter came to himself, he said:

"Now I know as a certainty that the Lord has sent his angel and has delivered me out of the hand of Herod, and from all that the Jewish people intended."

When he had considered this thing,

As Peter knocked at the outer doorway, a maiden named Rhoda came in answer. And when she recognized Peter's voice, her gladness was such that she did not open the gate but ran in and told the others that Peter was standing before the gate.

They said to her, "You must be mad." But she kept insisting that it was so. Then they said, "It is his angel."

Peter continued knocking, and when they had opened the door and saw him, they were astonished. But he, motioning to them with his hand to hold their peace, told them how the Lord had brought him out of the prison. And he said, "Go tell these things to the brethren." And he departed, and went to another place.

Now as soon as it was day, there was great confusion among the soldiers over what had become of Peter. And when Herod sought for him and did not find him, he questioned the guards and commanded that they should be put to death.

BARNABAS AND PAUL ARE CHOSEN

Now in the church at Antioch there were certain prophets and teachers, Barnabas, and Simeon, who was called Niger, and Lucius of Cyrene, and Manaen who had been brought up with Herod the governor, and Saul, who was also called Paul.

And as they were serving the Lord and fasting, the Holy Spirit said, "Set Barnabas and Paul apart for me for the work for which I have called them."

And when they had fasted and prayed together, and laid their hands on them, they sent them away. So Barnabas and Paul, being sent forth by the Holy Spirit, departed to Seleucia, and from there sailed to Cyprus.

he went to the house of Mary the mother of John, whose other name was Mark, where many were gathered together praying.

481

PAUL'S FIRST JOURNEY

 **A**FTER preaching on the island of Cyprus, Paul and Barnabas set sail again and went to the mainland cities of Perga in Pamphylia and Antioch in Pisidia.

They were at Antioch on the sabbath day and they went into the synagogue, and sat down. And after the reading of the law and the prophets, the rulers of the synagogue sent word to them, saying, "If you have anything to preach to the people, say it."

Then Paul stood up and motioning with his hands spoke to the congregation of Jesus and the history of Israel.

"Men of Israel," he said, "and you that fear God, listen. The God of this people Israel chose our fathers and gave strength to our people when they dwelt as strangers in the land of Egypt. He delivered them with great power from their oppressors and for about forty years he maintained them in the wilderness. When he had destroyed seven nations in the land of Canaan, he divided the land to them by lot, and gave them judges for about four hundred and fifty years until Samuel the prophet.

"The people asked for a king and he gave them Saul, the son of Kish of the tribe of Benjamin for forty years. Then he raised up David in Saul's place, saying, 'I have found David the son of Jesse a man after my own heart who shall do my will.'

"Of David's seed, God according to his promises has now raised to Israel a Saviour, Jesus. To you and to all who fear God is this saviour and this word of salvation sent."

And the following sabbath almost the whole city came together to hear Paul and Barnabas. But their enemies stirred up the chief men of the city against them, so they departed from Antioch.

They preached in the synagogues and in the streets wherever they went, bringing the message of Jesus to Jews and Gentiles alike, for, as they said, "The Lord gave us this command: 'I have set you to be a light to the Gentiles, that you should work for the saving of souls to the ends of the earth.'"

And it came to pass in Iconium that they went together into the synagogue and spoke so that a great multitude of both the Jews and Gentiles believed. But the unbelieving Jews stirred up the Gentiles and set their minds against Paul and Barnabas. The city was divided and part held with the Jews and part with the disciples.

When an attempt was made to stone them, Paul and Barnabas were aware of it, and fled into Lystra and Derbe, other cities of Galatia, and into the region that lies round about. And there they preached the gospel.

Now there was a certain man of Lystra who, being a cripple from

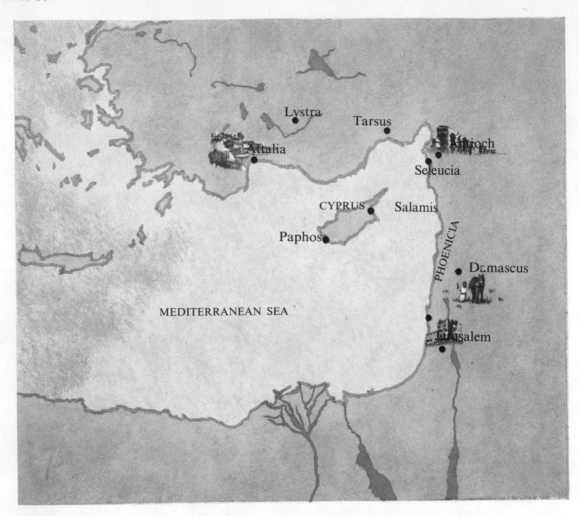

birth, had never walked. He heard Paul speak, and Paul, looking at him and seeing that he had the faith to be healed, said in a loud voice, "Stand up on your feet." And he leaped up and walked.

When the people saw what Paul had done, they lifted up their voices, saying in their own tongue, "The gods have come down to us in the likeness of men." They called Barnabas Jupiter and Paul Mercury, because he was the chief speaker.

Then the priest of Jupiter, whose temple stood in front of the city, brought oxen and garlands to the gates, to offer a sacrifice with the people. And when the apostles, Paul and Barnabas, heard of this, they tore their clothes and ran among the people,

crying out, "Sirs, why do you do these things? We are only human beings, with feelings like you, and are preaching to you that you should turn from these vain worships to the living God, who made heaven and earth, and the sea, and all things in them.

"In times past he let all peoples walk in their own ways, but he did not leave us without reminders of himself, in that he did good, and gave us rain from heaven and fruitful seasons, filling our hearts with food and gladness."

Even with those words, they barely restrained the people from offering sacrifices to them.

But there came there certain men from Antioch and Iconium who swayed the people. They stoned Paul and put him out of the city, thinking he was dead. However, as the disciples stood round about him, he rose up and came into the city.

The next day, he departed with Barnabas to Derbe, and when they had preached the gospel to that city, they returned again to Lystra, and to Iconium, and Antioch.

And after they had passed throughout Pisidia, they came to Pamphylia. And when they had preached the word in Perga, they went down into Attalia, and from there sailed to Antioch in Cilicia. And there they stayed a long time with the disciples.

THE EPISTLE OF PAUL TO THE GALATIANS

Some time after leaving the Roman province of Galatia, Paul wrote a letter (epistle) to the Christian churches he had helped establish there. It is one of many he wrote to different groups. In all, the letters form a little more than a quarter of the New Testament and are full of advice and encouragement concerning Christian life and worship. Paul wrote his angry letter to the Galatians, parts of which follow, apparently after hearing of severe discord over doctrine by Galatian church members.

From Paul and all the brethren that are with me to the churches of Galatia:

"O foolish Galatians, who has bewitched you that you should not obey the truth, you before whom Jesus Christ has been clearly set forth as crucified? Only one thing would I have you tell me: Did you receive the Spirit by the works of the law or by the hearing of faith?

"Are you so foolish to believe that having begun in the Spirit, you are now made perfect by the flesh? He therefore that ministers to you the Spirit and works miracles among you, does he do it by the works of the law or by the hearing of faith?

"Be sure that they which are of faith are the children of Abraham.

"Christ has redeemed us from the curse of the law. Before faith came, we were kept under the law, shut up until faith should be revealed. The law was our schoolmaster to bring us to Christ, that we might be justified by faith. But after faith has come, we no longer need a schoolmaster.

"You are the children of God by faith in Christ Jesus. There is neither Jew nor Greek, there is neither slave nor free, there is neither male nor female, for you are all one in Jesus Christ. And if you are Christ's, then you are children of Abraham and heirs to the promises of God.

PAUL'S SECOND JOURNEY

From Antioch, Paul and Barnabas returned briefly to Jerusalem where a meeting of the apostles and many elders of the church was held to try to resolve the problem which plagued the churches of Galatia: Did Gentiles have to become Jews before they could be Christians? Paul and others persuaded, temporarily, the church leaders in Jerusalem that Gentiles could be accepted directly as Christians, as long as they followed certain minimal rules of behaviour and worship.

Then Paul and Barnabas returned to Antioch and resumed teaching and preaching the word of the Lord.

AFTER some days, Paul said to Barnabas, "Let us go again and visit our brethren in every city where we have preached the word of the Lord, and see how they do." But a disagreement arose between them and was so sharp that they went separate ways. Barnabas sailed to Cyprus. Paul went through Syria and Cilicia and a part of Galatia. Then after passing through Mysia, he came down to Troas.

There a vision appeared to Paul in the night. A man of Macedonia stood and begged him, saying, "Come over into Macedonia and help us." And after he had seen the vision, immediately he set out for Macedonia. From Troas, he came in a straight course to Samothrace, and the next day to Neapolis, and from there to Philippi, which was the chief city of that part of Macedonia and a Roman colony.

And it came to pass as Paul and Silas (a disciple from Jerusalem chosen by Paul to accompany him) went to pray, a certain girl possessed with a spirit of clairvoyance which brought her masters much gain met them. She followed them and cried, saying, "These men are the servants of the most high God, who tell us the way of salvation."

This she did many days. But Paul, being grieved, turned and said to the spirit, "I command you in the name of Jesus Christ to come out of her." And he came out the same hour.

And when her masters saw that the hope of their gains was gone, they caught Paul and Silas, and brought them before the rulers of the city, saying:

"These men, being Jews, do exceedingly trouble our city, and teach customs which are not lawful for us to receive, being Romans."

PAUL AND SILAS ARE IMPRISONED

And the multitude rose up together against them, and the magistrates tore off their clothing and commanded them to be beaten. And when they had laid many lashes upon them, they cast them into prison. They charged the jailer to keep them securely, and he, obeying his orders, had them thrust into the inner prison and locked their feet in the stocks.

And at midnight Paul and Silas prayed, and sang praises to God, and

PAUL'S SECOND MISSIONARY JOURNEY

the prisoners heard them. And suddenly there was a great earthquake, so that the foundations of the prison were shaken. Immediately all the doors were opened, and everyone's bonds were loosed.

The keeper of the prison, waking out of his sleep and seeing the prison doors open, drew out his sword and would have killed himself, supposing that the prisoners had fled. But Paul cried with a loud voice, saying, "Do not harm yourself, for we are all here."

Then the jailer called for a light, and he sprang into the cell trembling, and fell down before Paul and Silas, and brought them out, and said, "Sirs, what must I do to be saved?"

And they said, "Believe in the Lord Jesus Christ, and you shall be saved, you and your house." And they spoke the word of the Lord to him, and to all that were in his house.

And the same hour of the night he took Paul and Silas and washed their wounds; and was baptized, he and all his family. And when he had brought them into his house he set meat before them, and rejoiced, believing in God with all his household.

And when it was day, the magistrates sent the sergeants, saying, "Let those men go." And the keeper of the prison told this to Paul, saying, "The magistrates have sent word to let you go. Now therefore depart and go in peace."

But Paul said, "They have beaten us openly, uncondemned, being Romans, and have cast us into prison. How do they thrust us out secretly? No indeed, let them come themselves and fetch us out."

And the sergeants told these words to the magistrates, and they feared when they heard that they were Roman citizens. And they came and begged their forgiveness, and brought them out and asked them to depart out of the city.

And they went out of the prison, and entered the house of Lydia; and when they had seen the brethren they comforted them and departed.

THEY PREACH IN THESSALONICA

Now when they had passed through Amphipolis and Apollonia, they came to Thessalonica where there was a synagogue of the Jews. And Paul, as his manner was, went in, and on three sabbath days reasoned with them out of the scriptures, saying, "This Jesus whom I preach to you is Christ." And some of the Jews believed and joined Paul and Silas. So did a great many of the devout Greeks and not a few of the chief women.

But the Jews which did not believe, moved with envy, took certain lewd fellows of the baser sort and gathered a company and set the whole city in an uproar, crying, "These that have turned the world upside down have come here also. And these all do contrary to the decrees of Caesar, saying there is another king, one Jesus."

THEY ESCAPE FROM BEREA

And they troubled the people and the rulers of the city, when they heard these things. So the brethren immediately sent away Paul and Silas by night into Berea.

Coming there, they went into the synagogue of the Jews. These were more noble than those in Thessalonica, in that they received the word with all readiness of mind and searched the scriptures daily to find whether these things were so.

But when the Jews of Thessalonica had knowledge that the word of God

was being preached by Paul at Berea, they came there also and stirred up the people. And then immediately the brethren sent Paul away toward the sea.

And they that conducted Paul brought him to Athens.

Then, after receiving for Silas and Timothy a commandment from Paul to follow him from Berea with all speed, they departed.

THE LETTERS TO THE THESSALONIANS

Arriving alone, a fugitive, in Athens, Paul must have worried about the threats to his work in the north. For, as he states in a passage from one of the two letters to the Thessalonians, he soon sent back one of his closest fellow missionaries to encourage them. That the news he received back from Thessalonica some time later was good is indicated from the two letters, parts of the first of which are given here.

"To the church of the Thessalonians: Grace be unto you, and peace, from God our Father, and the Lord Jesus Christ. We give thanks to God always for you all, making mention of you in our prayers. We remember without ceasing your work of faith and how you became followers of us and of the Lord. Having received the word in much affliction, you were examples to all that believe, in Macedonia and Achaia.

"For yourselves, brethren, know that our coming to you was not in vain. Even after we had suffered and were shamefully treated, as you know, at Philippi, our God made us bold to speak to you of his gospel in the face of much opposition.

"Then we, brothers, being taken from you—in person, not in heart—tried all the more to see you again. We would have come to you—I, Paul, again and again—but Satan prevented us. Therefore we sent Timothy, our brother and minister of God and our fellow labourer in the gospel of Christ, to establish you and to comfort you concerning your faith.

"Now as touching brotherly love, you do not need me to write you, for you yourselves were taught by God to love one another—but we beseech you, brethren, that you increase in this more and more.

"But I would not have you ignorant concerning those who sleep in death, that you sorrow not like those who have no hope. For if we believe that Jesus died and rose again, so also will God bring with him those who sleep in Jesus.

"For the Lord himself shall descend from heaven with a shout, with the voice of the archangel, and with the trumpet of God. And the dead in Christ shall rise first. Then we who are alive and remain shall be caught up together with them in the clouds, to meet the Lord in the air. And so shall we ever be with the Lord. Therefore comfort one another with these words.

"The grace of our Lord Jesus Christ be with you. *Amen*."

PAUL PREACHES TO THE ATHENIANS

Now while Paul waited for Silas and Timothy in Athens, his spirit was stirred within him when he saw the city wholly given to idolatry. Therefore he argued in the synagogue with the Jews and with the devout persons, and in the market daily with them that met with him.

Then certain philosophers of the Epicureans and of the Stoics encountered him. Some said, "What will this

babbler say?" Others said, "He seems to be a setter forth of strange gods." For he preached to them about Jesus and the resurrection.

And they took him and brought him to Areopagus, saying, "May we know what this new doctrine is of which you speak? For you are bringing strange things to our ears, and we would like to know what they mean." (For all the Athenians and strangers which were there spent their time in nothing else except telling or hearing some new thing.)

Then Paul stood in the midst of Mars' hill and said:

"You men of Athens, I see that in all things you are too superstitious. For as I passed by and beheld your

devotion, I found an altar with this inscription: 'TO THE UNKNOWN GOD.' Whom therefore you worship as unknown, him shall I make known to you.

"God that made the world and all things therein, seeing that he is Lord of heaven and earth, dwells not in temples made with hands. Neither is he worshipped with men's hands, as though he needed anything, seeing that he gives to all men life and breath and all things, and has made from one blood all nations of men.

"For in him we live and move and have our being, as certain of your own poets have said, for we are his offspring. Inasmuch then as we are the offspring of God, we ought not to think that the Godhead is like gold or silver or stone or images of man's devising.

"The times of ignorance God winked at, but now he commands every man everywhere to repent, because he has appointed a day in which he will judge the world in righteousness by that man whom he has ordained. He has given assurance of that to all men by raising him from the dead."

And when they heard of the resurrection of the dead, some mocked and others said, "We will hear you again on this matter."

So Paul departed from among them. However certain men followed him and believed, among whom were Dionysius the Areopagite and a woman named Damaris, and others with them.

HE CONTINUES TO CORINTH

After these things, Paul departed from Athens and came to Corinth. And he argued in the synagogue every sabbath and persuaded the Jews and Greeks.

When Silas and Timothy arrived from Macedonia, Paul was engaged in testifying to the Jews that Jesus was Christ. And Crispus, the chief ruler of the synagogue, believed in the Lord with all his household, and many of the Corinthians hearing believed, and were baptized. And he continued there a year and six months, teaching the word of God among them.

And after this Paul took his leave of the brethren and sailed from there to Syria. And he came to Ephesus, where he entered into the synagogue and reasoned with the Jews. When they asked him to stay a longer time, he did not consent, but bade them farewell, saying, "I must by all means keep this feast that is coming in Jerusalem. But I will return again to you, if it is God's will." And he sailed from Ephesus.

THE EPISTLES OF PAUL TO THE CORINTHIANS

When Paul left Corinth, he had established there a seemingly strong and healthy following. But as he travelled, news came to him of serious conflicts within the church. These prompted his stern letters to the Corinthians, his longest writings to any one church, passages from which follow.

"To the church of God which is at Corinth: Grace be unto you, and

peace, from God our Father, and from the Lord Jesus Christ.

"Now I beseech you, brethren, by the name of our Lord Jesus Christ, that you all agree and that there be no divisions among you. For it has been declared to me that there are contentions among you.

"I thank God that I baptized none of you. For Christ sent me not to baptize but to preach the gospel, not with the wisdom of words, lest the cross of Christ should lose its significance.

"For the preaching of the cross is foolishness to them that perish. But to us who are saved, it is the power of God. For it is written: 'I will destroy the wisdom of the wise, and will bring to nothing the understanding of the prudent.'

"Where is the wise? Where is the scribe? Where is the disputer of this world? Has not God made foolish the wisdom of this world? For the Jews require a sign, and the Greeks seek after wisdom. But we preach Christ crucified, a stumblingblock to the Jews and foolishness to the Greeks. But to them which are called, both Jews and Greeks, Christ is the power of God, and the wisdom of God. God has chosen the foolish things of the world to confound the wise, because the foolishness of God is wiser than men, and the weakness of God is stronger than men.

ROLE OF THE APOSTLES

"I think that God has set forth us the apostles last, as if sentenced to death. For we are made a spectacle to the world, and to angels, and to men. We are fools for Christ's sake, but you are wise in Christ. We are weak, but you are strong. You are honourable, but we are despised.

"Even to this present hour, we hunger and thirst and are naked and are buffeted and have no certain dwelling place. We labour, working with our own hands. Being reviled, we bless. Being persecuted, we bear it. Being defamed, we conciliate. We are like the filth of the world, the refuse of all things.

"I write not these things to shame you, but as my beloved sons I warn you. What will you? Shall I come to you with a rod, or in love and in the spirit of meekness?

"For to one is given by the Spirit the word of wisdom; to another the word of knowledge by the same Spirit; to another faith by the same Spirit; to another the gifts of healing by the same Spirit; to another the working of miracles; to another prophecy; to another discerning of spirits; to another divers kinds of tongues; to another the interpretation of tongues; but in all these works but one and the self-same Spirit, dividing to every man as he will.

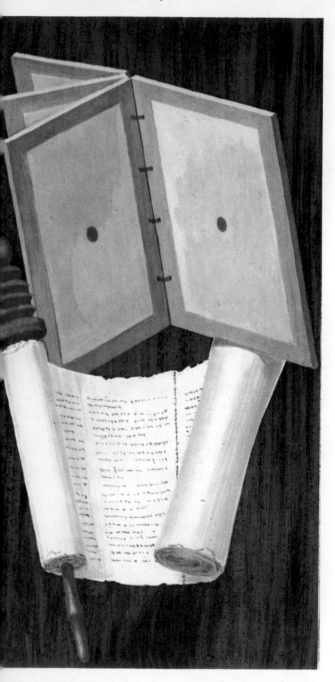

ther we be bond or free; and have been all made to drink into one Spirit. For the body is not one member, but many. If the foot shall say, because I am not the hand I am not of the body, is it therefore not the body? And if the ear shall say, because I am not the eye I am not of the body? If the whole body were an eye, where would the hearing be? If the whole were the hearing, where would the smelling be?

"But now God has set the members, every one, in the body as it pleased him to do. And if they were all one member, where would the body be? But now they are many members, yet but one body. And the eye cannot say to the hand, I have no need of you; nor again the head to the feet, I have no need of you.

"And if one member suffers, all the members suffer with it; or if one member be honoured all the members rejoice with it. Now you are the body of Christ, and members in particular. And God has set some in the church, first apostles, secondly prophets, thirdly teachers, after that miracles, then gifts of healing, helps, governments, diversities of tongues.

"Are all apostles? Are all prophets? Are all teachers? Are all workers of miracles? Have all the gift of healing? Do all speak with tongues? Do all interpret? But covet earnestly the best gifts; I will show you a more excellent way.

PAUL LIKENS CHRISTIANS TO THE PARTS OF A BODY

"For as the body is one, and has many members, and all the members of that one body, being many, are one body; so also is Christ. For by one Spirit are we all baptized into one body, whether we be Jew or Gentile, whe-

THE MORE EXCELLENT WAY

"Though I speak with the tongues of men and of angels, and have not love, I am become as sounding brass or a tinkling cymbal. And though I have the gift of prophecy, and the understanding of mysteries, and all knowledge; and though I have all faith, so that I could remove mountains, and have not love, I am nothing. And though I give all my goods to feed the poor, and though my body to be burned and have not love, it profits me nothing.

Love suffers long, and is kind, love envies not; love boasts not, is not puffed up, does not behave itself unseemly, seeks not her own, is not easily provoked, thinks no evil; rejoices not in wickedness but rejoices in the truth; bears all things, believes all things, hopes all things, endures all things.

"Love never fails. But where there are prophecies, they shall fail; where there are tongues, they shall cease; where there is knowledge, it shall vanish away. For we know in part, and we prophesy in part. But when that which is perfect is come, then that which is in part shall be done away.

"When I was a child, I spoke as a child, I understood as a child, I thought as a child. But when I became a man, I put away childish things. For now we see through a glass, darkly, but then face to face. Now I know in part, but then shall I know even as also I am known.

"And now abides faith, hope, love, these three; but the greatest of these is love."

THE LETTER OF CHRIST

"Do we begin to commend ourselves again? Or do we need, as some others, epistles of commendation to you, or letters of commendation from you? You are our epistle written in our hearts, known and read by all men. For you are manifestly declared to be the epistle of Christ ministered by us, written not with ink, but with the Spirit of the living God, not in tables of stone, but in fleshy tables of the heart. Not that we are sufficient to think anything of ourselves. But our sufficiency is of God who has made us

able ministers of the new testament, not of the letter, but of the spirit. For the letter kills, but the spirit gives life. Now the Lord is that Spirit, and where the Spirit of the Lord is, there is liberty."

"Finally, brethren, farewell. Be perfect, be of good comfort, be of one mind, live in peace, and the God of love and peace shall be with you."

PAUL'S THIRD JOURNEY

Sailing from Ephesus, Paul landed at Caesarea, and when he had gone up and greeted the church, he went on to Antioch. And after he had spent some time there, he departed and went over all the country of Galatia and Phrygia, strengthening all the disciples.

Then having passed through the upper coasts, Paul came again to Ephesus. And he went into the synagogue and spoke boldly for three months, disputing and persuading concerning the kingdom of God.

 OD worked special miracles through the hands of Paul, so that handkerchiefs or aprons were brought from his body to the sick, and the diseases departed from them, and the evil spirits went out of them.

Then certain vagabond Jews took it upon themselves to call the name of the Lord Jesus over those who had evil spirits, saying, "We command you by Jesus whom Paul preaches." They were seven sons of one Sceva, a Jew, and chief of the priests, who did so.

But the evil spirit answered and said, "Jesus I know, and Paul I know. But who are you?" And the man in whom the evil spirit was, leaped on them and overcame them, so that they fled naked and wounded.

This was known to all the Jews and Greeks dwelling at Ephesus, and fear fell upon them all, and the name of the Lord Jesus was praised. And many that believed came and confessed and told of their evil deeds. Many of them also who used magic brought their books together and burned them before all men. And they counted the price of them, and found it fifty thousand pieces of silver. So mightily did the word of God grow and prevail.

THE SILVERSMITHS' REVOLT

But at this time, there arose no small stir in Ephesus. For a certain man named Demetrius, a silversmith who made silver shrines for Diana, called together the workmen of like occupation and said, "Sirs, you know that by this craft we have our wealth. Moreover you see and hear that not only at Ephesus but almost throughout all Asia, this Paul has persuaded and turned away many people saying that there be no gods which are made with hands.

"So not only is our craft in danger, but also the temple of the great goddess Diana is in danger of being despised and her magnificence of being destroyed, she whom all Asia and the world worships."

When they heard these sayings, they were full of wrath and cried out, saying, "Great is Diana of the Ephesians." And the whole city was in uproar, and having caught two of Paul's companions in travel, they rushed with one accord into the theatre, where some cried one thing and some another. For the assembly was confused and most knew not why they had come together.

When the town clerk had quieted

PAUL'S THIRD MISSIONARY JOURNEY

the people, he said, "You men of Ephesus, what man is there that knows not how the city of the Ephesians is a worshipper of the great goddess Diana, and of the image which fell down from Jupiter? Seeing then that these things cannot be spoken against, you ought to be quiet and do nothing rashly. For you have brought here these men who are neither robbers of the temple nor even blasphemers of your goddess.

"Therefore if Demetrius and the craftsmen which are with him have a matter against any man, the law is open and there are deputies. Let them bring charges against one another. But if you inquire anything concerning other matters, it shall be settled in a lawful assembly. For we are in danger of being called in question for this day's uproar, there being no cause whereby we may give a justification for this meeting." And when he had thus spoken, he dismissed the assembly.

After the uproar had ceased, Paul called to him the disciples and embraced them and departed to go into Macedonia. From there he went into Greece where he stayed three months. And when his enemies laid in wait for him, as he was about to sail to Syria, he returned through Macedonia instead. From there he went to Troas where he stayed for seven days.

EUTYCHUS FALLS ASLEEP

And the day before his departure, when the disciples in Troas came together for the breaking of bread, Paul preached to them, and continued talking until midnight.

There were many lights in the upper room where they were gathered together. In one window sat a certain young man named Eutychus, who had fallen into a deep sleep. As Paul was long in preaching, he sank down in his sleep and fell from the third floor, and was picked up dead.

Paul went down and threw himself upon him, and putting his arms around him, said, "Do not worry, he is still alive."

When Paul came up again, he broke bread and ate and talked a long while, until break of day, and then he departed. And they brought the young man home alive and were not a little comforted.

PAUL HASTENS TO REACH JERUSALEM

Paul hastened in order to be in Jerusalem the day of Pentecost, if it were possible. Going from Troas, he sailed from Assos, and along the coast stopped at Mitylene, Chios, Samos, Trogyllium and Miletus, then Coos, Rhodes and Patara. From there Paul and his company sailed to Syria and landed at Tyre. Next they came to Ptolemais and the following day to Caesarea.

While they were there, there came down from Judea a certain prophet named Agabus. And when he had come to them, he took Paul's girdle and bound his own hands and feet and said, "Thus says the Holy Spirit, 'So shall the Jews at Jerusalem bind the man that owns this girdle, and shall deliver him into the hands of the Gentiles.'"

When they heard these things, they begged him not to go up to Jerusalem. But Paul answered, "Why do you weep and break my heart? For I am ready not only to be bound but also to die at Jerusalem for the name of the Lord Jesus." And when he would not be persuaded, they ceased, saying, "Let the will of the Lord be done."

And after those days, they went up to Jerusalem, together with certain of the disciples of Caesarea.

PAUL
IN
JERUSALEM

Paul wanted very much to visit Rome, the capital of the vast empire in which he had made his missionary journeys. Looking forward to this visit, he wrote a letter to the Christian community already established and active there. He planned to make the voyage after fulfilling his mission in Jerusalem. The unhappy circumstances under which he finally did were still to be determined as he wrote this letter from Jerusalem, parts of which follow, to his distant brothers.

 O all of God's beloved in Rome called to be saints: "I make mention of you always in my prayers, requesting that by some means through the will of God I might make a journey to come to you. I long to see you to impart to you some spiritual gift, even as I have among other Gentiles. I am debtor both to the Greeks and to the Barbarians, both to the wise and to the unwise. So I am eager to preach the gospel to you that are in Rome also.

THE LOVE OF GOD

"If God be for us, who can be against us?

"Who shall separate us from the love of Christ? Shall tribulation or distress or persecution or famine or nakedness or peril or sword? As it is written, 'For thy sake we are killed all the day long. We are looked upon as sheep for slaughter.'

"No, in all these things we are more than conquerors through him that loved us. For I am persuaded that neither death, nor life, nor angels, nor principalities, nor powers, nor things present, nor things to come, nor height, nor depth, nor any other creature, shall be able to separate us from the love of God, which is in Christ Jesus our Lord.

PRAY THAT I MAY COME TO YOU

"Now, having no place more to go in these parts, and having a great desire these many years to come to you, whenever I take my journey into Spain, I will come to you.

"But now I go to Jerusalem to minister to the saints. For it has pleased them of Macedonia and Achaia to make a certain contribution for the poor saints which are at Jerusalem. When therefore I have delivered this to them, I will come by way of you to Spain.

"Now I beseech you, brethren, for the Lord Jesus Christ's sake, that you strive together in your prayers to God for me, that I may be delivered from them in Judea that do not believe and that my service which I have for Jerusalem may be accepted by the saints; that I may come to you with joy by the will of God, and may with you be refreshed. Now the God of peace be with you all. *Amen.*"

PAUL IS ARRESTED

In Jerusalem, enemies of Paul from Asia, when they saw him in the temple, stirred up all the people and seized him with great shouts, accusing him of false teaching. Then the whole city was aroused, and people hurried together, and they took Paul and dragged him out of the temple, and at once the doors were shut.

As they were about to kill him, word came to the chief captain of the soldiers that all Jerusalem was in an uproar. He immediately took soldiers and centurions and ran down to the temple. When his enemies saw the chief captain and the soldiers, they stopped beating Paul. Then the chief captain came and arrested him and commanded him to be bound with two chains, and asked who he was and what he had done.

Some cried one thing, some another, and when he could learn nothing certain because of the shouting, the captain commanded Paul to be taken into the castle. And when he came to the stairs, he had to be carried by the soldiers because of the violence of the people. For the multitude followed after, crying, "Away with him."

501

HE MAKES HIS DEFENCE

As Paul was being led into the castle, he said to the chief captain, "May I speak to you?" He answered, "Can you speak Greek? Are you not that Egyptian who made an uproar and led out into the wilderness four thousand men that were murderers?"

But Paul said, "I am a man who is a Jew of Tarsus, a city of Cilicia, a citizen of no mean city. I beseech you, allow me to speak to the people." And when he had given permission, Paul stood on the stairs and beckoned with his hand to the people, and when there was silence, he spoke to them in the Hebrew tongue, saying:

"Men, brethren, and fathers, hear my defence which I make now to you." When they heard that he spoke in Hebrew, they kept all the more silent. "I am truly a man who is a Jew, born in Tarsus, a city in Cilicia, yet brought up in this city at the feet of Gamaliel, and taught according to the perfect manner of the law of the fathers, and was zealous toward God, as you all are this day.

"I persecuted to death the followers of Christ, binding and delivering into prisons both men and women. As also the high priest will bear me witness, and all the elders, I received letters to the brethren, and went to Damascus to bring them which were there to Jerusalem to be punished."

Then Paul told of his conversion and baptism and his presence at Stephen's death, and how the Lord had commanded him to leave Jerusalem, saying, "Depart, for I will send you far from here, to the Gentiles."

The people listened until this word, and then they lifted up their voices and said:

"Away with such a fellow from the earth. For it is not fit that he should live."

And as they cried and cast off their clothes and threw dust into the air, the chief captain commanded him to be brought into the castle and ordered that he should be questioned by torture, so that he might know why they cried so against him.

HE PLEADS ROMAN CITIZENSHIP

As they bound him with thongs, Paul said to a centurion that stood by, "Is it lawful for you to torture a man who is a Roman, and uncondemned?"

When the centurion heard that, he went and told the chief captain, saying, "Take care in what you do, for this man is a Roman." Then the chief captain came and said to Paul, "Tell me, are you a Roman?" He said, "Yes." And the chief captain said, "For a great sum I obtained this citizenship." And Paul said, "But I was born a citizen."

And immediately, they who were to have questioned him, departed. And the chief captain was also afraid, because he knew that he was a Roman citizen and because he had bound him.

On the next day, because the chief captain wished to know why Paul was accused by his enemies, he loosed him from his bands and commanded the chief priests and all their council to appear, and brought Paul down and set him before them.

But when there arose a great dispute, the chief captain, fearing that Paul would be pulled in pieces by them, commanded the soldiers to go down and to take him by force from among them, and to bring him to the castle.

The following night, the Lord stood by him and said, "Be of good cheer, Paul. For as you have testified for me in Jerusalem, so must you bear witness also in Rome."

HIS ENEMIES PLOT AGAINST HIM

When it was day, certain of his enemies banded together under a pledge saying that they would neither eat nor drink till they had killed Paul. They came to the chief priests and elders, and said, "Ask the chief captain to bring him down to you tomorrow, as though you wished to question him further. And we, as he comes, will be ready to kill him."

But the son of Paul's sister heard of their lying in wait and went to the castle and told Paul. Then Paul called one of the centurions and had the young man brought to the chief captain. And when he had told him of the plot, the chief captain let the young man depart, saying, "See that you tell no man that you have told these things to me."

Then he called two centurions, saying, "Make ready two hundred soldiers and go to Caesarea with seventy horsemen and two hundred spearmen. Go at the third hour of the night and bring him safe to Felix the governor."

Then the soldiers, as they were commanded, took Paul and brought him to Caesarea.

HE IS BROUGHT BEFORE FELIX

After five days, Ananias, the high priest, came down with the elders and with a certain orator named Tertullus who spoke to the governor against Paul, saying:

"We have found this man a pestilent fellow, and a mover of sedition among all the Jews throughout the world, and a ring-leader of the sect of the Nazarenes. He also has gone about profaning the temple. We seized him and would have judged him according to our law, but the chief captain came

upon us and with great violence took him away out of our hands, commanding his accusers to come to you."

Then Paul, after the governor had beckoned him to speak, answered:

"They neither found me in the temple disputing with any man, nor raising up the people in the syna-

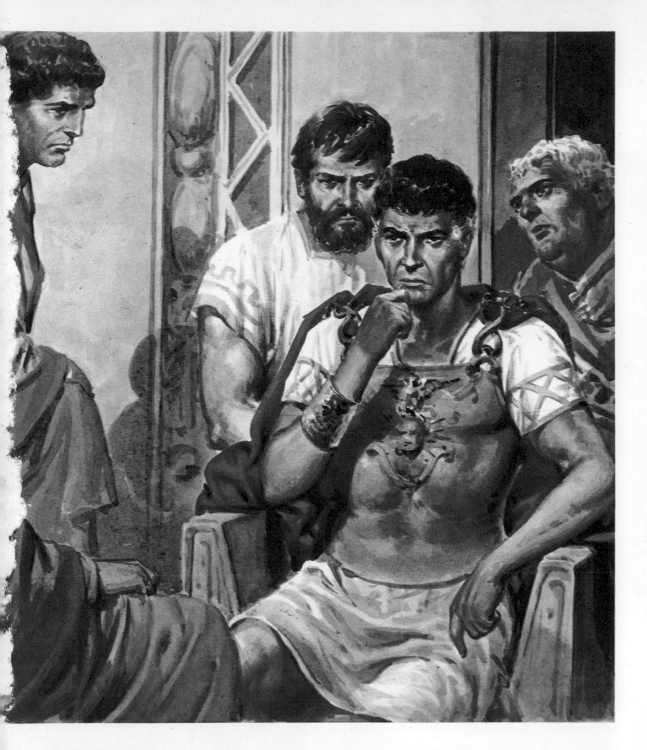

gogues or in the city. Nor can they prove the things of which they now accuse me."

When Felix heard these things, he said, "When the chief captain comes down, I will know more about your matter." And he commanded a centurion to guard Paul, and to let him have some liberty and that he should forbid none of his acquaintances to come to him and care for him. And Felix often sent for Paul to hear him.

Paul was still a prisoner when, after two years, Porcius Festus came to take Felix's place. And Felix, willing to do the Jews a pleasure, left Paul bound.

HE APPEALS TO CAESAR

Soon after Festus had come into the province, he commanded Paul to be brought to him as he sat on the judgment seat. And the Jews who had come down from Jerusalem laid many grievous complaints against Paul which they could not prove.

Paul answered for himself, "Neither against the law of the Jews, nor against the temple, nor yet against Caesar have I offended anything at all."

But Festus, willing to do the Jews a pleasure, asked Paul, "Are you willing to go up to Jerusalem and be judged of these things before me?"

Then Paul said, "I stand at Caesar's judgment seat, where I ought to be judged. To the Jews I have done no wrong, as you very well know. If I am an offender and have committed anything worthy of death, I do not refuse to die. But if none of these things are so, of which these men accuse me, no man may deliver me to them. I appeal to Caesar."

Then Festus, after he had conferred with the council, answered, "Have you appealed to Caesar? To Caesar you shall go."

KING AGRIPPA HEARS PAUL

Some days after, King Agrippa and his sister Bernice came to Caesarea to greet Festus. And when they had been there many days, Festus told the king about Paul's case. Then Agrippa said to Festus, "I would like to hear the man myself."

"Tomorrow," said Festus, "you shall hear him. Perhaps from your examination of him I may have something to write about him, for it seems unreasonable to send a prisoner to Rome without signifying the crimes laid against him."

The next day, in the place of hearings, Paul spoke before Agrippa and Bernice and many others, explaining how he was converted and preached repentance and the way of God.

Then Agrippa said to Paul, "You almost persuade me to be a Christian."

And Paul said, "I wish to God that not only you, but also all that hear me this day, were both 'almost' and altogether like I am, except for these chains."

And when he had thus spoken, the king rose up, and the governor, and Bernice, and they that sat with them, and when they had gone aside, they talked among themselves saying, "This man has done nothing worthy of death or of chains."

Then Agrippa said to Festus, "This man might have been set at liberty if he had not appealed to Caesar."

PAUL'S JOURNEY TO ROME

TEMPEST AT SEA

Nevertheless the centurion believed the captain and the owner of the ship more than Paul. And because the harbour was not well suited to winter in, most people advised departure, in order, if it were at all possible, to reach Phoenix, which is a harbour of Crete, and winter there.

When the south wind blew softly, thinking that they could reach their goal, they untied and set sail close to Crete. But very soon there arose a mighty gale. The ship was caught and could not face into the wind, so they let it run before it.

And running behind a small island called Clauda, they had much work in making fast the ship's boat. When the boat had been taken up, they ran ropes under the ship to secure it. Then, fearing that they might run on to the sand, they struck the sails and let the ship drift.

Being greatly tossed about by the tempest, the next day they lightened the ship. And the following day with their own hands, they threw out the ship's tackle. But when neither sun nor stars appeared for many days, and the great storm still raged, all hope of being saved was given up.

But after going without food for a long time, Paul stood up in the midst of them and said, "Sirs, you should have listened to me and not have loosed from Crete. But now I exhort you to be of good cheer, for there shall be no loss of any man's life among you, but only the ship. For there stood by me this night the angel of God, whose I am and whom I serve, saying, 'Fear not, Paul. You must be brought before Caesar, and, lo, God has put under your protection all them that sail with you.' Therefore, sirs, be of good cheer. For I believe God, that it shall be even as it was told me. However, we must be cast upon a certain island."

HEN it was decided that Paul should sail to Italy, they delivered him and certain other prisoners to one named Julius, a centurion of Augustus's forces. Boarding a ship of Adramyttium, they launched forth, meaning to sail along the coast of Asia.

The next day, they touched at Sidon and Julius courteously gave Paul liberty to go to his friends to refresh himself.

When they left there, they sailed along the coast of Cyprus, because the winds were contrary. They came to Myra, a city of Lycia, where the centurion found a ship from Alexandria sailing to Italy, and he put his prisoners on it.

When they had sailed slowly many days, without favourable winds, they came to a place which is called 'The Fair Havens,' near the city of Lasea. Much time had passed and seafaring was now dangerous, for the winter had nearly come.

Paul warned them, "Sirs, I foresee that this voyage will bring damage and loss, not only of the cargo and ship, but also of our lives."

THE SHIP RUNS AGROUND

When the fourteenth night had come, about midnight the men of the ship felt that they were drawing near to land. They took soundings and then cast four anchors off the stern. When they had let down the boat, about to flee the ship, Paul said to the centurion and to the soldiers, "Unless these men stay with the ship, you cannot be saved." Then the soldiers cut the ropes of the boat, and let her drift away.

While the day was coming on, Paul asked them all to take food, saying,

"This day is the fourteenth day that you have taken nothing. Therefore I pray you to eat, for this is for your health. For not a hair shall fall from the head of any of you."

And when he had thus spoken, he took bread and gave thanks to God, and when he had broken it, he began to eat. Then they were all of good cheer, and they also took some food. And they were in all two hundred and seventy-six souls on the ship.

When they had eaten enough, they lightened the ship, casting out the cargo of wheat into the sea. And when it was day, the land was unknown to them,

from their plan, and commanded that those who could swim should cast themselves first into the sea and get to land; then the rest should follow, some on boards and some on broken pieces of the ship. And it came to pass that they all escaped safe to land.

THEY WINTER ON MALTA

After their escape, they found that the island was called Melita (Malta). The natives there showed them much kindness, for they kindled a fire and welcomed them all to it, because of the rain and the cold.

When Paul had gathered a bundle of sticks and laid them on the fire, a viper came out because of the heat and fastened itself on his hand.

When the natives saw the poisonous beast hang from his hand, they said among themselves, "No doubt this man is a murderer whom justice will not permit to live, although he has escaped the sea."

But Paul shook the beast off into the fire and felt no harm. They looked for him to swell or fall down dead suddenly, but after they had looked a great while, and saw no harm come to him, they changed their minds and said that he was a god.

Now in the same area were the lands of the chief man of the island, whose name was Publius. He welcomed Paul and lodged him courteously for three days. The father of Publius lay sick with a fever and a flow of blood and Paul prayed and healed him. So when this was done, others on the island which had diseases came and were healed. They heaped honours on Paul, and when he departed, they gave him all he needed.

After three months, he left in a ship from Alexandria which had wintered at the island. He went to Syracuse, to Rhegium, to Puteoli and so to Rome.

but they saw a creek with a beach where they planned, if it were possible, to run the ship ashore. So they took up the anchors, loosed the rudder bands, and hoisted the mainsail to the wind and, committing themselves to the sea, made toward shore.

And falling onto a shoal, they ran the ship aground. The forepart stuck fast and remained unmovable, but the after part was broken with the violence of the waves.

Now the soldiers' plan was to kill the prisoners lest any of them should swim out and escape. But the centurion, wanting to save Paul, kept them

PAUL'S FINAL YEARS

When they had appointed him a day, there came many to him in his lodging. From morning till evening, he talked to them about the kingdom of God, persuading them concerning Jesus. And some believed the things which were spoken, and some believed not. And when they did not agree among themselves, Paul said, "Well spoke the Holy Spirit through Isaiah the prophet to our fathers, saying: 'Hearing you shall hear, and shall not understand: and seeing you shall see, and not perceive. For the heart of this people has become heavy, and their ears are dull of hearing, and their eyes they have closed.'

WHEN the brethren in Rome heard of Paul's arrival, they came to meet him as he approached, going as far as the Appian Forum and The Three Taverns. And when Paul saw them, he thanked God, and took courage.

And when he came to Rome, the centurion delivered the prisoners to the captain of the guard. But Paul was allowed to dwell by himself with a soldier to guard him.

After three days, Paul called the chiefs of the Jews together, and said to them, "Men and brethren, though I have committed nothing against the people or customs of our fathers, yet I was delivered prisoner from Jerusalem into the hands of the Romans."

They said to him, "We neither received letters from Judea concerning you, nor have any of the brethren that came spoken any harm of you. But we desire to hear what you think. For as concerning this sect, we know that everywhere it is spoken against."

"Be it known therefore to you that the salvation of God has been sent to the Gentiles, and they will hear it." And when he had said these words, the Jews departed and had great disputing among themselves.

And Paul dwelt two whole years in his own rented house, and received all that came to him, preaching the kingdom of God and teaching those things which concern the Lord Jesus, with all confidence, no man forbidding him.

THE LETTERS FROM ROME

During his long semi-confinement in Rome, Paul wrote to many groups and individuals, his letters making up some of the final chapters of the New Testament. Like his earlier epistles, these are full of spiritual advice from which many of the basic elements of Christian belief have been drawn. Some selected passages are given here with the name of the group or person to whom they were written.

OF THE ARMOUR OF FAITH
(EPHESIANS)

"Be strong in the Lord, and in the power of his might. Put on the whole armour of God, that you may be able to stand against the wiles of the devil. For we wrestle not against flesh and blood, but against principalities, against powers, against the rulers of the darkness of this world, against spiritual wickedness in high places.

"Stand therefore having your loins wrapped around with truth, and having on the breastplate of righteousness. Have your feet shod with the preparation of the gospel of peace. Above all, take the shield of faith, with which you shall be able to quench all the fiery darts of the wicked. And take the helmet of salvation, and the sword of the Spirit, which is the word of God."

THINK ABOUT THESE THINGS
(PHILIPPIANS)

"Brethren, whatever things are true, whatever things are honest, whatever things are just, whatever things are pure, whatever things are lovely, whatever things are of good report, and if there be any virtue and if there be any praise, think about these things. Those things which you have both learned and received and heard and seen in me, do; and the God of peace shall be with you."

SEEK THOSE THINGS WHICH ARE ABOVE
(COLOSSIANS)

"If you have been raised with Christ, seek those things which are above, where Christ sits on the right hand of God. Set your affection on things above, not on things on earth."

In a short letter to Philemon, an old friend of Paul's and a leader of the Colossian Christians, Paul asks him to receive back a runaway slave whom he has converted.

"For, perhaps, he departed for a season so that you should receive him for ever. Not now as a servant, but above a servant, as a beloved brother. If you consider me therefore a partner, receive him as myself. If he wronged you or owes you anything, put that on my account. I Paul have written it with my own hand; I will repay it."

OF FAITH WITHOUT WAVERING
(HEBREWS)

"Let us hold fast the profession of our faith without wavering, for he is faithful that promised: 'The just shall live by faith, but if any man shrinks back, my soul shall have no pleasure in him.'

"Now faith is the substance of things hoped for, the evidence of things not

seen. Through faith we understand that the worlds were framed by the word of God, so that things which are seen were made out of things which do not appear."

What happened to Paul after his two years in Rome is not certain. The Bible leaves off with him awaiting trial. Some scholars believe he was released and left Rome. But traditionally it is held that he was still there during Nero's persecution of Christians and that he was beheaded after being heard and sentenced by Nero himself.

In any case, among his very last writings must be counted his second epistle to Timothy. In this letter to his long faithful lieutenant, he talks of his death as an approaching certainty.

"I am now ready to be offered, and the time of my departure is at hand. I have fought a good fight, I have finished my course, I have kept the faith. Henceforth there is laid up for me a crown of righteousness, which the Lord, the righteous judge, shall give me on the day of judgment. And not only to me, but to all them also that love his appearing.

"Do your best to come to me shortly. The others have deserted me. Only Luke is with me. Take Mark and bring him with you, for he is profitable to me for the ministry. The cloak that I left at Troas with Carpus, when you come, bring it with you, and the books, especially the parchments.

"The Lord Jesus Christ be with your spirit. Grace be with you. *Amen.*"

THE LETTERS OF PETER

The later pages of the New Testament were written during the years of widespread persecution of early Christians by the Romans. They point to future glory as the reward for present suffering and warn against spiritual weakness. These pages, which follow the epistles of Paul, comprise letters by four other leaders of the growing church, among them Peter. This is Simon Peter, the apostle of Christ, who was crucified head-down in Rome, a martyred victim of Nero.

OW who is he that will harm you, if you are followers of that which is good? But even if you suffer for righteousness' sake, happy are you. And be not afraid of terror, nor be troubled. For it is better, if the will of God be so, that you suffer for well doing than for evil doing. For Christ also once suffered for sins, the just for the unjust, that he might bring us to God, being put to death in the flesh but made alive in the Spirit."

PETER COUNSELS HUMILITY

"All of you be subject to one another, and be clothed with humility. For God resists the proud and gives grace to the humble. Humble yourselves therefore under the mighty hand of God, that he may exalt you in due time. Cast all your care upon him, for he cares for you.

"Be sober, be vigilant, because your adversary the devil, like a roaring lion, walks about, seeking whom he may devour. Resist him, steadfast in the faith, knowing that the same sufferings are befalling your brothers throughout the world."

PETER SPEAKS OF THE COMING OF THE LORD

"But, beloved, be not ignorant of this one thing, that one day is with the Lord as a thousand years, and a thousand years as one day. The Lord is not slack concerning his promise, as some men count slackness, but is long-suffering, not willing that any should perish, but that all should come to repentance.

"But the day of the Lord shall come like a thief in the night, in which the heavens shall pass away with a great noise, and the elements shall melt with burning heat. The earth also and the works that are on it shall be burned up. Nevertheless we, according to his promise, look for new heavens and a new earth, where righteousness will dwell.

"Therefore, beloved, seeing that you look for such things, be careful that you be found by him in peace, without spot, and blameless. And count the long-suffering of our Lord as salvation, as our beloved brother Paul has written to you, speaking of these things in all his epistles.

"Grow in grace and in the knowledge of our Lord and Saviour Jesus Christ."

THE VISION OF JOHN

The final book of the Bible, The Revelation of St. John the Divine, tells in vivid images of God's final judgment.

The book is cast in the form of a vision and many of its prophecies are disguised attacks on Rome, the great power of the first century. Such is unquestionably the case of the references to Babylon. This ancient capital of paganism and persecution was comparable in the eyes of early Christians to the Rome of their day. Thus the following passages must have been clear and encouraging to many.

"And after these things, I saw another angel come down from heaven, having great power. And he cried mightily with a strong voice, saying, 'Babylon the great is fallen, and is become the habitation of devils and the hold of every foul spirit, and a cage of every unclean and hateful bird.'

"And I heard another voice from heaven, saying, 'Come out of her, my people, that you be not partakers of her sins, and that you receive not her plagues. For her sins have reached into heaven, and God has remembered her iniquities.

" 'And the kings of the earth, when they shall see the smoke of her burning, standing afar off for the fear of her torment, shall say, "Alas, alas, that great city Babylon, that mighty city." '

A NEW HEAVEN AND EARTH

"And I saw a new heaven and a new earth, for the first heaven and the first earth had passed away, and there was no more sea. And I, John, saw the holy city, new Jerusalem, coming down from God out of heaven, prepared as a bride adorned for her husband.

"And I heard a great voice out of heaven, saying, 'Behold, the tabernacle of God is with men, and he will dwell with them, and they shall be his people. And he shall wipe away all tears from

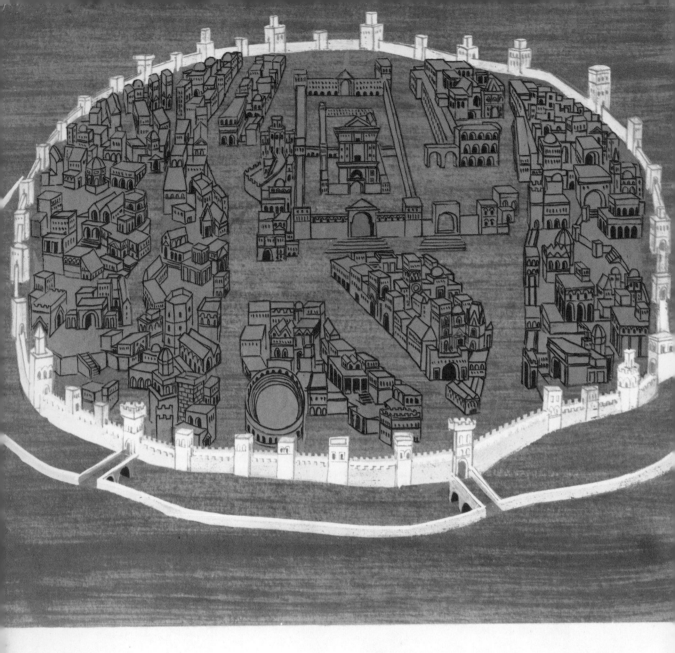

their eyes, and there shall be no more death, nor sorrow, nor crying. Neither shall there be any more pain.'

"And he carried me away in the spirit to a great and high mountain, and showed me that great city, the holy Jerusalem. And her light was like a stone most precious, even like a jasper stone, clear as crystal. And she had a wall great and high, and had twelve gates. The wall of the city had twelve foundations, and in them the names of the twelve apostles of the Lamb.

"And I saw no temple therein, for the Lord God Almighty and the Lamb are the temple of it. And the city had no need of the sun, nor of the moon, to shine in it. For the glory of God did lighten it, and the Lamb is the light thereof.

"And the nations of them which are saved shall walk in the light of it, and the kings of the earth bring their glory and honour to it. And the gates of it shall not be shut at all by day, for there shall be no night there.

"And I, John, saw these things, and heard them."